DAYS OF PLUNDER

Finding Light in the Darkness to Overcome and Recover All

DIANA LYNN ROGERS

ISBN 978-1-953223-00-5 (paperback)

Copyright © 2020 by Diana Lynn Rogers

All rights reserved. No part of this publication may be reproduced, distributed, or transmitted in any form or by any means, including photocopying, recording, or other electronic or mechanical methods without the prior written permission of the publisher. For permission requests, solicit the publisher via the address below.

Rushmore Press LLC
1 800 460 9188
www.rushmorepress.com

Printed in the United States of America

CONTENTS

DAYS OF PLUNDER Volume I
Finding Light in the Darkness Overcome and Recover All

Foreword 5
Introduction 7
Part I Corridor of Times 9
Part II Building Your Vision 68
Part III Pathways to Healing 90
Part IV Poetry 108
Epilogue 113

THE PROMISE Volume II
Finding Light in the Darkness to Overcome and Recover All

Prelude 117
Part I The Corridor of Times 119
Part II Covenant Talk 189
Part III Warrior's Battlefield 204
Part IV Celebrate Life 236
Acknowledgement 287
Index Reference 289

FOREWORD

"Many are the afflictions of the righteous. But the Lord delivers him out of them all." Psalm 34:19

There are many roads that one takes in this journey called life. Each path gives us insight and wisdom accompanied by pain, sorrow and sometimes, confusion. It is the wisdom of God that walks this life with us and gives us ears to hear and eyes to see. Thank God for His mercy!

In my life I have realized there are two major ways that one gains wisdom and understanding.

The first is education; lessons learned by studying and gathering information brings the student a working knowledge of life, most often without the experience that may accompany this factual information. As we garner more details, we "know" more about the subject, person, area etc.

The second is experience; the things that happen to us and around us that can change the course of our lives because of the face to face encounter with people and circumstances. When I first met Diana Rogers, I learned she had both working in her life. The education was evident, and one knew that she was learned and knowledgeable. But there was also a depth of wisdom she possessed through the many things she experienced. The loss of a marriage and tremendous trials through a debilitating accident could have taken her in many directions. Because of the Grace and Mercy of Almighty God she has found comfort, healing and a "hands-on" knowing in the Lord Jesus.

To be around her is to know that she is always encouraging and supportive of others, wanting them to succeed in life.

You will find that as you read *"Days of Plunder"* that out of some heart-wrenching pain and disappointment there come lessons shared that are both piercing and quite thorough in experiencing the Grace of God.

But I urge you; walk slowly through these pages so as to receive all the Lord might have for you. There is a reason why you are reading this, and God will use this as a tool in the shaping of your heart and life. What Diana has shared will cause freedom and strength that is borne from having lived through the experience and freely sharing it with all.

Your heart and head will be challenged, and your life changed as you allow the words to speak to your heart. The Lord will use that to adjust, heal and focus you on the life He has given you.

My dear friend has found some golden "nuggets" of wisdom that she has felt compelled to share for the purpose of freeing others. I believe she has succeeded!

Rick Smail
Pastor of New Life Church
Rochester, IN

INTRODUCTION

It is a new day! Have you ever just wanted to tell someone a secret so amazing you can hardly wait for them to know what you know? This morning I awakened to a new day; it is morning Lord!!!! A joy is flooding my soul! It is the gift of a new day.

When we are walking through the Valley of the Shadow of Death, it really doesn't feel like you really have much to laugh about or for that matter who even cares? Resurrection and healing blots out neither the death, nor sorrow of the loss. Moving beyond and rising up and healing doesn't leave us without making scars, and deep wounds on our heart and soul. Memories fade, something lingers, it is there to be left as a mark on your soul.

Whatever the loss or wound, it remains within you to miss that person; or a particular circumstance will remain with you, always to be a part of you. It doesn't have to be a physical death; it can be any loss or type of grief. Those grieving don't return to the old self; it is forever changed the "old life" is gone. The memory lingers but it is a new day. Life and loss has wrought and brought about change.

It's a new day. You now look through life with different eyes. You no longer presume you are always going to be here; nor do you think you can do it by yourself; in your own strength-you now realize life is a gift. A gift to be opened each day from the giver of life, God. You no longer take so much for granted you now know; and you rise up and receive it with a grateful heart—a heart filled with gratitude. Oh, give thanks, God has given you the gift of life.

He has heard your cry; and has answered you!!! You are humbled beyond all words to express the depth of your gratefulness and thanksgiving. Your soul now burns with a longing to share the amazing knowing that is now within you.

You see a friend or a stranger; they are hurting, or suffering. You know and think, "If I could just tell them the secret of what I know and have discovered when I walked through where they are, then they could be healed and not hurt." You want that badly, for them to find the answer. You want to share the secret to all…that is what this book is written about. To give you not only hope but open your eyes to come to know Him in greater ways than you could possibly imagine, as you discover the truth; He is an amazing God…Come join me as I share truths with you, my friend.

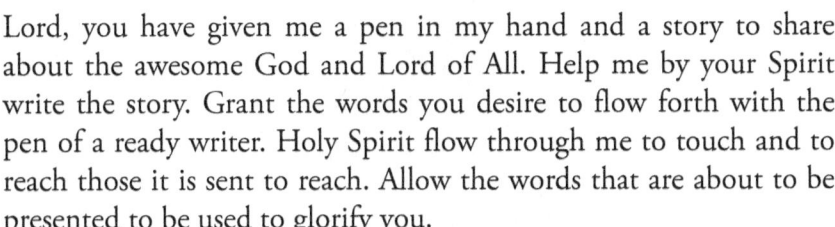

Lord, you have given me a pen in my hand and a story to share about the awesome God and Lord of All. Help me by your Spirit write the story. Grant the words you desire to flow forth with the pen of a ready writer. Holy Spirit flow through me to touch and to reach those it is sent to reach. Allow the words that are about to be presented to be used to glorify you.

The Hebrew word for "Plunder" is nasal meaning "to snatch away" (Strong's Concordance). [1] When God delivers His children, they never must simply escape, barely able to make it. Their deliverance leads to His glory in the most amazing and unimaginable ways. Uniquely it is His solution and to His glory alone.

The story I am about to share is about my plunder, the silver, the gold and the precious stones to be gathered. It is about what is meant for evil being turned to good. It is a song of triumph and discipline, deliverance and recovering that which has been stolen from me. This is not intended to tell of the seasons in humiliation, shame and self-imposed slavery but about the God who looked upon my ugliness and set this captive free.

For this reason, just as the Israelites built the tabernacle of God commanded to take back the plunder from their captors; I too shall in the following pages take my plunder back offering it back to the same God, the Ancient of Days.

---

[1] Plunder Hebrew Strong's Exhaustive Concordance 9571498

One final word before I revisit the ancient ruins of yesterday; this has not been an easy journey. Often it has been a time filled with great pain and suffering. It was a land filled with deep humiliation and shame; a depth of embarrassment I was unable to even speak about any part of it. There have been moments when I wanted to run, to hide and never to look back at any of it. Times of brokenness to the point I didn't want to go on, not even one more hour, much less a day.

Today the only place I want to run is into the arms of my loving Heavenly Father, to be near Him. He has turned my mourning into dancing and my weakness into His strength. Through all that I am about to share, He has given me peace and joy. In His love, mercy and grace my sins are forgiven and have passed away. It is a new day! Great is His faithfulness and His mercies are new every morning. My greatest desire is to share not just a story, but to help you find your way and release you from your own prison chains that hold you captive.

Let us now begin this journey. The ancient hinges groan as the door is pushed open and we begin our journey down the corridor of time. As we pass by many doors finally, we find ourselves standing in the middle of a delivery room scene. We are in the company of a young mother who appears to be in her late twenties and a young nurse who is frantically trying to remain composed as a baby's head is crowning and the doctor has not arrived. In a panic, she stopped the delivery by holding the mother's legs together, not allowing the newborn to enter this world, causing the baby to be suspended in the birth canal.

Suddenly, the surgery doors burst opened and the doctor pushed the nurse aside and began the delivery of the infant. It was born blue black and its cry was not much more than a whimper of WAA, WAA, WAA, comparable to a windup doll, stopping only to start the process over again. After several attempts as the minutes passed the infant was briefly able to be shown to the new mother and placed in an incubator and whisked away to the nursery to be attended.

Earlier in the same hospital perhaps within 24-48 hours a set of twins were born. Shortly after delivery, yet within that same window of time; the parents were told of the death of one of their newborns. With grief over the loss of the one newborn the attention was then focused on the remaining baby. In the days to come they returned home with their son. Their other baby was placed in the family cemetery only with the name "infant", no gender given. The grieving parents were told it was a boy which never was to be questioned, after all there was no reason to see for oneself their precious baby was gone, why would anyone lie about that???

There the deception began, and the switch occurred. The mother of the twins had said goodbye to her baby, believing it had died. The parents of the newborn infant with the breathing difficulties were never told it actually had died. However, she had seen the baby and deep within herself knew this was not her child, but she remained silent. This baby was important to her because it was a girl and the one thing to keep her troubled marriage together.

A name was given to the baby girl, and this began the switch to live in a family she didn't belong. The doctor signed the record book at the Board of Health using the name Diana; not the one chosen by the family the infant was going to be with. Maybe someday someone would discover the truth by the difference of first names and then question why. Perhaps he justified this as he erroneously wrote the birth family name further justifying there would be no lawsuits involved. Realizing his error he crossed out the beginning letters of her birth family name and wrote the name of the family's surname she had been given to removing her from those she rightfully belonged with. After all, he would possibly be gone before this would ever be discovered. This was the actual turn of events along with all the hospital records being destroyed in a flood.

No one knew beyond those in the hospital delivery room and silence was sworn by all to seal the truth. The truth was to be hidden away for years to come that a wrongful event had occurred by those involved in this switch and not likely ever to be found.

Many years later…I needed a birth certificate to travel to the Cayman Islands. There was not enough time to get a passport, but I could legally go with a certified birth certificate. I had a baby footprint document given by the hospital, but it was not acceptable legal proof.

Pushing the door open at the office of the Board of Health, I entered the room and began discussing with the clerk my need. Because of my interest in genealogy, I asked to see the book of birth records while I waited. At first, I was denied, and then with further discussion it was agreed upon to allow me to look with the other entries below and above my entry being covered with paper. As I began looking right to left musing over the entry information, I reviewed it all with interest. Then came the entry of my first name stunned by the realization the name was Diana, not Linda! I pushed the papers away only to discover there was no Linda, only another Diana and we were friends. Because of my discovery I discussed my identity difference with the clerk. After several minutes and a phone call or two, I accepted the incorrect document and left, allowing me to go on my trip. There wasn't anything I could do about it now before I was to leave for my trip, there was no time.

I resolved I would try to find out the answer to why the two different names. I had decided it most likely was a changing of minds after the name had been given, or something just as simple that was the reason for this issue.

Later I was to discover prior to my returning, my birth name was crossed out and "Linda" red lettered in. This action is tampering which is an illegal falsification of public records. The illegal event remains in the birth record book and the name above mine was taped out. This was discovered at the time when I returned to make legal corrections and change my name to what was actually my rightful identity. Someone knew something enough so to risk making these illegal changes.

A few weeks later, having returned from my trip, I drove to see the woman who I knew as mother. Carefully asking if she had any idea why I would have a different name in the record book than what was told to me. Immediately, she reacted, becoming extremely agitated and upset. When her husband entered the room, she continued to explode again telling him the issue. I knew then by his lack of concern and reaction he knew nothing. Just as much so that something was definitely known and not being told by her.

Several times in the months to come I made attempts to discuss this with her. Yet the time came when I made another attempt to discuss our relationship. This time however, she picked up her car keys, put on her shoes and winter coat and walked out, closing the door. I stood watching her, asking her not to go. I told her I would leave it wasn't necessary for her to leave. After all this was her home, but if she left, I wouldn't be back.

Acting as though I had never spoken a word, she turned her back and walked out, leaving me standing there. In disbelief, I watched her get into the car and back out. As she departed, I bowed my head and asked for forgiveness for her.

In the years to come, I would not see her again for many years, as the Lord instructed me to let go and not return. Ironically, I was never to see or speak to the father I was raised with again as no one contacted me to let me know of his illness. Only after his death did I know he had been ill and was gone.

GOODBYE...

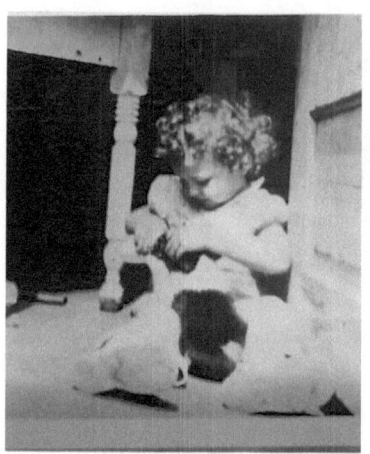

Goodbye morning glories blooming in the lane.
Goodbye to yesterday's shadows of sorrow and pain.
Goodbye to the wounded child of three or four,
Your journey of sorrow has come to an end
Your life of trust is now in the I AM who lives within.
Only precious memories of a sackcloth bleached white for your gown,
A harmonica and organ playing
"The Old Rugged Cross" are to be found.
"The Sweet Bye and Bye .... Hush Little Baby ...Don't you cry."
Your tasseled curls of silvery white
How you have grown. You are precious in my sight.
Child of God, you are my delight. I bid you now go my child.
Come follow me to that distant land.
Come follow me true life just began.[2]

Since then, the passing has occurred of the one I called mother for so many years. Once again, never was I told of her death, but left to discover that as well. Although, at two different times I did make attempts to see her and allow her the opportunity to discuss the truth with me before her passing. Because of her health, the time was not such to ever allow me any further discussion with her. I was told by her that she only wished to see family, no one else, to include visitors. The family I since knew has become hostile and there is now no further need to have conversation. I have been told I am not family, it was admitted at the end of her days.

---

[2] International Library of Poetry

Father God, we forgive those who have known the evil deeds that they do and thank you that those things hidden in darkness are exposed to the light. Into your loving hands we release all.

Gently we close the door to this ancient room as we leave those unanswered questions in the hands of the God who sees. Perhaps to yet another time and place as the echo of our footsteps rings out as we continue along our way.

Along the corridor of ancient ruins are many doors of which we will pass, leaving them for yet another day or time. Over the doors are written many names; Abuse, Sorrow, Suffering, Loss, Brokenness, Failures, Shame, Regret, Embarrassment, Humiliation, each with their own stories to tell.

Down the corridor of these ancient ruins, our attention is drawn to yet another door. Silently turning the knob, we glance up. The name above this door is "Lost and Found". There is a curiosity about this strange name as we step into this room; what can this possibly mean or what story can it possibly have to tell?

It is written that if one loses a coin, won't we go searching for it? Or if you have 100 sheep and one is missing, won't you go in search of it, leaving the 99 sheep to find the one? How much more He loves each of us. How very strange to consider leaving the 99 for just one but yet I remember the day when the Great Shepherd went looking for me.

I had just come through one of the most traumatic events of my life. I found myself searching for some meaning or something to fill the void of all that I had just lost. Sitting in the chapel with the sunshine filtering through the beautiful stained glass, I bowed my head. I knew I needed this One who was calling my name and drawing my heart to receive His love.

As a small child, I was raised mostly by a godly grandmother I adored. She too has long since gone from my life but the faded memories of the One she taught me about now are calling me and remain hidden away in my heart. Yes Lord, I come as I welcomed this One into my life. I was lost and now I am found.

In previous weeks I had walked through a devastating divorce, losing my home, my daughter moving away to school after graduation and my son temporarily remaining in his childhood home with his adopted dad. Adding insult to injury, I felt the need to leave my dog with my son to comfort him. All that mattered to me was gone.

My heart was so broken I didn't know how I was going to go on any further. So much had been so suddenly taken out of my, life resulting from the lack of a heartbeat, my entire life was to be changed from that moment of time.

Life remained difficult as the memories of each event played in my mind. The awful, painful day that was to become the beginning of the end of my marriage. A note was left for my children to find and bring to me telling of his leaving. It was our wedding anniversary day, how very cruel. The end of the marriage came as did attack upon attack until I was emotionally almost destroyed.

The memories of that day would flood back and hold me as a captive. Would I ever be able to move past the time when the one I loved so greatly was changed before my eyes as death came suddenly near? Memories flash back in my mind as I recalled that day. My husband came in the living room and said he felt dizzy. I looked up at his ashen face and told him to lie down and I would take his pulse. No, that couldn't be right, 39 beats. I glanced up at him and told him I was going to take it again; I had miscounted. As I looked up a second time, I was just in time to see his eyes roll back and hear the air leave his lungs. He was gone!!! I yelled at my daughter who was watching all of this telling her to get help. I ran for the phone as she ran to the neighbors.

Before the ambulances arrived, I returned to his side. His jaws had locked, and I kept calling his name over and over again, firmly patting his face, trying to get a response. Our dog was trying to get to him and as I would push him away, suddenly I knew the death angel had entered the room. The room turned cold and clammy and our dog began running frantically through the house and then back to us.

Finally, the arrival of the ambulance! By then my husband's lips were blue black and he was cold and still no pulse was to be found. I stepped away as the attendants started checking him, but never doing anything to try to get a heartbeat.

A second ambulance attendant arrived and as they came up on the porch and saw what was happening, I heard one say to the other, "He is gone. Do you want to go or wait?" They decided to wait, not realizing I was his wife and heard all that was spoken between them.

They assisted in loading him into the ambulance rear and I took the front seat. Astonishingly enough, as we were near arrival at the hospital, suddenly, my husband began to regain consciousness. Repeatedly, as he tried to sit up, he would ask, "Where am I?" The attendant told him he was en route to the hospital and to lie back down. By the time we arrived, he was back to a normal conscious state.

No explanation could be found for what had just happened. He was admitted and the next day a cardiologist examined him and ran some tests. I determined I should wait to check in later at home on the children and stay with him. As I sat in the lobby waiting for the tests to be completed, the doors exploded open. Then a gurney was rushing by when suddenly I realized it was my husband! He had coded. His heart stopped during tests and they were rushing him to the intensive care unit. After hours of waiting, he was transported to Indianapolis Hospital and remained for over 6 weeks in critical condition.

He finally received a pacemaker and was permitted to come home. Somehow, he was different; the loving, close marriage and devoted husband had changed. He had transformed into a cold and indifferent person. The change was like an angry Jekyll and Hyde personality.

Finally, months changed to three years and the distance became greater as time passed. I denied it by saying it was his heart and that he would get better, in total denial of that not happening. My life spiraled downhill as our marriage ended. I moved to the town I had previously lived in, letting my son remain while I tried to find work and adjust to the changes and losses. Little did I realize the turn of events that were to come and what the new normal was to become.

Spring turned to summer and then fall was upon us and it was drawing time for school to begin. I was struggling to find work and did not know where I would end up living. Reluctantly, the decision to let my son remain in his childhood home was made.

I prayed and prayed for an answer and help. I was forced to sell my little house I had only recently bought and rent from a friend. Finally, a door opened for work. As I began working, I had to go to school for training out of state for window design besides the diploma I already held.

Life was spiraling out of control. I would cry until there were no tears left and fall asleep as I kneeled in prayer. Over and again I would say, "Jesus if I could just touch you, I believe whatever is wrong you would heal me." I would see myself crawling on hands and knees always reaching, trying to touch the hem of His garment. I just believed He would do that for me.

In agonizing emotional pain, I would work, coming in late and exhausted. Working was the only time I would stop crying. Gone was the time of hoping my son would be with me. The hope of change coming forth had now been taken from me. The pain was so great, I was dropping excessive weight as I grieved all that had been taken from my life. I just wanted it to end. I knew I couldn't go on this way, yet I didn't know what was happening to me. I couldn't stop crying, I was heartbroken.

It finally came to a point I would say, "Here he is Lord." And I would try to release my son, who represented the last emotional thing I had to hold on to. Then I would pull him back from The Lord. This emotional pain went on for almost three years until finally one night looking across the table at my son, I gave him to the Lord in my heart and I knew I meant it. I couldn't go on the way things were.

A dead calm entered my heart, I knew at last it was over. I let go and gave him to the Lord. This was in late January and the days passed on. Only this time I never tried to take him back but at long last released him into the hands of the Lord in a total surrender.

I continued to work, but now the tears had ended and were replaced by numbness. I remember sitting in the church I attended when the Pastor ask to have the song "Unfailing Love"[3] sung. As the song began, I suddenly felt the presence of Jesus standing immediately in front of me. I sensed what felt like a river of current flowing through my body. As the words were sung "Unfailing love, unfailing love, He touched my soul". Suddenly I felt the heat of Jesus' touch as He began touching my soul as I literally felt the entire inward area of my chest moving as though being knitted and kneaded, double my fist in size. As the song ended, so did the healing. No more crying, no more pain, only the peace of the Lord remained.

In the fall, I was to take my son to college to begin his first semester. After hugging him and telling him I loved him and goodbyes were said, he turned and walked away while I got into the car. As I started to back away, I realized I almost forgot to look back to watch as he crossed the campus.

---

[3] Unfailing Love source: Musixmatch

With the healing came a shield that covers my heart so that things of this world hit and bounce off, and things of His Kingdom will go beneath the shield. That remains so even to this day.

As we turn to depart from this room of Lost and Found, I leave you with these thoughts. Letting go of those we love comes with great cost but remember God knows, He let go of His Son for us. Many changes have come to my life since that time, but the unforgettable truth of Jesus as a healing Jesus remains with me as clearly as the day when He touched me. We can trust Him and can let go and He is faithful to heal us in His time and His unfailing love. It doesn't always come in the way we want but He will never leave or forsake us. Because of these things you can trust Him with those you love and walk on with Him.

The echoes of our footsteps ring out in the Ancient Ruins as we turn to walk down the corridor. The door quietly closes, leaving these great sorrows behind. The lessons of trusting and letting go of those we love and leaving them in His hands remain fresh in my heart even to this day.

Mark 5:24-34 (NIV)

24 So Jesus went with him. A large crowd followed and pressed around him. 25 And a woman was there who had been subject to bleeding for twelve years. 26 She had suffered a great deal under the care of many doctors and had spent all she had, yet instead of getting better she grew worse. 27 When she heard about Jesus, she came up behind him in the crowd and touched his cloak, 28 because she thought, "If I just touch his clothes, I will be healed." 29 Immediately her bleeding stopped and she felt in her body that she was freed from her suffering. 30 At once Jesus realized that power had gone out from him. He turned around in the crowd and asked, "Who touched my clothes?" 31 "You see the people crowding against you," his disciples answered, 'and yet you can ask, 'Who touched me?' 32 But Jesus kept looking around to see who had done it. 33 Then the woman, knowing what had happened to her, came and fell at his feet and, trembling with fear, told him the whole truth. 34 He said to her, "Daughter, your faith has healed you. Go in peace and be freed from your suffering.

Should you find yourself in a similar place in your life with great assurance I can tell you beyond any shadow of doubt this truth; Jesus loves you and He will come to you at His appointed time. Never give up but continue to hold on to His unchanging hand.

There are many lessons to be learned in the most painful and difficult places of your life. Keep your focus on God and during your trouble sing praises to His name yes, I know you don't feel like praising but just do it! This will release the power and presence of God to move in your life as you trust Him with your sacrifice of praise.

Once more we resume our journey as we walk on. In the distance from this door we pass by many doors and events in the Ancient Ruins. At long last we come to a door; its name is Eternity. The light inside this door is brilliant with light radiating all about. As we enter this room, we remain standing there looking about as our eyes adjust to the brightness. This room holds shelves filled with many books, all with varied titles. As we scan the many titles a few that we see are Shepherd, Deliverance, Truths, Courage, Faithful, Sorrow, Suffering, Shame, Provider, Righteousness to name a few. I stood looking for a special book amid the many titles. While searching my eyes are drawn to the book Remembrance. Ahh! Yes, this is the book we must look at.

As I begin to open its pages my attention is immediately drawn to these writings that I am about to share. How very well I remember this time. Let us sit down and read these writings and prepare to glean all of the lessons to be learned and how to find the hand of God in the midst of our troubles. Lessons filled with teachings of who He is and the faithfulness of God. Let us begin this story now.

SO BEGAN THE JOURNEY

So began the journey. A winter storm began to arrive in north central Indiana as I started to leave the house. As I prepared to back out, I was impressed to text my daughter, telling her I loved her. The thought occurred to me how important it is to tell those we love that we do love them…you never know!

After a brief stop to purchase some winter boots, the clerk had several difficulties placing the order. He and his manager struggled, both frustrated because of delaying me. As we talked, I told them not to worry about it; sometimes God causes delays to protect us.

After driving for a short distance, the sleet and snow had begun to pick up intensity. A Semi and SUV had slid off into the median. As I continued driving, I prayed for their needs. Minutes down the highway, perhaps a mile or two, I looked over to the north bound lanes as I watched with alarm. I realized a white pickup truck was entering into the median.

No time to react and nowhere to go! Without any doubt, I was going to hit the vehicle head-on as his truck shot out in front of me, I couldn't avoid him. I cried out," No God! No! Help me!!!"

I was lying slid down in the front seat in the corner of the driver seat, pushed against the door, half under the steering wheel. No air would enter my lungs. No sound would come forth from my mouth. In my mind I called out, "Jesus, help me!!! I can't breathe!!!" Repeatedly, I cried out as I was coming to the end of consciousness, I asked the Lord… "is this the end???" Slowly like that of a tire with a slow leak, air began to enter my lungs.

As I looked about, I saw my arm was extended into the passenger seat. My bone was sticking out. As I slowly moved my way toward my hand it was obvious it was completely separated away from the rest of my arm, connected only by flesh. As I began to reach with my left hand to move my arm to my lap when clearly these words entered my mind, "Diana, be very careful you have shattered bones wrapped around veins and arteries and you could bleed out."

Carefully, I began to lift my hand and move it into my lap. As I lifted and moved my arm slowly, the thought occurred to me, and I asked, "God, how will I know if I am bleeding out, will I just be gone???"

I arrived at the hospital in critical condition. My heart rate was bradycardia with my heart rate dropping to the twenties (20s) then accelerating in excess of 180 beats per minute. My heart remained in this condition for several hours to come. As soon as I was stabilized, I was taken to Indianapolis, although, due to the weather I was transported via ambulance where for the next several days I remained in intensive care with a Trauma Team of twelve doctors working to stabilized me.

My journey has included a broken back, a crushed sternum, all my ribs but two broken, a compound fracture with two plates and a strap attaching my hand to my arm. Additionally, there was a tear in my right shoulder, cervical damages, nerve damages to my hands and spine, a bruised kidney and liver.

As I laid on the Edge of Eternity, I sensed lying in the palm of His hand as I grasped His finger, the faithfulness of God hearing my cry. My question for you is, do you know in your time of trouble who you are going to call upon for help??? Do you know that you know the answer to this question????

Quietly we walk out into the light, away from the ancient ruins. Let us set to the side all of this and allow me the opportunity to share beyond these writings some of the plunder that is to be taken as some of the greatest lessons have come forth in knowing God because of these life experiences. These are truths that I personally could never have known had I not walked through the valley of the shadow of death.

Nor could I have known had I not entered the valley of sorrow and suffering that literally broke my heart, shattering it into a million pieces, filling me with grief. This includes finding I didn't belong and heart break from all the losses including knowing who I really am. My natural family has yet to be discovered but who I am in Christ Jesus has been the greatest discovery and plunder that no one can possibly take from me.

Romans 8:38-39 (KJV)

38 For I am persuaded, that neither death, nor life, nor angels, nor principalities, nor powers, nor things present, nor things to come, 39 Nor height, nor depth, nor any other creature, shall be able to separate us from the love of God, which is in Christ Jesus our Lord.

MIRRORS OF THE SOUL
International Library of Poetry

WHO AM I?
Diana Lynn Rogers

Who am I Lord, but a piece of clay?
Molded and shaped, being created new each day?
Who am I that you should care, even to the numbers of my hair?
Who am I that you should send your beloved Son
That His blood would cover my sins?
Who am I Lord that the Holy Spirit would dwell within?
How can it be, that in your infinite love and wisdom for me?
That even in my most unloveliness you love and care for me?

Who am I Lord? I am unworthy even to speak your name.
Yet you have granted me mercy and grace to forgive and forget the past.
Who am I Lord that you would touch and heal my broken heart?
You in your holiness and purity would touch me,
Give me a new name and grant me a new start.

Lord I cannot grasp the infinite wisdom,
Nor know your ways.
But to this I am committed and do know,
Where you lead, I will follow all of my days.
My heart doth sing, I love you Lord,
Whither thou wilt go, there also will I go.[4]

OVERCOMER

Overcomers[5] are followers of Christ who successfully resist the power and temptation of the world's system. An Overcomer, is not sinless but holds fast to faith in Christ until the end. He does not turn away when times get difficult or become an apostate, requires complete dependence upon God for direction, purpose, fulfillment, and strength to follow His plan for our lives (Proverbs 3:5–6; 2 Corinthians 12:9 (KJV).

The Greek word most often translated "overcomer" stems from the word "nike" which, according to Strong's Concordance, means "to carry off the victory. [6]The verb implies a battle." The Bible teaches Christians to recognize that the world is a battleground, not a playground. God does not leave us defenseless. Ephesians 6:10-24(KJV) describes the armor of the Lord available to all believers. Scattered throughout this narrative is the admonition to "stand firm." Sometimes all it takes to overcome temptation is to stand firm and refuse to be dragged into it. James 4:7(KJV)says, "Resist the devil and he will flee from you."

An overcomer is one who resists sin no matter what lures Satan uses.

---

[4] International Library of Poetry
[5] Overcomers http://spoke -word-church.com @Spoke BibleStudy.com
[6] Strong's Concordance Overcome

Lessons to be learned as an Overcomer

1. Fixed focus on Christ Jeremiah 29:13.
2. Letting go and trust in God as you exchange your strength for His. Not by might, nor power, but by His Spirit...Zech. 4:6(KJV)
3. Recognize God is in control of all situations He allows or permits. Isa: 41:10 (KJV)
4. All things work to the good. Romans 8:28(KJV)
5. Lord is my Shepherd Ps 23(KJV)
6. Give thanks and praise Proverbs 4(KJV)
7. Not my might nor power Zach 4:6(KJV)
8. Yield and surrender Ps. 37:7 (KJV)
9. The power of prayer. John 14:13-14 (KJV)
10. Finding the gold. Job 23:10(KJV)
11. Come out from among them. 2 Cor. 6:17 (KJV)
12. More than conquerors. Roman 8:37(KJV)
13. Confront the situation and apply the word. 2 Sam 22-19(KJV)
14. All things are possible! Only Believe! Mark 5:35-36 (KJV)
15. Praise in adversity releases Gods power. Heb.13:15 (KJV) Sacrifice of praise.

Some of my most life changing lessons taught me by the hand of God have been because of the head-on wreck. For this reason, I would like to begin at that point of time and share with you the lessons of coming to know Him during this time.

After being in a drug induced coma for the biggest part of a week, I was brought to consciousness. I have very little recall, but I do remember the incredible bright lights of eternity and loving hands that surrounded me. Much later it was revealed to me in a flashback that I was in eternity.

I was placed in a full body brace while remaining on oxygen with my right arm in a soft cast and splint. Several hours passed before I was stabilized and ready to transport. I was moved from the Trauma Center via ambulance to the Rehabilitation Hospital.

In the coming days, I was to remain in this condition with limited ability to turn or stand or do anything on my own without assistance of a nurse. During the night hours, I would ask that my drapes were to be opened that I might lay looking out into the heavens. I always had a great awareness of God being near me at all times. I sensed laying in the palm of His loving hand and holding onto His finger as He watched over me.

The time came when I began therapy twice daily. On the days when the pain was so intense I could barely function, I began a process of counting my blessings. When I was working out and alone on the equipment, I would sing songs to the Lord as I worked out. I continually was aware and sensed His nearness and presence. I would reflect on His words to me and promise to "never leave or forsake me". I would recall the precious gentle voice when I heard his audible voice and the love in it. During the night hours, the Lord would send to my room nurses from all parts of the hospital so I could talk to them and tell them to be ready for eternity.

The time arrived when I was to be transported to see my Orthopedic Surgeon, then later appointments to see the Brain and Spine doctors. The weekend prior to the appointment a friend was to visit. Because of the winter storms and work my daughter had been unable to visit this entire time. I had what I came to call my uniform to wear which consisted of two sets of hospital pants, and two T-shirts given to me to wear under my brace sporting the brace company logo. (This was totally laughable as I was very much into fashion and clothing. I now laugh with God at the vanity and self-importance as He humbled and stripped away the layers.)

This particular evening Indianapolis was hosting the Super Bowl and my friend got turned around making it impossible for her come to see me as a result of the heavy traffic. I wasn't worried about it at all as I had decided I would wrap up in a blanket since my coat and all my clothing had been cut off of me in the ER. And I could wear my uniform as normal and socks to cover my feet. I would be fine.

In the evening, my night nurse came and was talking to me, asking about what happened with my friend; I laughed and told her. We said our goodnights after discussing my situation. She was off the next two days. Monday came, while during my shower time I heard the rustling of paper while I was showering. The same nurse called out telling me she was there, and she would be back after signing onto duty.

Before she returned to help me dry and dress, I saw the three bags sitting on the vanity. Finally, I was able to reach them to see what was in them. Inside the bag were tennis shoes, a sweat suit, and in the last bag a winter coat. God had provided for me and I hadn't even asked!!! That night as I lay in my bed, I considered all that had taken place. His words in Matthew Chapter 6 flooded my soul.

Matt: 6:25-28 (KJV) Therefore, I say unto you, take no thought for your life, what ye shall eat, or what ye shall drink; nor yet for your body, what ye shall put on. Is not the life more than meat, and the body than raiment?

Behold the fowls of the air: for they sow not, neither do they reap, nor gather into barns; yet your heavenly Father feedeth them. Are ye not much better than they? Which of you by taking thought can add one cubit unto his stature? And why take ye thought for raiment? Consider the lilies of the field, how they grow; they toil not, neither do they spin: And yet I say unto you, that even Solomon in all his glory was not arrayed like one of these.

Consider the lily of the field, it doesn't toil or spin and the fowl of the air our Heavenly Father knows our every need and care. Praise God for His loving care and faithfulness.

DAYS OF PLUNDER

Each step of the way He has shown His faithfulness. Provisions came forth one after another, never early but always just at the point of need. Each and every need was met. From the necessity to have an attorney, to the Rehabilitation Hospital I now laid in as well as Doctors and Surgeons, my every need was met.

When it came time to move once again, in split second timing, the need was met. Only days before had I began walking with assistance. My daughter arrived and transported me to my next stop along my journey.

I was taken to Wynnfield Crossing Assisted Living, where I was to be near family and was to remain for three months. Again, in perfect time I was to move to a rental property with the assistance of a local realtor. How thankful I was to have her assistance as the need was not one, I could do on my own.

The day came when I moved to what was to become home for me. The weeks turned to months as I had been able to get a car and drive myself to therapy in Kokomo. My cast had been removed and at long last my body brace was. Then therapy and traction began to recover use of both of my hands and body strength as the entire core of my body had collapsed because of the spine and rib fractures.

My days for the next year were spent mostly sleeping both day and night as my body recovered. One day at a time, one step at a time. When not sleeping, I began studying and reading my Bible for hours as I had strength to do so. Some of the most critical times as I passed through all of this were teaching me to fix my focus on God. My days became filled with praise and giving thanks unto Him. Continually I surrounded myself with praise and worship music, mostly instrumental.

Many times, I was to be asked why I thought this happened to me, or wasn't I mad it happened? The answer to this is simple because it pleased Him. Lessons to be learned aren't always apparent when we are in the midst of our troubles and distresses. The one thing I can assure you, if you dig in the ashes of these situations you will find where the fire lily grows; and out of it you can and will come to know God in amazing ways. You will discover life lessons of His faithfulness and how very trustworthy He is. You will learn to know Him as your Shepherd and provider, ever present help in times of trouble and He will become your strength I am only giving you but a few of my own experiences of coming closer to Him and knowing Him in ways I never could have without these trials.

Romans 8:28(KJV) And we know that all things work together for good according to them that love God, to them who are the called according to His purposes.

This doesn't state anything about life being easy or you will never suffer, contrary to popular opinions that are misguided into believing that the life of a Christian is easy. This isn't true. Every sorrow as well as every suffering is not lost in the teachings of God.

Matt: 16:24 (KJV) Then said Jesus unto his disciples, if any man will come after me, let him deny himself, and take up his cross, and follow me.

His Word states, we are to deny ourselves, pick up our cross and follow Him. He went to Calvary for our sins. Are you willing to let go and follow Him???

Some of my greatest growth has come through this last three and half years of pain and suffering. I have passed through some of the most excruciating sufferings I have ever known where it took every ounce of my strength to move, walk or stand. Yet, although I wouldn't want to repeat this ever again, I would never want to have missed all of the ways I have learned to know God.

I'm not someone who especially likes being hurt or tortured in some strange way. I do know that this has most assuredly stopped my life, putting it on complete hold, not only to teach me to know Him and

His ways but also for the privilege to share with you, as you read these pages.

We all have choices in life and when you come to a place in your life that makes no sense or you don't understand the why, don't ever give up but look up and trust the Lord. My prayer is for you to discover the lesson He has for you, as you read my journey.

Proverb 3:5-6(NAS) Trust in the Lord with all of your heart, and do not lean upon your own understanding. In all your ways acknowledge Him and He will make your path straight.

Trust is often not an easy thing to learn, and it comes with the companions of suffering and sorrow accompanied by patience and waiting. This isn't something we want to hear as we are spoiled and taught often to give it to the Lord, and it will be alright. In our presumption, we think it means now.

LETTING GO

Letting go of my son and learning to trust God was one of the greatest tests that I was to face. I loved my son. I really thought something would change and I would be able to have him with me. I just believed God would help me, and He did, just not in the way I thought He should answer.

The way for me was to surrender my son, my only son; to let go and trust God. I held on clutching to my desire to have my son with me as if I was clinging to a 220 wire and unable to release it. Emotionally I knew I was going to see my daughter move away to school, so I had learned to accept that. I had even somewhat accepted the end of my marriage after three years of struggle to keep it glued together. But my last emotional hold I grasped onto was my son. I have shared my experience in letting go and trusting God; how He touched and healed me. I must tell you it came with great suffering and brokenness. Any parent who has lost a child or found themselves grieved by the loss of someone whom they loved can identify. Allow me to tell you I understand and know the pain of loss, but I also know the answer, and that lies in trusting God. I don't write these words lightly, nor do I not know how very difficult it is to let go. I took me months and months to finally come to brokenness to the point of not being sure I could go on another day.

With great assurance, I can tell you to trust the Lord with those we love is the only decsion will make a difference to you and allow you to move forward from the suffering. He will not fail you, trust Him. I will also tell you, getting it from our head and actually, knowing it in our hearts is a very difficult journey. It is well worth the pain to find the answer and know it for yourself. Once you know it nothing can take it from you. Healing may not come in the way that mine came yet it will come forth. When we lay our Isaac down, we have one who will "never leave or forsake you." Hebrew 13:6 (KJV) is a promise and an absolute you can cling to with all of your heart. Our loving Heavenly Father gave us His Only Son. He knows our pain. If you can't trust the One who died for us, who can you trust????

SWITCHED

At the time of my discovery of being switched I would ask God over and again, "Who am I??? Did my mother just not want me???" Why??? A thousand times over the thoughts entered my mind as I grasped to find understanding. Nights I would wake up crying and talking to God about it all.

There was no one to turn to but the Lord. My family had been removed from my life and all of my self-identity taken from me as well. During those painful days came the awareness I had only one I could trust and turn to. Realization began to take hold I belonged to God and no one could take Him from me I was His child. To His hand I clung, I would see myself climbing up onto His lap and being held in His loving embrace.

Romans 8:38-39 (KJV) For I am persuaded that neither death, nor life, nor angels, nor principalities, nor powers, nor things present, nor things to come, nor height, nor depth. Nor any other creature, shall be able to separate us from the love of God, which is in Christ Jesus, our Lord.

These are not words to me written in a book. These are the very essence of life I cling to then and now. Nothing can separate us from the love of God or tear us away from Christ. We will always have the choice and decision to choose our way.

Anyone who may read this and has found themselves stripped of their identity or who has been abandoned, rejected, orphaned or adopted; hear me well. This is a truth. Let no one be allowed to remove this truth from you ever. It is an anchor in every storm. This is your hiding place to run to when those who are supposed to love, care and watch over you fail.

During this time of discovery there is a scripture which was given to me and I want to give to you. May it comfort and keep you in your times of trouble as greatly as it has me.

Isaiah 43:1:4 (NAS) 1 But now thus saith the Lord your Creator, O Jacob, and He formed you, O Israel, "Do not fear, for I have redeemed you; I have called you by name; you are Mine!

2 When you pass through the waters, I will be with you; and through the rivers, they will not overflow you: when you walk through the fire, you will not be scorched; nor will the flame burn you.

3 For I am the LORD thy God, the Holy One of Israel, your Savior: I have given Egypt as your ransom, Cush and Seba in your place.

4 Since you are precious in My sight, since you are honored, and I love you, I will give other men in your place, and other peoples in exchange for your life.

FIXED FOCUS

The following are Lessons learned in gaining a fixed focus. When you focus your heart, mind and soul on the Lord it is critically important as that is where you gain your strength in God.

Zechariah 4:6 (NIV) So he said to me, "This is the word of the Lord to Zerubbabel, 'Not by might, nor by power, but by my spirit,' says the Lord Almighty.

1. As you focus on the Lord you will gain His perspective and the mind of Christ as you pray for wisdom and seek understanding.
2. Pressures will lessen as you focus on the Lord and His truths concerning your present situation.
3. Fear of loss or change will begin to fade away as you begin to find your peace as you continue to focus.
4. As you focus on the Lord, if you will begin to praise Him and count your blessings, giving thanks for all He has done. Soon you will find yourself entering His rest.

John 16:33(KJV) These things I have spoken unto you, that in me ye might have peace. In the world ye shall have tribulation: but be of good cheer; I have overcome the world.

With each trial that comes your way the quicker you can learn to develop the habit to keep your eyes upon the Lord and not look upon your circumstances; no matter how overwhelming they may be. The quicker you are able to overcome, withstanding fear and dread of what may happen; you realize that God is able to do exceedingly and abundantly beyond your need or situation.

AVOIDING CONFRONTATION

1. Many times, we create walls or barriers not allowing others to see through us. At times, we may be guilty of projection of our faults on others.
2. Acquiescence is when we give in to avoid facing the truth of our feelings, attitude, or behavior.
3. By lying we hide our guilt to be more acceptable and loveable.
4. Conformity is a cover to allow ourselves to blend in rather than to run the risk of being rejected when in truth we want to be acceptable.
5. Reliance and dependence upon others doesn't work. Striving to meet the need on your own will not work. You must shift your focus off yourself onto God.

ANXIETY

1. Anxiety comes in self-striving. It causes you to think too much about wrong things, self-desires, efforts, and concerns.
2. Depression comes from a sense of failure or a desire unmet.

Philippians 4:6-7(NAS) Be anxious for nothing, but in everything by prayer and supplication, with thanksgiving, let your requests be made known to God; and the peace of God, which surpasses all understanding, will guard your hearts and minds through Christ Jesus.

James 1:5-8 (KJV) instructs us to ask God for wisdom who will freely give it to us. James also tells us to ask in faith, not going back and forth in the question or we will become tossed about like a wave on the sea. We will become driven by the wind.

Matthew 14 writes of Peter, who was found walking on the water along with Jesus. The instant his focus was broken, and he looked about Peter began to sink.

As you bring your troubles before the Lord and become transparent in all of your concerns, you will become less self-focused and more kingdom focused. Stability comes in the presence of the Lord. An interesting thing when you stand in two different places you will become unstable and unable to receive. You can have what you say. If hell can get you in agreement by your words, there is power in your words. It isn't only about your believing but what you say. There is life and death in the tongue (see Proverbs 18:21 KJV). It is a proven fact whatever you say goes out into the universe and continues without end.

During each step of my journey attacks have come in a variety of unending ways. There have been multiple attempts to try to get me to move in my own self-efforts. The flaming darts have assailed me to get me to react, to huddle in agreement in fear, doubt, temptations, anxieties, anything to cause confusion. Darts are meant to try to get me to take the situation or need into my own hands, rather than to trust God for the need or situation.

There have been times of false accusations accusing me of disobedience and not hearing from God to cause me to take the problem on my own. Many times, there may be friends who love and mean well but just need to give you a word. Most of the time God's way versus common sense and logical ways are entirely different.

Be careful in the counselors you are hearing from. Carefully and prayerfully take it before the Lord. Let the Word of God act like a filter to any word given to you. Let His Word and His peace guide your steps.

There have been many harsh lessons learned, but well worth the pain and disappointments to come to know the truth and surrender and yield to God's way.

Prov.3:5-69(NAS) Trust in the Lord with all your heart and do not lean to your own understanding. In all your ways acknowledge Him and he will make your paths straight.

We have been taught to do-it-yourself and along with the independence of self-sufficiency is the way we are to walk through our life's journey. Yet in all of this, God repeatedly teaches by example and the written Word. The pattern in following God is to deny ourselves and pick up our cross and follow Him.

Our success is not going to happen by self-efforts and ways. Watchman Nee, in his writings of the soul's release describing it as a bean that has a hard-outer shell and with each blow, the shell slowly begins to crack until it releases the inward part of the bean. Such as it is with our souls as God, blow by blow, begins to break away the things of this world from our life and allow our souls to be released.

COME OUT FROM AMONG THEM

II Corinthians: 6:17(KJV) Wherefore come out from among them, and be ye separate, saith the Lord, and touch not the unclean thing; and I will receive you.

Gal.5:1(KJV) Stand fast therefore in the liberty wherewith Christ hath made us free and be not entangled again with the yoke of bondage.

Recently, I was asked the question by a fellow Christian concerning bondages and captivity of believers. Yes, I do believe it is possible to be in bondage and still be a Christian. Although many Christians are reluctant to admit it, they still struggle with hidden areas of their life. Much of captivity comes from childhood trauma or victimization, various yokes of bondage or generational curses. These are not immediately dealt with but are exposed in layers. Many children of God have fought the battle of a wounded child and will have cycled patterns of sexual sins, homosexuality, and fear of men (women) as a direct result of child abuse. They will find themselves unable to love people or their spouse. They may find themselves involved in a pattern of lying or some other form of dishonesty or cycle of behavior.

Some will be critical or judgmental or have issues of anger, either toward their parents, God or some other offender. These all are believers who have found Christ, yet the battle continues. It may be any number of issues to include depression, doubt, discouragement, loneliness or a chronic lack of satisfaction.

Many of the issues of the wounded child are intertwined with the one who is abusing. They have suffered by similar encounters as a child and it is being handed down from one generation to another either directly or linked into the family history. It may not be the parent but the grandparent, etc.

As God begins dealing with the issues of our life and puts us on the infamous potter's wheel, we begin to confront truths. As Watchman Nee describes, our soul begins to be released with each turn of the wheel as the Master Potter reshapes and restores life to become what we were designed and created to be.

As we yield and surrender our will and release our control, yielding to God's will and way, steadily and continually, the chains are broken. The former becomes released and as Isaiah 61 (KJV) states it, Christ came to set the captive free.

Isaiah 61:1-4 (NAS) The Spirit of the Lord God is upon me, because the Lord has anointed me to bring good news to the afflicted; He has sent me to bind up the brokenhearted, to proclaim liberty to the captives and freedom to prisoners; 2 to proclaim the favorable year of the Lord, and the day of vengeance of our God; to comfort all who mourn; 3 to grant to those who mourn in Zion, giving them a garland instead of ashes; the oil of gladness instead of mourning, a mantle of praise instead of a spirit of fainting; that they may be called oaks of righteousness, the planting of the Lord, that He may be glorified. 4 Then they will rebuild the ancient ruins, they will raise up the former devastations, and they will repair the ruined cities, the desolation of many generations.

This isn't an easy process and it will take your deciding you're tired of living the same pattern over and again, always ending in failure. I know, because I struggled through many areas of my life to come through to the end of the former and break free from all those painful, humiliating and shameful issues in my own life. I can tell you this, it is well worth the struggles to be set free! But God!!!!

Should you fall down, get up immediately, repent, seek God's forgiveness and move on. Never, never stay down; you are not defeated. It is only a temporary setback. God will meet you right where you are. Don't even consider letting it rest for a day. It is too easy to slip off the pathway and wander away. God is big enough to handle your failure and His love and mercy are able to get you right back on track. Run to your Heavenly Father!

Remember, the very things you are struggling with now are the very things God will use to help others to be set free. There is no lesson more powerful than when you know with certainty it is true. Whether it is a lesson concerning the reality of your healing, or your deliverance and being set free. God's Word states, 'What the Son sets free is free indeed"! We all have choices and decisions to make. I know that I know, and it is my desire that you experience God in these areas as well.

The enemy brings things to our minds to break our focus. Busyness and distractions of all kinds, even church activities are things that take us away from our time alone with God. The lack of quiet time spent with God is the root of all failure and the struggle to find time is often difficult, and one must become desperate to find it.

HIS MIGHT AND POWER

Ephesians: 6:10(NAS) finally, my brethren, be strong in the Lord, and in the power of his might.

In other words, our strength and keeping from failure is in His might, not our independence and own strength.

Zechariah 4:6 (KJV) Then he answered and spake unto me, saying, this is the word of the Lord unto Zerubbabel, saying, Not by might, nor by power, but by my spirit, saith the Lord of hosts.

I have always been an, "I can do that!" kind of person. One area the Lord has taught me during my recovery from my wreck has been lessons in self-effort, while learning to lean on Him and not do things in my own strength.

If I expect to gain victory over the enemy I must learn to lean on the Lord and trust His ways to lead me by His Spirit. This is a learning curve is difficult to yield and surrender for most all. The letting go of control of one's life and yielding to the Holy Spirit to direct our steps isn't easy. But here is the thing, we aren't actually in control at all. God's sovereign hand moves continually about us. The very things we grasp tightly to may be the very things can become idols and separate us from the love of God.

With each issue, as God has brought to my attention areas He desired to cleanse, change and heal, these areas have required my yielding to Him. Yielding and surrendering to His will and way has ultimately brought the power of God into the situation and then the complete deliverance and closure from the issue.

I have learned in coming to know God that as I trust Him, I surrender my will. In my feeble efforts to make things happen in what I think is best; I have discovered His way far exceeded my expectations and brought success in ways I hadn't begun to consider as a possibility.

Transferring our control and releasing to His way is a process, and easy to fall back into the bad habit of self-reliance as we struggle in our daily walk and issues. God has given us free will and choice. However, when you receive and do His will and way you divert many hurts, failures, and heartbreaks. You can stumble around in the dark or you can allow God to direct your paths. This is your choice. He will not force His way upon you. However, don't blame God when you have bruised knees and skinned elbows because you thought you could do this without His help! Sadly enough, the rebellion in your heart grieves the Holy Spirit. Unfortunately, it isn't as simple as "Oops, I blew it!" but a serious issue of the matters of your heart.

As difficult as it is to sometimes wait, better to tarry an hour longer and know the way of the Lord than to find yourself standing alone. Obedience is a step by step learning process. Not every circumstance or person who comes to you is sent by God. The enemy uses every opportunity that he can to distract and break your focus.

I have discovered the sense of urgency, feeling that I should do it right now, and most pressure is not of God. An experience I was taught early on in my walk happened as I was looking for an apartment having been transferred to the Indianapolis area to work. I really had no information to go on, but I needed to move soon. I visited an apartment complex and there was an apartment available. Uniquely enough, a man came in as I was talking with the salesperson and it became a do it right now decision. I sensed pressure with it, and decided to wait, knowing if God desired for me to have it would be there when I returned. I lost the chance for the apartment, only to learn months later someone in that very apartment was shot in a robbery situation. We can always trust Him! He will not fail you or let you miss what He has for you. He will gently nudge you along as the Shepherd does his sheep. When you know God says do it, then move and move now!

YIELDING AND SURRENDERING

Earlier I shared my healing and how it did not occur until I yielded and surrendered emotionally to let go and trust God for the outcome. This lesson has been tested in various ways. Will I let go or hold on to something important to me even if it means I may lose it? Can I trust God to provide for me?

Line upon line the tests have come forth. When the time came to purchase my little cottage house, I really liked and needed the next step to move forward. As I continued to seek His way, I sensed guidance to let go after having placed a deposit on the property. I knew it was possible to lose the deposit I had given yet I was determined to obey. After several weeks, I felt released to return to the seller. Now I write from the little cottage I call home.

Each yield and surrender that has happened along the way has always come with the check of my heart requiring me to release and trust the Lord. There have been situations that have challenged my trust in God and whether I would do it myself or wait in obedience. I have learned over and again that the walk of self-denial is always a dying of my desires and yielding to the Holy Spirit.

It isn't necessarily something that is a popular thing. The truth is, it isn't intended to be pleasing, but rather choosing to die to self to gain in Christ.

When you keep your focus on Christ not the immediate circumstances you will succeed.

Unrest and anxieties prevent or hinder God's working on our behalf.
1. Never act until these three things agree with each other:
    a) When you sense an impulse or desire to decide. Pray.
    b) Look for the Word of God to direct you.

    c) Then as circumstances move, watch for doors to open or close.

Although there are many wonderful opportunities that will open along the way, the time spent alone with God is critical. We will fail if we don't take that time and as a result, do things in our own strength.

2. Self-efforts, self-denial, self-sufficing, and independence draw us away from obedience to God. To deny ourselves and to lay down our desires will cross the very nature of the flesh
3. Frustration can easily slip in as we shift our focus off Christ to the issue we are dealing with. Immediately adjust your focus away from the problem and onto the Lord. He knows the way we are to take.

One of the tests you may find yourself facing is not being forced into a situation but to make the choice to do God's will or take an easier way out. To your mind it would seem reasonable, involving less risk.

A test of self-effort came my way to reach for an opportunity to go to work. I decided to put an application in, and the door immediately slammed in my face. Then yet another opportunity opened there really wasn't anything wrong with it except again this was not the way of the Lord. It was another self-effort situation. Then a third opportunity arose, and it would have been so easy to do this and could have provided a lessening of the financial struggle as would any of the other situations.

When I felt a conviction in my heart on the second opportunity to not do it, I immediately stopped. When the third situation arose, I started to move toward it and after prayerful consideration realized I couldn't do that either as it would be in conflict to building code regulations.

As easily as not I could have justified my action. I could have justified and turned my head to the acknowledgement of the violation, but

I would immediately have been walking in disobedience. Rebellion always wants to raise its ugly head and try to convince you it will be alright to just ... and reasoning will quickly follow behind.

My pastor in his love and concern desired me to apply at the benevolent fund at Church. I was not working and struggling desperately to stay afloat, and I was not able to meet all my bills. I thanked him and based on the conviction the Lord had put on my heart concerning a similar situation, I knew this too would be a self-effort on my part. The final test came as I was down to $1.00 and still several days to go before, I would receive any money again. Sunday I took my last $1.00 bill and placed it in the offering plate. Before the day ended, I had received $100.00 and the following days brought forth in the mail money to pay my gas bill. When meeting with a friend, the Lord placed it in her heart to give me both money and canned goods as part of her Christmas gift and loving concern for me. Then my daughter called and offered to give me meat to help me as she too had felt impressed to help. Yet to none of these had I mentioned how bad my financial situation was.

As we yield and surrender in obedience, the Lord will lead guide and provide. Great is His faithfulness. I am beginning to realize and find that the safest prayer I can pray is, "Not my will but Thy will be done."

God's ways and thoughts are so much higher than what we can even begin to conceive or imagine. Even when the very outcome seems to be perilous and we are straining to hold on to see the hand of God move we can and should trust him for his best. He will not fail.

A lesson which has repeatedly brought me through has been keeping my focus fixed on God and not my circumstances. When I was in the Rehabilitation Hospital and it was nearing time to make a move, I had a nurse who would tell me it might be God would simply put me in a homeless shelter as I had no ability to finance my housing and the Insurance Company was dragging their feet in deciding for this need. I was still in a wheelchair and body brace and my hand had a cast on it. I couldn't walk or stand much less use the bathroom or shower facilities without assistance. How the enemy would try to get me to panic or not trust God to provide. I would smile and say to her, "You know I understand and appreciate what you are saying to me, but that isn't the God I know". Praise God, always in last-minute timing He has provided every step of my way.

Ps 91:2 (KJV) I will say of the LORD, He is my refuge and my fortress: my God; in Him will I trust.

BECAUSE[7]
Diana Lynn Rogers

Because the storm has come, I walk in a new way.
I walk with the Holy One; each day is a new day.
No longer looking back or wandering astray.
Counting my blessings one by one …
Remembering all that God has done.
Shattered and broken I have lain
As the self of my life daily was slain
Through suffering and sorrow, I came.
Trusting the Lord, I shall never be the same.

When our security is in God and we show convictions about His promises, peace follows. Our calm and peace will waver however if we mix trusting with self-reliance. We can lose our confidence when we focus on our circumstances. When Peter walked on the water, when his focus remained on God, he had no fear, but as soon as he took his eyes off the Lord, fear rushed in.

The instant you find your peace shifting away, refocus on the Lord. Let the peace of God direct your pathway. Where there is no peace,

---

[7] Because Diana Lynn Rogers

wait on the Lord until it returns. Remember, when the way is rough your patience has a chance to grow.

James 1:3 (KJV) Knowing this, that the trying of your faith worketh patience.

Patience is a process causing your character to grow and helps you trust God more each time you use it until finally your hope and faith are strong and steady. Don't try to squirm your way out of your problems. For when patience has finished her works you will be ready for anything and strong in character and complete.

THE LORD IS MY SHEPHERD

Psalm 23:1(NAS) The LORD is my shepherd; I shall not want.

2) He makes me to lie down in green pastures; He leads me beside the quiet waters.

(3) He restores my soul; He guides me in the paths of righteousness for His name's sake.

As I listened to the gentle lapping of the waters of Lake Manitou against the seawall, I realized I had been led to rest by the still waters. Still waters are that of quiet rest.

Psalms23:4-6(NAS)

(4) Even though I walk through the valley of the shadow of death, I fear no evil, for Thou art with me; Thy rod and Thy staff they comfort me.

(5) Thou dost prepare a table before me in the presence of mine enemies; Thou hast anointment my head with oil; my cup overflows.

(6) Surely goodness and loving kindness will follow me all the days of my life, and I will dwell in the house of the Lord forever.

He brings thoughts of peace. Philippians 4:7(KJV) tells you about the One who goes before you. God's care isn't just for the wounded but for the weary and worn.

THE SHEPHERD

Diana Lynn Rogers

The Lord is my Shepherd upon Him I trust and wait.
Alone I stand at the lonely garden's gate,
Trusting and waiting for His answer and the outcome of my fate,
Upon Him I cast my every care.
My every burden to Him I bring and share.[8]

Anything that takes precedence over the Lord can send you down the wrong path. Families, jobs and pleasures can become obstacles. The goal is to fix your eyes on Jesus not the path or to try to find your own way. He is your guide and destination.

As I sat listening to my Pastor this morning as he was teaching out of John 19 (KJV) "Behold the Man," [9]my attention was drawn to the questions he began to speak about. Speaking of the DNA in Christ he began to question, "Is your DNA on the cross you carry??? Are your footprints at the cross you are to be, or is someone else carrying it for you??? Where is your focus??? Is it on the Lord or gazing at the past, or perhaps searching for answers for tomorrow? Possibly, you are caught up with the things of this world."

---

[8] The Shepherd Diana Lynn Rogers
[9] Behold the Man/ John 19/ Pastor Rick Smail New Life Church Rochester, IN

DNA is always a significant question as to who you belong to. Does your DNA reveal the blood of Jesus in your daily living??? Do you reflect Christ in all your ways, or when your DNA is revealed, will it be a weakened linage polluted with the world? As he continued to speak the next question was," Is your DNA going to convict you or will it validate your walk with God". Where is your focus??? Is it on the Lord or gazing at the past or searching for answers for tomorrow?

As I listened, my mind wandered back in time to the mystery surrounding my birth and who my family really is. DNA is always a significant question as to whom you belong. I remember the day I stood in the clerk's office looking at my own records. Then came the discovery in addition to the shock which was followed by realizing I wasn't who I thought I was. But my name was an entirely different name. I can recall the shock, followed by the realization I literally had to make an identity correction one way or the other. Is it time for you to make a DNA correction???

Consider this; what if you go for years and think your identity is as a Christian to realize your walk is far removed from what truly is the will of God. What if you have listened only to those things having tickled your ears and have taken shortcuts? Are you laying down your plans and denying yourself or taking the broad road of the world? Will you be one of those who, as you stand at the door of eternity, is told "I know you not".

Every person has a choice to make. Death is an inevitable encounter when exiting this world. Will our choice be to enter eternal torment or everlasting beauty of God's presence forever and ever? Clearly, what you believe about heaven or hell will not influence God in the slightest but rather what His word says. Remember this, nothing can hold you captive without your permission. Be careful what you think, it can lead your mind and direct your footsteps along the wrong pathway!

Where is your focus??? Is the Lord your shepherd? Does He carry all your needs or just some of them?

ALL THINGS WORK FOR THE GOOD

Romans 8:28(KJV) And we know that all things work together for good to them that love God, to them who are the called according to his purpose.

1. Consider as we reflect on the way the gospel is spread how we learned. We grow and learn through Biblical examples and patterns.
2. How you respond to painful circumstances can lead to understanding God uses every experience for good whether it is a loss, a wreck, or a tragedy.

We must focus on God's will not man's will or way. To rise above the experience, we are to trust God wherever or whatever we are in is under the authority of God always! Consider, as we remember Paul in prison, the outcome of his imprisonment was he developed better and greater fruit. He was chained to a Roman soldier and one after another soldier, he witnessed to the goodness of God. Have you ever considered where you are now these chains may be preparing you for a higher purpose?

As we turn our attention to Christ, He reveals opportunities for imparting the gospel to people. Often there are circumstances when we don't even realize people are watching. I remember near the end of my stay at the Rehab Hospital I was wheeled up to the door area to wait for someone to take me back to my room after my therapy. This day I was placed near the area where the Therapy Supervisor was standing. He walked over to me and began a conversation. During the conversation, he told me he had daily watched me in my sessions and observed whether it was a difficult day for me, or the workout was extremely painful. Throughout each session he noticed and would observe me at times smiling and singing. He was curious as to what caused me to be different. It was God and God alone with His ever-present help in times of trouble. You never know who may be watching you just as he was. Whether it be in a Rehab Hospital counting your blessings, or in therapy, or in a hospital bed chained in a body brace; God may send people to you to share His grace and mercy. God never allows anything to touch us that He will not turn to our benefit and the good of His Kingdom.

1. Look to the Lord, focus on Him for direction in all areas and will to obey.
2. Identify the Lord's plan. Give attention to the Word of God continually.
3. Search His Word and learn His pattern for living; then identify the steps necessary to take. It all requires effort and commitment but great is the reward.

Keep your focus on Christ, not your immediate circumstances and you will succeed. The solitude and times alone with God cause you to rely on Him and strengthening comes. As you wait, God's power comes forth.

MY GRACE IS SUFFICIENT FOR YOU

2 Corinthians 12:9 (NAS) And he said unto me, "My grace is sufficient for thee: for my strength is made perfect in weakness." Most gladly therefore will I rather glory in my infirmities, that the power of Christ may rest upon me.

Pain isn't something any of us want to go through. However, recently I walked through an area of my life I want to share with you. I personally stand in awe of the Lord's power and strength to take the things that are meant for evil to literally use them as a tool to transform our hearts to walk in His love and forgiveness.

Lessons of pain are used to change us to the likeness of Christ. Pain is a tool used to bring the ungodliness to the surface. It causes us to be sifted, shaken and pruned. Stressful circumstances are used to reveal our true convictions. Do our actions and words reveal our attitude of trust? One of the greatest obstacles is the flesh nature and the "I, me, we four and no more" barrier. It is easy to become "me-centered". Our attitudes mixed up priorities, ungodly self-control habits are some of the obstacles we are challenged to overcome.

The pressures that come our way bring impurities to the surface. These hardships are not intended to cause us to drown but rather to purify and redirect our footsteps away from the ungodliness. It teaches us how to help and comfort others which equip us for serving others. We also learn through suffering as we endure the sufficiency of God. Before long we are learning the very nature of God and becoming Christ-like as we come to know Him.

We are much like the wonderful story by Margery Williams, about The Velveteen Rabbit[10], and the question of can a toy become real? With each tear disguised as adversity, trials, hardships, and many difficulties, we become more "real", until we ultimately become a reflection of Christ. Our testimony during the times of trouble becomes authentic and gives us an understanding of the one we are reaching to help.

In recent months, the Lord has brought into my life many who are suffering from being subjected to various forms of abuse. You may be unaware of the fellow worker, a neighbor or a friend who is hiding the pain in silence and trying to deal with it alone. They may be hurting, suffering alone hidden away from eyes to see. There is more than one form of abuse as you well know you yourself may have experienced, or perhaps you are suffering through now. As a child, I was exposed to sexual abuse, as an adult I have experienced physical and emotional abuse.

This brings me to a most recent event when the Lord walked me through an area of my life where I had been physically abused. I was

---

[10] The Velveteen Rabbit Margery Williams

held hostage at gunpoint with a hand revolver laid against my temple and kept hostage for hours. Needless to say, my first marriage ended both violently and abruptly.

Now years later, after God had walked me through the areas of forgiving, as well as seeking forgiveness, I was placed in a position by the Lord to pray for my captor's salvation as he faced certain death from terminal cancer.

The last week of his life the Lord instructed me to send him a card. I recall only two important things I was to share. One was if the Lord could love me in all my ugliness and forgive me, what made him think He wouldn't love him? Secondly, I was to share my experience during the hours following my wreck and to tell him that heaven was real; I knew for certainty, I had been there. I was to also tell him to make the right choice. By the grace of God, I believe in the last hours of his life he chose to enter eternity and be with God. Amazing Grace how sweet the sound!!!

John19:18 (KJV) relates the story that there were three on the crosses. Jesus was in the middle. One hanging next to him accepted Jesus and entered paradise. The other thief chose not to and went down into the torments of hell. We all have a choice. The ultimate decision is left to each one to determine their eternal destination, it is an eternal choice.

As for myself, I stand in awe of God. The fact he could take the anger and resentment out of my heart and put his love and forgiveness into my heart to the extent I would pray weeping and interceding for his salvation. All glory and praise to God! It is not His will that one will perish.

The song rising up in my heart is, "Can You Imagine", [11]envisioning the love, the patience, the mercy and grace, He has extended to each

---

[11] Can You Imagine song title

of us. Can you imagine the countless times we have received mercy and grace when we rightly deserve to burn in hell for eternity? Can you imagine the love He has for the one lost He will continue to the very last moments to reach out to bring this one home? As I write I think of the one who was next to Him at Calvary.

Remember, there was a time you and I were there or perhaps you may be lost now, and He is standing with His arms wide open. Run to the One who loves you so greatly He gave His life for you. These aren't just words but rather truths.

Ezekiel 36:26 27 (KJV)

A new heart also will I give you, and a new spirit will I put within you, and I will take away the stony heart out of your flesh and I will give you and heart of flesh, and I will put my Spirit within you, and move you to walk in my decrees, and you will be careful to keep my laws.

The amazing thing in all of this is His grace is sufficient for each of us. He gives the grace to change our hearts just as He has mine; from one of stone filled with hostilities to one that is transformed and filled with His love and compassion.

I am learning to live with this new heart as He continues to work through me as I surrender and yield to His ways. How true that is as He works in each of us by His grace to change and reflect more of Him and less of us.

Just as a side note, don't let the hypocrisy (one who claims to have a moral belief or standard but doesn't conform) [12] of someone cause you not to enter into the love of God and His presence.

It is hard to imagine His grace comes with no charge, unlike love from another person or money for work. There is no bartering or

---

[12] Webster Merriam Dictionary

system of one sort or another to balance it out. It is as simple as "here it is", freely I give to you. For whatever reason, we seem to think we need to do something to receive it and that isn't true at all. Grace has been described as extending your hands under an automated water faucet. When we pray, and by faith trust God to answer, His grace flows freely toward us and ultimately, we trust Him for the answer.

His Word says, "Only believe." (Mark 5:36 NAS) Yet many times we pray with little confidence He will answer us. So, then my question becomes, "If I don't believe why I am bothering to pray at all???"

As I have come to know God, I have found myself more and more letting go of the things of this world and what I thought was best. As I have learned to yield to His ways, I gradually have entered a rest and peace as I have come to surrender and yield to Him.

With each step of my journey I have found myself more and more in a place where peace has become a guidance tool to me as I depend upon His peace and rest to direct my steps. Without the peace of God, I have no desire to step out or run forward. In the times I have found myself moving without that assurance I will immediately stop and refocus to find His hand amid my situation. No peace, no go! That doesn't mean there won't be any struggles, but it does mean you have the assurance of God's presence during trouble or decisions. Confront situations and apply the Word.

Something I have found significant is to become as transparent with God as I can possibly be and to realize we all have areas of weakness and we must bring them to God to ever move past them. There is no hiding place He does not see all.

Just as it is recognized to begin healing you first must confess you have an issue and that you need help; same as with God. If you were an alcoholic or drug addict you first must recognize the problem. By His grace, you can come totally clean and seek His help to be restored to what He created you to be before life has caused its damages. God can and will change you if you will let Him. In His time you will discover you have become free and whole to walk in His love and grace.

In the middle of the word sin is the letter "I", so it is in the self-centered word pride. Sin is selfish and always without exception, it leads to death. All that glitters isn't always gold but may be fool's gold leading to destruction and death.

With David, his sin led to the death of his innocent son. So often others are wounded or killed because of the acts of our sin. The answer is atonement, which is satisfaction, reparation, or expiation given for an injury or wrong

The decision of Abraham to have Ishmael by his wife's servant cost him the right to a relationship with his son. He attempted to bring about the promise given to him by his own self-effort.

When David tried to conceal his adulterous relationship with Bathsheba, God revealed. David had her husband sent to battle when he was told Bathsheba was pregnant, to cover up his sin.

The dirt of the world always leaves us with the need to be washed continually in the Word of God and to be transparent. There are the wavering and blurred lines and the little hidden roots of rebellion as we travel along in life. Then we must use the bronze laver, which is the Word of God, as it reflects our souls tainted with things that try to attach themselves to our lives. In the tabernacle, the bronze laver was used. It was made from the bronze mirrors of the women. Exodus 30:17-2 (KJV) The priest would wash their hands upon entering and once again before coming out again.

By the mercies and goodness of God, His loving kindness and the sacrifice of His Son Jesus we can come to Him with a contrite and broken heart to confess our sins and He is faithful to forgive us.

God desires for us to become transparent and open to admit our weaknesses and mistakes, shortcomings and sins to Him. He desires us to be open and honest, confessing all before Him and seeking His forgiveness. As each layer of your soul is cleansed and the world removed from you, then you will have the reflection of Christ for this world to see.

Psalm 51:17(KJV) The sacrifices of God are a broken spirit: a broken and a contrite heart, O God, thou wilt not despise.

Often the enemy attempts to cause us to believe we have everything in control. When we rely on God all things are possible in His time.

Entering sacrificial worship is not a half-hearted attempt to sing praises or enter the church services. The meaning of sacrifice is something you place upon the altar that costs you something and means a great deal to you. For me, it was letting my son remain with his father when I wanted to have him with me. It became a true sacrifice as the Lord led me to release him and entrust my son to Him.

Is there something in your life that God is asking you to trust Him to lay down??? Trust Him, the price of obedience sometimes requires giving all to Him. Our Father is waiting for us to come to absolute abandonment and surrender. He is waiting to restore our joy and salvation, waiting to remove the pain and chaos in our life. He is waiting for you and me. Forget the opinions of man, possessions, applaud of man or of life reputations, what the budget is or what the calendar or the issues of the times we are in. Embrace Him and yield to His call. Eternity is calling and He is coming soon.

Today I was messaging with a dear friend who recently moved to another country. In our conversation, she was sharing the simplicity of the lifestyle and the changes her family were making and the adjustments required. That is much as it is with God. He desires for us to simplify our lives and follow along the pathway He has for us to fulfill our destiny. We all need to discover what God requires of us and not man. We are to fix our focus on Him and walk continually closer with Him.

DIGGING FOR GOLD

Often the question arises, would God allow us to undergo a crisis if it meant He would teach us about Himself and the things we need to change? Absolutely!! During some of the most painful times of my recovery it took every ounce of me to hold on to the faithfulness of God and to trust Him. Every circumstance and detail of my life was to be shaken.

As I laid there, I knew I was totally physically, emotionally and spiritually dependent upon His hand providing. With that realization, I was in a place of utter dependence. Such a place I had never been before. The reliance on knowing only God and God alone could bring me through caused me to continuously fix my focus upon Him.

Physically for weeks I was unable to stand without help or to even turn from side to side as I lay completely confined to my bed in a full body brace. The only exceptions were when I showered or was taken to therapy or the dining room via wheelchair.

My hands had to be desensitized to even tolerate touching things. It took all my strength to hold a pencil and literally impossible to try to cut my food, I was barely able to feed myself. During this frightening and incredibly painful experience, I continually fixed my focus on Jesus, meditating on how He loved and care for me. I would remind myself constantly that God was with me, watching over me and I sensed His presence was with me as I leaned upon Him.

As nighttime would come, I insisted my curtains always remain open so I could look to the heavens as I would lay there thinking about Him. On the most difficult days, I would cling to His promise to never leave or forsake me. The pain was excruciating as the entire core of my body had collapsed from all the breakage in my back and ribs, all but two being broken, my right side crushed. There were extensive neck damages and severe whiplash. Because of the whiplash my cervical (neck) bows into my esophagus. But God, my ever-present help in times of trouble, has continued to heal me. The incredible lessons I have learned in knowing God in these unbelievably painful circumstances far outweigh the suffering I am walking through.

Many lessons I have experienced to come to know Him in a greater way. I have learned to know Him as my Provider, Keeper, Strength, my Sun and Shield. He has become my Beloved whose banner over me is love. There have been lessons of mercy, the sufficiency of His grace and learning to lean on His might and power.

There were teachings of how all things work for the good of those who love the Lord, and foremost the lessons of His love and care for me. These have come as layer upon layer of my life and the things I have loved and cared so greatly about have been removed.

Those things also include all that I desperately held on to and clung to so tightly. Those I loved, possessions of every kind, all things of this world, one after another I have yielded and surrendered. All to Jesus I freely give. There has entered my heart a knowing that it has cost me all, yet I have found all. I have found and entered peace and rest that the world cannot take away through all the letting go.

No matter what happens to me, nothing can take me away from the love of God that abides in my heart. The Lord is my Beloved and I am His.

JACOB'S TEST

Have you ever found yourself struggling and wrestling to be obedient and resisting the will of God to let go? I have many times through the years, only to find later the very thing I grasped so tightly to was the very thing that had the potential to harm me. God knew His ways were far above my thoughts and ways.

Gen 32:24-25(KJV) And Jacob was left alone; and there wrestled a man with him until the breaking of the day. And when he saw that he prevailed not against him, he touched the hollow of his thigh; and the hollow of Jacob's thigh was out of joint, as he wrestled with him.

The changing of Jacob's name was his character being changed from deceiver to the transformation meaning God prevails. The Hebrew word is Yisra'el. [13]

In the account, in Genesis 32 (KJV) we see Jacob wrestling. The wrestling that took place brought Jacob to a place of full surrender of his will to God. I have come to realize, as perhaps you have as well, the wrestling with God has been pressing/pushing my old life from me. By "daybreak" at the end of the trial and wrestling, I now desperately cling to God as the old life has completely fallen away. From now on I may be broken and weak as a result of this time from others' perspective.

Gen: 32:28 (NAS) And He said, "Your name will no longer be Jacob but Israel, for you have striven with God and with men and have prevailed."

During the time of crisis, when all your resources fail, you can fall into ruin or you can fall into the hands of God and receive something better than you ever dreamed possible. Become willing to surrender completely to Him. Let go and cease striving from your own wisdom, strength, and righteousness. Let go and surrender all. To be crucified with Christ as it is written in Gal. 2:20(KJV), is to be alive in Him, The God of Jacob. It all comes with a price.

What are you holding onto, are you willing to let go and trust God and surrender all? Have you come to realize that no matter what you

---

[13] Strong's Concordance 415 Hebrew Yisra'el the mighty God, http;//biblehub.com.

are gripping so tightly to, it can in a moment be gone from your life? Outside of God and eternal life there is nothing here that is permanent, it is all temporary down to your own very life.

One of the most startling realizations was how temporary life is. This came as the result of a cardiac arrest of my former husband, as clinically speaking he lay lifeless. I had remarried and was blessed with a wonderful marriage. It was a marriage filled with love and happiness, when suddenly all was taken from my life. This was a result of the lack of one heartbeat; and the presence of the death angel which eventually destroyed our marriage. The weeks and months that followed as a result, of this incident, ended our marriage as he literally walked out of my life.

At first, I was left for months in denial, saying it was his heart and things would be better. Our marriage moved from a close loving relationship, the kind most people really long to have, to one where I became the "Chosen Frozen One".

After months of trying to fix the situation, I too became reactive to the cold indifference. It was like Humpty Dumpty, no one could put it back together again. The man I loved so much had changed, and I now was living with a stranger. Basically, my husband died the day it happened and never returned. A stranger entered my life.

My heart was broken into a million little pieces. All I loved within a short period of time was taken. First came my marriage, then my daughter moving to go to school. The final blow came with being forced financially to do what was best for my son. The decision was to allow him to remain in his childhood home and school.

Life has so many twists and turns. Perhaps the reason this was even more devastating came because of my having to decide when early on I was given a diagnosis of having six months to live. I made the heart-wrenching decision to allow my daughter to stay with her father, only later to discover that the diagnosis was inaccurate.

Although I had a serious blood issue, I did become stable and it went into remission with treatment. Months later I was to be blessed with having my precious daughter returned home. My life became much more stable as did my health.

Love truly sometimes means letting go. Love sometimes will do what is best for others. It will forget about the pain it will bring, even when it costs you all. People will judge and criticize you, ridicule, and perhaps even say evil against you. Remember this love will never fail, it began at the cross with Jesus. In the months following our divorce, I was to come to the Healer of my soul as life moved on and the new normal was a life emptied out of my home and family.

PATHWAYS OF BROKENNESS

There were days and hours of brokenness. The pathway of my life was strewn with loss as my life has been sifted in every way. There were countless nights I would be awake all night reading my Bible. For many weeks, this became my life. Then one night as I sat in the darkness of another night, I was reading my Bible when suddenly I became aware of the room smelling like roses. My windows were open, it was a warm summer night. I got up and walked over first to the window then the screen door and yet the odor wasn't coming from either area. When I sat down and opened my Bible once again, I began to read, the fragrance returned. Twice this was to happen. Then the third time I opened my Bible I knew the fragrance was The Rose of Sharon that was filling my room with His presence.

I found myself dreading Sunday afternoons; after church was the most difficult time for me. My family always was together and now all was gone. One Sunday I returned home after church, I was under so much emotional attack I called a friend who had become my prayer partner and I went to her house. The attack was incredible on my mind. I sensed as if I was falling down a spirally tunnel trying to grab on to something but nothing was there. The entire time the attack lasted my prayer partner was being told by the devil, "See! If there is a God, why isn't He helping your friend???" It was all I could do to hold on mentally to any reality. Finally, in panic, she called another friend, telling her she thought I was losing my mind as I basically stared out in space. Suddenly, I managed to break through enough to ask for a Bible. When I opened it, I read one word at a time. I fixed my eyes on the scripture until somehow, I would grasp the word I was reading then move on to the next word. This lasted for several minutes when suddenly just as quickly, the attack ended. My mind was completely clear as though it never happened. Make no mistake, there is a real devil; but rather than to confirm, that I write this to give you an insight into the power of the Word of God. When you are in a place of darkness you can reach for the Word of God and it will deliver you from the enemy's attacks.

HOPE [14]

The dictionary defines hope as follows:

1. A feeling of expectation and desire for a certain thing to happen.
2. A feeling of trust to want to happen or be the case. Hope in the Lord is to expect or anticipate.

Ps. 33:22(KJV) Let thy mercy, O Lord, be upon us, according as we hope in thee.

The Hebrew definition of hope (yachal) is to wait and hope [15]

Ps. 130:7(KJV) Let Israel hope in the Lord: for with the Lord there is mercy, and with him is plenteous redemption.

---

[14] Hope Merriam Webster Dictionary
[15] Strong's Concordance 3176 Yachal wait

Ps. 39:7 (AMP) And now, Lord what wait I for and expect? My hope in thee.

The Hebrew word (*towcheleth*) [16] is the same root word but meaning expectation.

This reveals God's faithful reliance and trustworthiness of the Lord.

The Greek word for hope is (*elpis*) [17] meaning to expect or anticipate with pleasure that the Lord can be trusted to keep His promises.

Romans 5:2(KJV) By whom also we have access by faith into this grace wherein we stand and rejoice in hope of the glory of God.

Col 1:5(KJV). For the hope, which is laid up for you in heaven, whereof ye heard before in the word of the truth of the gospel.

Hope is not a maybe but an absolute and definite guarantee by the Word of the truth of the gospel.

Titus 1:2 (KJV) In hope of eternal life, which God, that cannot lie, promised before the world began;

Eternal life is guaranteed and promised by the God of the universe. He cannot lie and will not. You can know that God promises heaven and He promised eternal life when you trust in Jesus Christ as your Savior. It is as simple as a decision. When you decide to follow Jesus, your spending eternity being in heaven is secured; believe in His Word. Jesus died, that is history. Jesus died for me, that is a decision. Your hope of heaven is guaranteed eternal without end, beginning the moment you trust Christ as your Savior.

---

[16] King James Bible Dictionary Strong's Lexicon H8431 towcheleth hope
[17] King James Bible Dictionary Strong's Greek 1680 elipis expectation hope

HEALING

The question is, "how does healing occur"? The Word states that healing comes by faith, believing God's Word, and applying it to our circumstances. Only believe!!! What you say you can have, but you must not doubt. Doubt brings us into an agreement with hell that it won't happen and cancels faith.

Even though all this truth applies, never put God in a box. I want to take you through some of my journey and experience before I was physically touched and healed of a broken heart. The days I walked through were filled with darkness and pain. I was grief filled with immeasurable suffering both mentally and emotionally as the incredible loss plagued my mind and emotions. There was the shocking trauma of my former husband when both his heart and breathing stopped. Clinically speaking he died while was I taking his pulse. There was more trauma to see him survive and have a stranger enter my life. The final blow was to have him walk out of our marriage and my life, abandoning me. Then my children through circumstances were no longer in my life. Part of life's circumstances and every emotional stablizer taken away. My family, my identity unknown, my life all I loved gone.

This started a three-year process that almost destroyed me as I was literally grieving myself to death. I lost down to a child's size. My life became shattered into a million pieces. I couldn't even begin to know what to do as the pain was an all-consuming grief. I truly would have been happy to die; the pain was so great. I had just returned to God and was led to believe that everything would be alright. That just wasn't true, in fact, it led to greater suffering. I would sit on the stairway in a state of emotional shock and post-traumatic stress trying to hold on to and make sense of what was happening to me.

With tears streaming down my checks I would tell God I didn't know what was wrong with me. I couldn't quit crying, but I believed if I could just touch Him somehow, I would be alright. At times, I would sit just simply in praise and give thanks for His help.

Many nights I would collapse in prayer at the foot of the bed and find myself still there in the morning. During this time of suffering God gave me a prayer language. There were no words to describe the depth of suffering and loss I was enduring. During these times I would pray using this language only God knew.

For the ones who don't believe such a language exists or the prayer language is evil allow me to share this with you expressly. There is such a place of grieving there are no words to describe your pain. When I was going through the valley of death of all I knew, God literally lifted me out of my body to allow me to watch myself singing in church while worshiping in song, "How Great Thou Art" [18]in a language I knew not but was totally fluid as I sang. To this day when there is suffering, I pray using this gift from Him knowing He alone knows my heart. This opened the revelation knowledge of truth that caused me to know Him in a greater way. This is a gift pure and true from God. As well as the gift of a prayer language, God also allowed me the gift of a quest that continues to last a lifetime.

I read the story, "The Life of Samuel Morris" [19]who was a prince in the deep and remotest parts of Africa. He was staked to the ground and left to die with honey in his mouth to be killed by killer ants. This punishment was to pay for the crime his father the King, had committed. The crime was he was unable to repay a debt. He literally was rescued by the Holy Spirit and led through the darkest parts of Africa to a missionary family, later to be led to the United States.

It was such an incredible story of his life. The unimaginable way he was rescued by the Holy Spirit placed such a hunger and thirst down in my soul to know Him. To this day I intensely continue seeking and longing to know the Holy Spirit in all His ways.

---

[18] How Great Thou Art song title
[19] The Life of Samuel Morris by Kjersti Hoff Baez; Ken Save

In I Kings17(KJV) Elijah the Tishbite, a prophet from Gilead, decreed no rain to fall. For three years no rain fell. After he was tested by the false prophets, he called forth fire to fall from heaven and it did. If you take a minute and read the account, you will see this prophet of God focused and prayed to God. Following the Lord's instruction, he decreed rain, yet nothing was seen. Elijah didn't pray once or twice but sent his servant out to look seven times until a cloud the size of a man's hand at a distance was seen. Once this occurred, Elijah then sent his servant to tell Ahab to get his chariot ready. Elijah spoke this in faith, not by the evidence of the rain. It is written soon the sky was black, and the rain fell

In many ways healing may come in a similar way by prayer, supplication, praise and thanksgiving. We must by faith, believe and speak it forth, to receive. Many feel if the manifestation doesn't occur it is evidence that God failed. No, it means he has a different way and it may mean it will be answered in eternity. His ways are far higher than our ways. But notice too, when instructed to call forth the rain it took praying seven times before the rain occurred. This may apply to healing as well.

The intriguing thing about knowing something is when you know it, all heaven and earth cannot move you from that place of knowing. Such as it is with the things I have shared here. I truly know that I know, God still heals, speaks, and delivers his children. That has never changed, and I know it.

REACHING YOUR DESTINY

Earlier I shared a few of the battles the Lord has brought me through. In this section of the book, it is my desire to help you build a bridge to cross over the gap to live the life God has created and purposed for you.

There is the story of Elijah who was exhausted from battles. Perhaps, you too find yourself exhausted as well. In the story as related in

1 King 19(KJV) he had fled from Queen Jezebel for his life. He went into the wilderness and sat down under the Juniper tree and requested to God that he might die.

Exhausted and spent from all he had been through, he fell asleep. Then the angel of the Lord touched him and told him to arise and eat. There was a baked cake on the coals and water at his head, so he ate and drank. Twice the angel of the Lord came to him telling him the journey was long and to eat and drink again. As he did, this food and drink sustained him for forty days on his journey. He came upon a cave while hiding there the Word of the Lord came to him, and said to him," What are you doing here?"

IDENTITY

Notice Elijah was hiding in the cave. Have you been hiding in a cave?

Why are you hiding in the cave? Pause to notice what you are noticing about your cave.

What does your cave look like?

What caused you to hide in your cave??? Was it fear, lack, discouragement, rejection, abandonment, abuse?

Does your cave have a familiar pattern to it? Does it have a repeat pattern?

What triggered your emotions?

What messages are you telling yourself?

Are you angry at yourself? Why???

THE PRINCIPLES OF GOD

Wisdom is the principle thing; therefore get wisdom and with all thy getting get understanding. (Proverbs 4:7)

As I have continued to study and listen intently to the Lord, there are very important issues I desire to clarify for my readers. In the effort to teach and give you clarity I wish to be perfectly clear that I as a writer am a child of the most high God. I am in no way or manner advocating the Law of Attraction only the principles and teachings of Jesus that are used in the world today.

Jesus came and is the law. You will discover every one of these laws Jesus is the one who has taught these principles and the world has come to recognize them through the Law of Attraction. There are many secular and religious leaders of various faiths that use these teachings, even those who practice various types of witchcraft and ungodliness.

I desire to "ghost bust" the myths and mythology as well as the religious spirits to teach you the real truth, these are all biblically based teachings. For these lessons the intent and purpose are to give you an understanding of how to apply these principles. In an upcoming book I write an in-depth study to recognize the various spirits and activities of Satan and the minions of darkness.

In Matthew 16, Jesus was confronted by the Pharisees and Sadducees for signs. There are always going to be religious spirits, soothsayers, witches and foreign gods in this world. When in question chew it up and spit it out much like a bone in a fish. God is always in the background sifting moving and teaching us to know Him. It is simple to discern in the life of an individual is God working in their life. You don't need a sign you simply need to trust Him and learn to know Him.

The Pharisees, and Sadducees came up, they asked Him to show them a sign from heaven. v.2 But He replied to them, "When it is evening, you say, 'It will be fair weather, the sky is red.' v.3 "And in the morning, 'There will be a storm today, for the sky is red and threatening.' Do you know how to discern the signs of the times? v.4 An evil and adulterous generation seeks after a sign; and a sign will not be given it, except the sign of Jonah." And He left them and went away.

What signs have you been seeking God for when the Lord is working all around you? Seek God for His understanding and wisdom, not a sign. There are many adages and sayings but at the end of the day there is only one thing that matters, to know Him.

THE UNIVERSAL LAWS OF ATTRACTION

There are physical laws that we can see, and spiritual laws that are invisible.

1. Notice your thoughts.
2. Let go of what you want to be and submit to a higher plan and purpose. Think God's will and way. You have a choice.

PRACTICE

Notice what you are thinking. The choice is yours to choose. Life and death are in the tongue so guard your word and your mind.

Proverbs 3:5-6 (KJV) Trust in the Lord with all thine heart; and lean not unto thine own understanding. (6) In all your ways acknowledge Him, and He will direct thy paths.

LAW OF THINKING

Hebrew 11:11(AMP) Because of faith Sarah herself received physical power to conceive a child, even when she was long past the age for it, because she considered God who had given her the promise to be reliable and trustworthy and true to His word.

God's Word frames the Universe. He spoke it into existence in Genesis 1(KJV) at the time of the foundation of the earth, putting all creation into place. He also set the laws of the Universe into place during this time by His Spoken Words. When you focus on the Word of God, and the Word's infinite power; faith is released by agreement of what you speak forth. This releases the action by faith to be (according to our measure of faith) into what you are saying. The power of speech is the same power God has within you as He flows through us.

Equally so, fear and worry negate your faith in agreement with the Word of God. Your speech and thought will come into agreement with the Devil by the framing of your words and thoughts. Further on we will see the magnetic power that frames our words and thoughts set in the Universal Laws.

Have you ever really been frightened you would lose something, or something bad would happen, and you are worried about it? You agree with the negative thought.

You have a choice in emotionalizing a thought. What we give attention to is the ruling mental state.

During my recovery, I learned a very valuable lesson regarding pain. When I began to become conscious after my drug-induced coma; during the days following I was told I had a broken back and was placed in a full body brace. I couldn't feel the pain of it at all because the overriding pain was my broken ribs. The secondary pain was my hand recovering from being broken completely free of the arm itself. Only after the pain began to reduce in these areas could I feel the pain of my broken back.

Many times, our mind will overrule the lesser pains of our emotions. The same principle of physical pain applies to our emotional pain. Our mind will mask the secondary pain, an equally important emotional pain, allowing us to ignore the hurt. This can be true in an emotional crisis. It is much like the individual that lifts weights multiple times greater than his normal strength, only later to be unable to do so. The mind is an amazing instrument created to guide and protect us. The paramount mental state of being will draw life-living performance energies, drawing the power from a sense of well-being. As a result, either this creates a drain on your life or an influx of positive performance.

The seed of thinking has power and is planted into the universe. These laws that God created read the intent by the attention given to your thoughts, receiving it as a proper request! Just as the power given to your words is critical and continuously at work, just like gravity, it is hidden from sight but actively at work. For that reason, you don't want to jump off a building, ignoring the law of gravity. You will fall! Change negative thoughts to positive ones, try to consider thinking that things are working for your good.

Romans 8:31 (KJV) What shall we say then to these things? If God be for us who can be against us.

- Focus on the fact that all things work for our good. What will you put your attention to??? Focus your thoughts. What are you thinking about? Turn to the Lord. Bring all your concerns to Him and rebuke fear.

Proverb 1:33 (AMP) But whoso hearkens to me (wisdom) shall dwell securely and in confident trust and shall be quiet without fear or dread of evil.

Matthew 10:31 (KJV) Fear ye not therefore; ye are of more value than many sparrows.

Cling to your Heavenly Father and keep your eyes focused on Him. What are you putting your attention and actions to?

THE LAW OF SUPPLY

The law of supply is based on the infinite supply of creation. In the Kingdom of God, the Creator's Word says to Ask, Seek and Knock according to Matthew 7:7-12 (KJV). Limited supply is simply not true. God is limitless, boundless and able to meet all creations need. With the simple speaking of His command, "Let there be, and there was". There is no lack in God's economy, only in our thinking.

The Law of Attraction draws its own type, much as does the mental magnet that draws from its thoughts. Fear, doubt and worry; each of these draws negative power. When we change our thoughts, moving from can't and don't to a positive charge of can, we are connecting into the infinite power of greater things into our life. We are connecting with the power of God; removing the negative charge while infusing the power of greater things into our life.

Phil 4:13(Amp) I have strength for all in Christ who empowers me (I am ready for anything and equal to anything through Him Who infuses inner strength in me: I am self-sufficient in Christ's sufficiency)

If God says I can who am I to question that???? The next question at hand positions us to open the infinite questions as to greater things.

THE LAW OF RHYTHM

Eccelesiastics 3:1 (KJV) To everything there is a season, and a time to every purpose under the Heaven:

All energy vibrates according to its own rhythm, it establishes cycles and patterns. Learn to harmonize.

What do I have in my hand?

The Law of Rhythm again creates a draw. As you picture those mental images you create a mental image in your mind. Once more the negative images will draw the negative. Much like the seed principle, an orange seed doesn't produce an apple or a peach; like brings forth like. So are your thoughts doing the same in the Universal Laws which are invisible to your sight yet are very much in existence!

As you construct thoughts of "what do I have?" they are creating a positive flow toward you. Positive desire creates images of those things you seek. What do you desire? From the position of desire, we can draw from our creative images to create expectations. This is the principle of the proton/neutron of the atom.

From Desires to Expectations:

When we have a desire, how do we generate a level of expectation? When you have a desire, and your expectations are of barely getting by, you struggle, and you are out of harmony with the Law of Attraction. Where is my attention? What am I putting my actions to?

LAW OF RECEIVING

The Law of Receiving is the reverse from what we are taught in the world system. Thinking from our resources is backward. What I have in my hand is the lesser, the teaching of giving from what you have is a lower level of attraction.

LAW OF THE SEED

The principle here states "Give and it shall be given, pressed down". If you desire money, you give money. Money can be represented in various forms. It may not be represented in coins only, but also as time. As time represents how you earn money. The way to access resources is by giving.

Luke 6:38 (NIV) "Give, and it will be given unto you. A good measure, pressed down, and shaken together and running over, will be poured into your lap. For with the measure that you use, it will be measured to you."

Give in the form you desire. If money is your desire, give in that which represents money. If you want an apple you don't plant a fig tree. It is the Law of Reproduction. It attracts and draws that form of giving to you.

LAW OF GENDER

The Yen (male) and the Yang (female) require space, time and nurturing; the male is represented by the seed, the time to manifest is by the female. This requires time and persistence to succeed. Seed time to harvest is represented in this law. This tells us to not give up before the goal is reached.

LAW OF INCREASE

Life is seeking ideas to discover more of the abundant life, bringing forth expanded expressions of your discoveries. The mentality to get more is backward thinking. You are the Law of Increase. What you have been given you are to give back to other's lives.

LAW OF COMPENSATION

Give in the form you desire to receive. This invisible law governs what we think if we think fear we will receive fear. It creates the exact likeness of our thoughts. The Law of Compensation will show you ever-increasing good!

LAW OF NON-RESISTANCE

The Law of Non-Resistance is about understanding when you find an obstacle work our way around the problem. Just like a stream facing to your biggest problems are at the beginning. If you can't do something about it, release it, resist it; a river flowing and a rock being in the way of it, causing it to flow around it. Similarly speaking when you try to force something into your life you personally aren't designed and created for, you will have disastrous results.

LAW OF FORGIVENESS

Forgiveness is to remove a block in my awareness of life's presence of God. When we pick hot coals to throw, we are the ones whose hand gets burned. When we refuse to forgive, we remain attached, much like that of gum to your shoe. Forgiveness is for you to create a release in your life. God's word says; "forgive that you shall be forgiven".

UNFORGIVENESS IS THE POISON YOU TAKE HOPING SOMEONE ELSE WILL DIE." (Linda White)[20]

"FORGIVENESS IS UNLOCKING THE DOOR TO SET SOMEONE FREE TO REALIZE I AM THE PRISONER!!!!" (Max Lucado)[21]

---

[20] http://www.great-quotes.com/quotes/author/Linda/White
[21] http://www.great-quotes.com/quotes/authorMax Lucado

Refusal to forgive causes you to remain attached to that person emotionally, giving them control over you. While the continued holding on to resentment attracts and draws more negative to you. This creates a cycle attracting more of resentment until the root of bitterness takes hold. Choose not to carry on. Forgive your debtors. With every action, there is a reaction. You choose how you handle the offense.

With whom are you wrestling with today? Who comes to mind and makes you lose your peace? You find yourself with feelings of anger or resentment when considering that person. If this is occurring, you are attached to them. This is causing you to lose your peace and this places you out of harmony immediately. Lord, I choose to forgive_____.

The choice to forgive does not mean it is ok, but rather you have chosen to release your right for the greater good and set yourself free from the offense and person or persons.

LAW OF SACRIFICE

Let go of the lesser for the greater good; the present good gets in the way of the greater good. Let go of the lesser and former doesn't fit with your peace. I have discovered many times a person truly is in your life for only a reason or a season. Once the time ends, you will find strife or continued struggles with the individual will continue to pop up its ugly head until you recognize and choose to release and move on.

Let go and move on. Life is calling you, and that person is no longer a part of that image. You need to let go and make room for what God has for you and your desires. When there is no peace you are out of the law of harmony; immediately forgive, release and move on. Let the peace of God rule your heart!!

LAW OF OBEDIENCE

Gravity is supernatural power and a powerful law all nature obeys. Thought seeds are energized to produce more of the same seed. The Law of Obedience is a purifying law leading to sacrifice and consecration. This is a law you will seek to become pure in heart. This is something to be considered as a sacrifice and willingness to become meek. You are gaining a willingness in spirit. This will cause you to become capable of giving at any given time while you help those about you. The Gift of Sacrifice also allows insight to learn about yourself, and what you are willing to offer to the Lord through obedience.

THE LAW OF SUCCESS

Success in the world's system is based on financial increases. In the Bible, only twice is success mentioned, both in the book of Joshua. With each step, along our pathway to our dreams and desires, there will be distractions and delays. Use them as stepping stones, not as stumbling blocks.

There will be those who will not agree with you. Don't let their littleness keep you from your greatness that God is calling you to. Ask yourself if this is what I believe or think that is being said. Bring it before the Lord and move forward. Let it go. Let the peace of God direct your footsteps. If you have no peace, don't move until you find it! Let the peace of God rule in your heart to direct your steps.

What brings you joy is an affirmation of the truth of what you desire. A proof of success is revealed in your joy. You will meet many challenges disguised and sent as opportunities to change your thought patterns.

What do we really love and desire to have in our life?

Your desires become a good indicator as to what you are longing to move toward. If it is a true God vision it will always require you to grow. Your destiny and plans will always cause you to rely on God. Circumstances will remove your emotional props of self-reliance and self-efforts disguised in many variations of lack and needs.

One of the many lessons I have come to learn has been in all things we desire, there always will be a required time of growth. This will cause us to expand and trust God to help us. This all is teaching us to have a greater reliance upon God along our journey.

The fact you have a longing and a desire is an indicator you are entering a season of growth. Consider longings and desires, using them as tools to become. What do you really want to do or become? Take a minute to pause and reflect on what you really want to have in your life change.

Write those things down. These are the things I would love to have changed. Make a page for each of these areas.

1. Relationships
2. Health
3. Vocation/ Work
4. Finances

There are no limitations to your dreams, only self-imposed boundaries, many of which have been learned boundaries. Give yourself permission as you work through this process to dare to dream the seemingly impossible dream that you long for and desire. There will be time to re-adjust as you grow and change from where you started.

I love the story of The Velveteen Rabbit by Margery Williams. [22]It is a story about becoming. We are to learn together in becoming who

---

[22] Velveteen Rabbit Margery Williams

God desires, as you stretch, grow, and identify those things you long to change and become.

Along the pathway strewn with obstacles known as difficulties, you are going to learn they are only stepping stones. These are not the end of your journey, neither do failures define the person you are becoming. Much of the things you find as roadblocks, in fact, are times to stretch and work your muscles, thus you will become stronger and have a greater persistence in overcoming trials. They are simply a storm cloud passing through your life, to teach you to depend on and trust God along your way.

A strange thing happened during one of my many trials as I struggled to survive so many losses that had entered my life. I had a very unusual dream where I heard in the stable next to me the roaring of a lion. It roared and roared with a terrifying volume. There I stood shaking in fear. Finally, I gathered my nerve, and stepped out of the stable. Stepping into the aisle I found myself face to face with the roaring lion. Just as suddenly, it turned into a "paper tiger", and poof it was gone. As in the dream, fear so much of the time is like the roaring lion; those things we fear don't happen, they are "paper tigers". The enemy floods our minds with things to break our focus.

I Peter 5:8 (KJV) Be sober, be vigilant; because your adversary the devil, as a roaring lion, walketh about, seeking whom he may devour;

Joshua 8 (KJV) Joshua was told to fear not; the battle was the Lord's. Most all know the story of Daniel who was placed in the lion's den, as related in Chapter 6 of Daniel. As a child of God, we are promised in Deuteronomy 31:6 (KJV) He will never leave or forsake us. If we can't trust the one who died for us, who can we trust?

2 Timothy 1:7 (KJV) tells us that God did not give us a spirit of fear but a sound mind. We all are subject to some fear. Fear is a Delilah in your life intended to stop you. If you allow it, it can destroy you. Doubts are traitors that cause us to miss the good that is ours when

we become fearful to try something, or merely stop our steps in mid-course. You will either choose to move toward a life designed by you with God's help; or you will by default, accept that which comes along. Either way, each day of your life you will have the choice. God gave us all free will to choose the pathway you are along.

It is impossible to not have some fear. Utilize it, asking it not to go away but rather use it as a tool of caution opposed to a driving force in your life. Doing this can result in fear becoming a friend to guide you along the pathway of perilous times. Then fear can allow you a safe place to cross over your situation. The greatest have all suffered fear. Those who don't experience fear are staying in their comfort zones. Fear is simply a border of the reality you have known. Your dream and destiny are beyond that border. People who are successful in reaching their destiny and dreams aren't successful in the absence of fear. In the same way distraction can be used as a memo and turned into a to-do list to serve you. Fear is the enemy of your dream. Face the fear and use it as a stepping stone; a vehicle to cause you to be insightful of potential hazards. Move forward from it.

Failure too can be an opportunity to redirect and rise above the situation; it isn't your destination. It just means change is needed. Change your perspective to see what you can do differently and still get the results you desire.

We use our faith to redirect and channel our efforts to move forward and try again. Many times, it is a redirection, and at the end of the pathway, there is something far greater and better for us. We may be moving toward the lesser and God has a far greater plan for us that we can't see. Isaiah 55:99(KJV) tells us that God's ways are far higher than our ways. When the road turns or changes we simply need to look up and be thankful He knows best. Always!

Question what possible good can come from this and what can I do differently.

Romans 8:28 (NIV) "And we know that in all things God works for the good of those who love him, who have been called according to His purpose".

Step back, pause and consider what to change.

UNLOCKING THE DOOR OF THE VISION

Habakkuk 2:1-3 (KJV), 1 Again I will stand on my watch, and set me upon the tower, and I will watch to see what He will say unto me, and what I shall answer when I am reproved

2 And the LORD answered me, and said, "Write the vision, make it plain upon tablets, that he may run that readeth it.

3 For the vision is yet for an appointed time; but at the end it shall speak, and not lie; though it tarry, wait for it; because it will surely come, it will not tarry.

Matthew Henry Commentary says of Habakkuk: Habakkuk 2:1-4 (KJV) "When tossed and perplexed with doubts about the methods of Providence, we must watch against temptations to be impatient. When we have poured out complaints and requests before God, we must observe the answers God gives by His Word, His Spirit, and providences; what the Lord will say to our case."

God will not disappoint the believing expectations of those who wait to hear what He will say unto them. All are concerned with the truths of God's word. Though the promised favor is deferred long, it will come at last, and abundantly recompense us for waiting. The humble, broken-hearted, repenting sinner, alone seeks to obtain an interest in this salvation. He will rest his soul on the promise, and on Christ, in and through whom it is given. Thus, he walks and works, as well as lives by faith, perseveres to the end, and is exalted to glory; while those who distrust or despise God's all-sufficiency will not walk uprightly with him. The just shall live by faith in these precious promises, while the performance of them is deferred. Only those made just by faith shall live and shall be happy here and forever.[23]

The vision is much like a racehorse. When at the start line, if it jumps the line prematurely it is disqualified to win the race. A vision or promise of God requires patience to wait upon the Lord. God's will has held within it a vision to accomplish His will and purposes. Guard the promise. If we are the initiator, the vision lacks integrity. It is easier to function in self-efforts than to wait on God for His desired direction.

The "faith gap" [24]is evidence we are placing our trust in God for His provision for the vision. Within the vision, there is a Law of Attraction of Focus that is implemented. The Laws of Thinking and Intent are also activated as we begin to see and visualize the vision. The greater the focus the closer to the vision we come. In the process, we remove hindrances and distractions intended to delay or completely abort the vision that God placed as a seed to grow within our soul. During this time, the vision seed is hidden away to grow much like that of a natural seed.

During the time of recovery from my wreck at the beginning of my first awareness following the wreck, I became intensely aware of the presence of God with me. His presence was continually by my side day and night. I would see myself like that of a newborn infant grasping to his hand, clinging with all my being.

Every minute was critical for me to keep my mind focused and centered upon God. With my continuous focus, God gave me moment by moment the strength to endure the excruciating pain, and the struggle to breathe or ability to move my body at all. Because of this focus on God, I experienced an awareness that I was not alone. But rather God's presence was with me continually, never leaving or for-

---

[23] Matthew Henry Hab.1-4 commentary http://biblehub.com
[24] Overcoming The Attacks Of The Jezebel Spirit author Don Richter

saking me for a moment. In this state of brokenness, I discovered the truth of God inhabiting the praises of His children. As I would fix my mind and focus on God. I would sing songs riveting my focus on Him. It was taking every ounce of my strength to workout. I knew my condition was so critical it was essential to workout regardless of the pain involved.

On my most difficult pain-filled days, I would attempt to stand from my wheelchair. Dressed in my daily uniform of a full-body-brace with my arm in a cast and sling, I would tell my therapist, "Today we are going to count my blessings". As she and I would begin my struggle to stand and walk, we would begin thanking God for all the good I could find in all of this. I would begin by giving thanks in all things God had done for me. With each step taken I would find something to give thanks or praise for, drawing God's presence nearer to surround and sustain me.

The Law of the Universe reads your intention by the attention given; it hears it as a proper request. Drawing God nearer to me, and His power strength and might into my situation was the heart motive in these struggles. Just as a side note, remember God is the creator of this universe and He is the one who put these laws in motion; so, it is not something that should be particularly peculiar to anyone regarding these principles and laws of the universe. We serve an amazing God, almighty and all-powerful.

Additionally, as I write this, I would like to point out to you the same principle applied in my healing that was discovered earlier when I was healed of a broken heart. Focus and continued believing and trusting are critical. One last point; what you see and what you truly believe matters greatly. The promise of God is as we draw near to him, He will draw near to us. He also promises to inhabit the praises of his children.

DIANA LYNN ROGERS

STEPPING STONES AND GAPS ALONG THE WAY

As I am sitting writing this, I am thinking about what I have in my hand as I Consider my present situation. How am I feeling about it? At first, I had peace over it but as the situation has continued and the lack is ever-growing greater, creating financial chaos and crisis, I feel a great deal of concern. I find myself questioning myself over and again. What am I doing? What is obedience? Where is the answer that directs me toward the path of my destiny and will of God? What created the situation?

I remain sensing this is a stepping stone taking me out of my comfort zone and normal way of doing things to follow the pathway of obedience into my next season.

1. What is around me and how am I feeling about what is happening? I am uncertain of the will of God and what I am to do.
2. Where do self-effort and passivity begin and stop?
3. Does it have a pattern to it?
4. Yes, work and loss of a job to restart over and over, there is a pattern.

Notice what you are noticing, write it down in your journal to consider. A new question has occurred; is it possible the operation of the Jezebel Spirit is attempting to strip me over and again? Could it be to bring discouragement to cause me to let go of the vision and promise from God?

What is causing this to occur and what do I do differently to end this cycled patterning? Stop, look about, take a deep breath here amongst all these questions. What is causing this? Do you notice confusion, doubts or uncertainty entering your thoughts? Let's take a closer look.

What was the purpose of Elijah being fed by the Raven and why did it dry up in I King 17? When the brook dries up our security is gone. It means God has something better! We need to be thankful for the brook and the season of provision. When the brook dried up, it was to end the supernatural supply preparing Elijah to move as he went first into the wilderness, exhausted and desperately alone. There he journeyed.

Was it the will of God for Him to move? Absolutely! He had a word of instruction to him when he exited the cave. Could it be your time of lack is a stepping stone to your next place in your journey?

Psalms 46:10 (KJV) Be still and know that I am God; I will be exalted among the heathen; I will be exalted in the earth.

BLOCKS

Identifying blocks of origin. What type of block is this? If this is a block, where is it coming from? Parental blocks are often time brought on by limiting beliefs. Perhaps the question blocking your belief was established by your parents with questions such as, "was that on sale? How much did it cost you? Was there a coupon?" These unconsciously create a sense of undeserving.

A Cultural/Religious block such as the belief that money is the root of all evil. These are a few more adages; "easier for a camel to go through the eye of a needle,

Money doesn't buy friends, love or happiness "One other example is to compare using failure as an example. These are intended to create a fear of success.

Low self-esteem is a lack of confidence creating a sense of not being good enough. Others can do this but not you. Every set back is judged personally, and you perceived it occurred because of shortcomings or you did something wrong. False accusations, criticism, judgmental comments are all intended to create a sense of wrongness and lower self-worth.

INABILITY TO RECEIVE

It is far easier to give than to receive. Many times, it is selfish not to receive; it 'stops the flow of allowing others to give, even so simple as receiving compliments. Unfortunately, the sense of undeserving or unworthiness to receive is involved in this situation. If you only allow yourself to plant and never harvest your fruit will die on the vine not creating a cycle.

Mind blocks are the issues stop success. When noticing the lack of success, our mind draws the conclusion that what we desire is where our greatest focus remains fixed. This cause a blockage seeing the opportunity I focused upon. By this reaction, our mind thinks that is what we are most interested in rather than the successes we desire. This blockage causes us to be in a negative state, and instinctively gathers evidence of why we can't do that, finding ways to not measure up and abort the very thing we desire.

SELF EXAMINATION

Is this what I really think or feel regarding this concern?

Is this something that someone or parents influenced by their opinions or is it mine?

1. Where are these thoughts coming from? How do I really feel about this?
2. Is this my feeling moving toward my desires/dreams or away from them?

Take actions toward success, move forward and get rid of the negative thoughts as you notice them. It is far easier to move pebbles before they become a stone wall block. removing them one stone at a time keeps our pathway clear to move on.

As a reminder, the law of attractions has a force field polarity of either being drawn to a negative or a positive vibration. These are dependent on your thoughts. An interesting thing about your thoughts, it will come out in unexpected ways. Just as what you really feel will be exposed as well when you are placed under pressure when pressed. If you take an orange and put it under great pressure what will come out? Orange juice. The same way things come out when you are put under great pressures. What you think and believe will come out in your words and actions. The way you act, and your reaction are truth-tellers, exposing much of what you truly believe and feel. Take a minute and examine yourself. What comes out of you under excessive pressure?

The point of Nexus [25] is the point where destiny and opportunity collide where God's call and man's courage will intersect. Some will call this the Quantum Leap. Merriam-Webster's definition is as follows: A quantum leap is a sudden large change, development. [26]

SETTING CORE VALUES

Take a minute to write your core values. Core values are the fundamental beliefs of a person or organization. For this particular exercise write those things that are really of greatest importance to you in the area of life you are leaping toward, whether it is your relationships, health or finances. Is my cup half empty or full??? What do I have in my hand that I can take and use to begin to fill my half empty-cup to overflowing???

1. I CANNOT GO FORWARD IF THESE ISSUES ARE VIOLATED
2. THESE ISSUES ARE IMPORTANT TO HAVE IN RELATIONSHIPS

---

[25] Nexus Merriam-Webster Dictionary
[26] Quantum Leap Merriam-Webster Dictionary

These items you have listed are what you will use as a filter to move forward in relationships, this filter applies to work, personal relationships or anything you choose to apply them to that will help you determine what is personally important to you.

INVENTORY

Take a separate piece of paper and list every type of life experiences and talents you have that might be used to fill the empty cup to overflowing. Bring these prayerfully into consideration weighing and pondering these in the presence of God our Creator who took from the inventory and created us into the persona and unique abilities, talents, gifting we possess. How can we bring this thing that we are created to for the unique purposes in the Universe to give back to others and bring forth the purpose driven life we were created to become? God created you for a plan and purpose.

Psalm 139:13 (NIV) For you created my inmost being; you knit me together in my mother's womb.

GETTING TO KNOW YOU

Take an additional piece of paper and write down all you would love to do or accomplish. Remove all barriers from your thoughts. If you always wanted to paint, write it down. Whatever desire you would like to see or fulfill write it down. What would my most incredible dream in life look like? Visualize it. Find pictures to remind you of it. If it is a new house then get pictures, designs, layouts, things you desire in your house. Consider how it looks. What rooms do you want? If it is a new truck, what color is your truck? What features does it have? What is the size of the engine, the style? Find pictures of your desired truck. Create a vision wall. What do you love to do? What can you immediately do to bring life to that? If you love to garden, buy a starter seed tray to begin. Water your seeds and watch them grow. Look at your list and see all you have accomplished, how amazing you are and so gifted and talented.

Fill your bucket list full of all the things you would love to do in a new opportunity. Open your mind to consider the pathways to take to reach that dream. Dare to dream and receive all God has for your life and see the unlimited possibilities of unique gifts and extraordinary talents.

Jeremiah 29:11 (KJV) "For I know the thoughts that I think towards you," saith the Lord, "thoughts of peace, and not of evil, to give you an expected end."

WHEN THINGS SEEM IMPOSSIBLE

The mind is the control of your life. Our thoughts greatly influence not only successes, failures and choices, but also a relationship with God. Changing ungodliness comes from changing our thinking to the way God does. Negativity impacts your thought life and is influenced by past negativity.

Remember, God gave us a new spirit and new life to start over, but that doesn't blot out our past experiences. Draw from the positive experiences of the past, you have been rescued from the negative. Unsuitable input of self-thoughts, and recycled experiences of negative situations greatly impact our thinking. When we think wrong thoughts, we create wrong appetites, creating conflicts within ourselves causing feelings of tension and guilt.

REPROGRAMING YOUR MINDS

1. You have the capacity to think right.
2. Seek spiritual thoughts and study the Word of God.
3. Filter your thoughts through the Word of God.

4. "Watch your thoughts, for they become actions. Watch your actions, for they become habits. Watch your habits; for they become character. Watch your character for it will become your destiny." Frank Outlaw[27]
5. You many times react instead of act. You do this without consideration of the outcome or regard for God's instruction or purposes.
6. Choose to refuse certain thoughts. You aren't responsible for thoughts popping in your mind but accountable for your response to them.
7. Ask God to redirect your thoughts; removing evil, harmful thoughts is a choice.

THE WHITE ALABASTER BOX

The white alabaster box... as I write this I am thinking of our men and women in the military and other branches of service "All that I have, all that I am." They have spilled out their lives for this great country, giving the freedom to be allowed to worship and pour out our praises for God. Not only do I think of them, but also, my mind turns to the wives, children and families. All these have paid great prices for this nation to be celebrated as the home of the free and land of liberty and justice for all.

For this reason, I would like to dedicate this section as an acknowledgement to one and all of those who have sacrificed for this nation.

May God help me pour out to you from His healing hands into your life, as I begin to share from my heart to yours from my alabaster box. Fill my cup Lord to pour out to the hurting, the suffering and broken, in Jesus' name. Amen.

---

[27] Goodreads-13466663.Frank Outlaw

Matthew 26:7 (NIV) A woman came to Him with an alabaster vial of very expensive perfume and she poured it on Jesus' head as He reclined at the table.

What is the alabaster box? It is a container, a vial or a box of perfume. The name came from Alabastron, Egypt where a soft white marble could be found. What is the significance of it? [28]

According to the Matthew Henry Commentary: pouring the ointment on the head of Christ was a token of the highest respect. Where there is true love in the heart to Christ nothing will be too good to bestow upon him.[29]

As we begin to unpack this and the different events in this section, take time to examine the events closely in your own life to find the keys to brokenness.

POST-TRAUMATIC STRESS DISORDER

What is Post Traumatic Stress Disorder[30]? It is a severe anxiety disorder that develops following exposure to extreme psychological trauma. About 10% of women compared to 5% of men develop PTSD. About 7 to 8% of people in the US will have PTSD at some point in their lives, 5.2 million adults suffer from PTSD each year. Often with both anxiety disorders and PTSD you will discover you are repeating patterns. The re-cycling pattern will continue until you recognize change is required causing breakthrough in your circumstances. You will find your action sabotaging the very thing most important in a relationship or situation.

---

[28] Alabastron, Egypt ebible.com
[29] Matthew Henry Commentary Matthew 26:7 http;//biblehub.com
[30] PTSD www.anxietysymptoms.com

Life has many traumas, all of which in one form or another affect your emotions and behavior patterns. All have causes and effects on how you grow and develop. Your behavior patterns which cause negative patterns and re-patterning in your life are good indicators that you have been wounded in one form or another.

God has led, healed and delivered me in each area of my life. These areas started as a wounded child which caused many damages in my life. These areas continued to be healed as recently as my head-on wreck. It is all part of life and God is able to bring us through it all. I would encourage you to seek counseling as well as spending time with God to become healed and whole.

There are physical causes such as heart issues, overactive thyroid, and hypoglycemia. In addition to these, stimulants, amphetamines or drugs similar to caffeine, and medication withdrawal can also result in some of these symptoms. Abnormal blood changes can affect your mental and emotional responses as well.

When I worked for FEMA assisting on the Disaster hotlines, and also in the Disaster Housing area we had Crisis counselors available at all times. Disaster and injuries are some of the most traumatic stresses that are constantly happening. In the news, today most all of the victims, of the recent hurricanes, floods, fires and earthquakes will be in some form of shock and trauma affected emotional state.

Disaster isn't selective in where or who it strikes down. Because of the many levels of shocks and injuries, often we take for granted that it really isn't a big deal, then all of a sudden something is happening, and you are having a really hard time putting it together. You realize something is wrong with you, perhaps you just can't quit crying, or you jump out of your skin at every turn. You anger easily, or you just feel numb, guilty, ashamed. Maybe, you just can't remember what happened or other simple things. You may have flashbacks and nightmares over and over again. All of a sudden you feel despair and hopelessness. You just want all of it to stop. You may find yourself angry when someone doesn't listen to what you are telling them, and you feel consumed with rage.

Look deeper, these are all indicators of PTSD; you may be a victim of it and suffering from it. Over 30% of Vietnam Veterans suffer from PSTD. While 10% of the Desert Storm Veterans suffer from this disorder and 11-20% of the Iraq Veterans and Afghanistan Veterans are battling this problem.

Cause of a traumatic event[31]

1. Witnessing a death or injury
2. Physical Assault
3. Combat
4. Sexual Assault
5. Accidents
6. Natural Disasters
7. Child Sexual Abuse

Because it comes in many variations, families struggle to understand that the person is struggling just to keep going daily. They too get hurt and angry because they don't realize this is an illness and needs medical attention just as much as the broken back or the amputated limb such as my daughter experienced.

My grandson had a Traumatic Brain injury caused by being hit in the head and had amazing amounts of medical side effects even to loss of hearing. Family, friends, patient pay attention; you may need help and that is alright too. Sometimes, you just can't handle it by yourself you need medical attention.

As an example, following my wreck, I would get milk out of the refrigerator to pour a glass of milk and simply walk away. I would have flashbacks of my wreck. I could remember very little of events

---

[31] Charts PTSD neurogym.com

in my life and would have to ask my daughter to tell me what it was about. These types of struggles happen when trauma occurs. It is like having a record that suddenly skips when it occurs.

As a second example, a certain member in the family I was raised in drove to a store and stopped for gas on his return trip home. He filled his car with gas. When he returned to the car, he sat down in the back seat of the car he was driving, later to discover he was a severe diabetic. These types of incidents occur as a medical event. When you are dealing with different types of blood issues this is not uncommon at all. Confusion occurs when not getting proper blood oxygen flow.

My daughter suffered a hand injury and finger amputation. After multiple surgeries, she needed anger management. She dealt with anger as a result of her injury with PTSD. It is not unusual to find responses similar to this as a result of physical or emotional traumas. Don't allow yourself to feel guilty; this is a result of shock, and your injury. You saw, felt and endured pain, shock or suffering because of the loss and trauma you experienced.

I have two straps and a plate holding my right hand onto my arm. That, too, is traumatic, to witness your hand separated from your arm, compounded with all the other injuries I sustained. My purpose in mentioning these are for you and your families to realize you may all need help to adjust to what you are experiencing.

Please verify with a physician if you are having any of these conditions as they can actually be red flags to medical issues and not just in your mind. Many times, it can be hormonal imbalances, or nothing more than adrenaline related medical conditions. Trust the medical advice given to you. Never assume it is in your mind because as easily as not it can be directly related to your body. It is critical to get the help you need to move forward whole and well.

Jeremiah 29:11(NIV) "For I know the plans I have for you," declares the Lord, "plans to prosper you and not to harm you, plans to give you hope and a future".

The Word of God is powerful as I demonstrated in a spiritual attack, I was under that I shared earlier. The reality is when something happens you can rely upon His Word, it works! I share that with you as I know this to be an absolute truth! It does work. The important thing is always to stay focused, whether in a personal injury or an emotional assault which can in fact be the far more damaging event. The most important words beyond… "but God", are never, never, never, give up!!!! Absolutely never give up, as long as you have air to breathe and a heartbeat; there is hope, and God truly is able to deliver you. Hold on and remember all things are temporary; you are going to make it!

ANXIETY

Anxiety causes the brain to wander. the frontal part of the brain region is the impulse control center where critical thinking, judgment, learning from experiences, attention span and perseverance are formed. Most are imaginary but still physically affect the brain.

Carl Jung said, "What you resist, persists". [32]

Neale Donald Walsch, "The act of resisting something is the act of granting it life [33] **Trying to resist or avoid situations causes panic, leaving one feeling defeated and exhausted."**

Using resistance alone has no forward progression. The act of resisting something is the act of granting it life. The more you resist the more you make it real that you are resisting.

---

[32] Carl Jung Goodreads quotes 485998
[33] Neale Donald Walsch Goodreads 9374

You need to start by changing your perspective. When you look at anxiety as a disease, that is what it becomes to you. What if you decided to change your thoughts and look at it as a friend that you can actually learn to accept? Just as I use distractions as a memo to remind myself later to do something; so, you can use this just simply by writing it down, it clears your mind. As you reframe and acknowledge it has a purpose, it can actually be of help to you.

It can be used to let you acknowledge that something is wrong, and a change is needed to bring you back into a balanced place in your life. It is much like running a fever, that alerts you that something is wrong.

What is causing the stress? Start looking at what needs to change. Are you overworked, lacking sleep, not eating properly? This can give you a clearer understanding of yourself and others. Look at your problem, confront it head on. What is causing the fear/anxiety? Then ask yourself wouldn't it be funny if…? Or wouldn't it be awful if …? then you can find something to laugh about. Make an appointment for 3 days from now with yourself and then be certain to keep it. In the midst of adversities, you can find the strength to overcome with a greater understanding and compassion for others.

Isaiah 41:10 (NAS) "Do not fear, for I am with you; Do not look anxiously about you, for I am your God. I will strengthen you; I surely will help you. Surely, I will uphold you with My righteous right hand."

2 Chronicles 20:17(NAS) "You need not fight in this battle; station yourselves, stand and see the salvation of the LORD on your behalf, O Judah and Jerusalem "Do not fear or be dismayed; tomorrow go out to face them, for the LORD is with you."

Stress unmanaged becomes anxiety. When anxiety is unmanaged it becomes a full-blown panic attack. It can come as a mild shock like a plug into a light socket. Panic attacks in a mild form will cause you to feel uneasy and you need to do something, but you can handle it.

DAYS OF PLUNDER

A full-blown panic attack causes you to feel like you are holding on to a 220 wire and you are going to die. Some of the symptoms of panic include nausea, shortness of breath, hyperventilation, feeling of choking, chest pains, heart palpitations, racing heart, trembling, shaking, sweating, fear of dying, losing control or going crazy. Panic can be brought on by radical life changes such as loss of a loved one or job loss. It may also include major life transitions such as moving, graduation, marriage, divorce, starting work, trauma, accidents, exhaustion or malnourishment.

How to Overcome Anxiety

1. Write down your fears. What can you change?
2. What is outside of your control?
3. Accept what you are unable to control, act on what you can control.
4. Recognize that most worries and things you fear don't happen; they are paper tigers.
5. Live in the now. Stay focused and look toward your goal, what you desire to happen.
6. Write down your end vision of where you are going; stay focused on God.
7. Trust God to help you. You are not alone in this battle.
8. Praise and focus on the promises of God to strengthen you and trust Him to guide you to the other side of your troubles.

When stress hits us, and it does all of us at one time or another, I personally use praise music to re-focus on God and off of my troubles. David, throughout the Psalms, would use music to release his soul from fear and discouragement to take his focus off of his dangers. It will bring rest to your mind and peace to your soul.

If you find yourself as I have written, perhaps you have realized you have been there. Maybe you are there right now, at the end of your strength. Remember and turn to God; you never walk alone.

He was there with me when I was a child that was sexually abused, and during my discovery of being switched at birth. He was there when my husband died while taking his pulse to only revive to become a different person. He was there during the loss of family, and lastly my head-on wreck. Through all the pain, sorrows and suffering, it has brought me to know Him in greater ways and now I can to stand and tell you He will help you and bring you through if you trust Him.

MARY DID YOU KNOW?

Luke 1:26-38 (NAS) 26 In the sixth month the angel Gabriel was sent from God to a city in Galilee, called Nazareth, 27 to a virgin engaged to a man whose name was Joseph, of the descendants of David, and the virgin's name was Mary. 28 And coming in, he said to her, "Hail, favored one! The Lord is with you." 29 But she was greatly troubled at this statement and kept pondering what kind of salutation this might be. 30 And the angel said to her, "Do not be afraid, Mary; for you have found favor with God. 31 And behold, you will conceive in your womb and bear a son, and you shall call Him Jesus. 32 He will be great, and will be called the Son of the Most High; and the Lord God will give Him the throne of His father David; 33 and He will reign over the house of Jacob forever; and His kingdom will have no end." 34 And Mary said to the angel, "How can this be, since I am a virgin?" 35 And the angel answered and said to her, "The Holy Spirit will come upon you, and the power of the Most High will overshadow you; and for that reason, he holy offspring shall be called the Son of God. 36 And behold even your relative Elizabeth has also conceived a son in her old age; and she who was called barren is now in her sixth month. 37 For nothing will be impossible with God." 38 And Mary said, "Behold the bond slave of the Lord, be it done to me according to your word." And the angel departed from her.

DIVINE ENCOUNTER

Mary was confronted by the unknown. She was highly favored and called by God. *Blessed is she that believed, for there shall be a performance of these things that had been told her from the Lord.*

How is this to happen? What is this to look like?

Did you know it would cost you all when your journey began?

Did you know each step of your way the great I AM walked by your side?

Did you know your tears that have fallen like rain, He has seen?

Did you know your teardrops are bottled in heaven to water the souls of the harvest to come?

Did you know with each day of brokenness that you have suffered, He was standing watching over you through each long and lonely night?

Did you know He has been there sitting by your side as you cried?

Did you know He saw your broken body as you have lain in pain?

Did you know He has been there?

Do you know how greatly He loves, you even to laying down His life for you?

He hears your every cry when there is no one else to care. When those you loved betrayed you or forsook you and walked away, He was there.

Do you know He is standing with arms open wide, inviting you to walk with Him?

Do you know His resurrection power can wash away every sin when it is confessed to Him?

Do you know the door is open wide welcoming you? Won't you reach and come to truly know Him???? Do you know Jesus loves YOU?

Luke1:45-49(NAS) "And blessed is she who believed: that there would be a fulfillment of what had been spoken to her by the Lord."

Luke 2:14(KJV) Glory to God in the highest, and on earth peace, good will toward men.

Live in peace and thanksgiving; these are weapons of sure victory. Change is difficult. Sometimes it is hard to change as it causes us to be uncomfortable. There will be dangers. You may find yourself with a Judas (betrayer).

PARADIGM SHIFT

English /Cambridge Dictionary defines a Paradigm shift as, "A time when the usual and accepted way of doing or thinking about something changes completely."[34]

LETTING GO OF THE FORMER

There comes a point in time when a metamorphosis will require a step change or change over. A shifting of your focus from yesterday's failures, losses, victories, and defeats is an essential requirement to close the door. Give yourself permission to let go; say goodbye to old habits, wrong relationships and yesterday's beliefs. It will with certainty require irrevocable change.

---

[34] Paradigm English/Cambridge Dictionary

There was a time that came to let go and trust God to always provide and care for my son. I had prayed endlessly, believing God would work it out for my son to remain with me. I had lost weight until I now wore a child size; my tears were endless. The tipping point came when the pain to hold on became greater than the pain of change. With the letting go, the new reality in God began.

Ultimately, God had a different plan. He desired to remove my Isaac and take me through a divine healing. I mention all of this to give you an understanding that God's way is far higher than our way. We must trust Him always for our best. He is a good God.

The quantum leap has cost me letting go of most of all that has mattered to me and led to a total reliance and trust of God. When you find your pathway being changed and you face a heartbreaking letting go, you may rely on God totally. You are in a belief test; will you trust God for His best and way?

Such was the case when the children of Israel were backed up against the Red Sea; only then did they learn that God was their provider. Another example was when Abraham had a knife drawn, ready to kill his only son and suddenly there was a ram in the thicket.

GOLDEN KEY

The Golden key to enter the promises is the key of obedience.

1. You need to be courageous, not deterred by pain, fearless and heroic.
2. Be regulated by God's Word.
3. Do not turn to the left or right; walk to please God.
4. In times of uncertainty and not understanding, wait upon the Lord.
5. Possess the land with assurance, being faithful to adhere to God's Word and you will conquer.

6. You will then have a life of victory and peace instead of anxiety; joy instead of mourning; strength instead of weakness.
7. Victory in Christ is our promised possession.
8. Meditation on God's Word is another way to enter into success.

Joshua 1:8 (KJV) Joshua reminds all the importance of these laws. You yourself, must ponder these continually so you will obey all of them, for your success.

Hebrew 4:11(KJV) Let us labour therefore to enter into that rest, lest any man fall after the same example of unbelief.

1. The same formula for walking in rest is walking in obedience.
2. Meditation words we read are spiritual. They are planted into the soil of our hearts for our souls to get strength from.

That which is in the spirit is mirrored in the natural. If we plant the seed (Yen) into the soil of our hearts (Yang) and let it grow, it will manifest a harvest. Earlier we discussed the Law of Gender; it applies in this discussion as well as the Law of Reproduction. What we plant in our minds will produce its likeness. We will have what we say and think. There is also power in our thoughts and words. We have found evidence of it as we discovered in the Law of Attractions, these laws were set into motion from the foundation of the earth.

Just as the atom, electron, neutron, proton and molecule all are parts of the composition of structure in our universe; the laws and principles of God were established long before our time began.

Often the misperceptions are based on misguided thinking, or unfounded beliefs. We all have been there, where we have realized we are wrong in our thinking. Failure or being wrong isn't a permanent condition, but a time to grow. When you look at what God says, then apply the Laws you have been studying, it gives you the help to get moving forward again. Also, this application causes you to begin to develop a habit of applying God's words and patterns to your issues. Many of the cycled patterns in your own life become broken, freeing you of many personal struggles. You will discover both insights and the revelation of God's Word that will open your mind to creative ideas and alternate ways to a solution as you pray and wait for guidance.

Immediately, turn from your ways; ask forgiveness for whatever you feel is in error. Next start digging to find the pattern and answer that applies to you! You aren't the only one who has believed wrongly or wanted to be of greater importance or significance. Easily, we can point to very clear examples. Eve ate the apple, but Adam knew better. Lucifer was the head Song Leader in Heaven; his pride literally cost him God's best. Judas, in his greed, ended his own life. The good news is God does give us a second chance. You do have a choice to stay in your pig pen or get out of it and seek His ways.

God is a good God and loves us. He also is a holy God. Just as your earthly father gives good gifts, so does He. Equally so, we can find ourselves being disciplined. Realize, the choice is yours and you are the one responsible for your actions, no one else.

Without exception one and all are hard-wired to know Him. That is a part of your intuition when you become aware you are doing something wrong or a stirring in your heart something is missing. You all have a place reserved for God alone. It all becomes a matter of choice your choice!!!

You now have learned a few Spiritual and Universal Laws to apply to your life. We have discussed a few of the guidance tools. We have studied the why of these laws. We have learned in Matthew 6:25(KJV) about our being anxious; its causes and effects. You now know the golden key to success lies in obedience.

You now have been given a greater understanding of the laws and princples which apply to you and the universe. You also have discovered unforgiveness is a roadblock and the significance of release is for you, not the offender.

The challenge is to realize it will take God's power as stated in Zech.4:6(KJV) for your passage and successful arrival. You will be successful as you focus on God for your journey's end. Your daily bread is important for your strength and reliable truth. It is important to have a proper diet to sustain you along the journey to include the Bible and the Universal Laws which are tools to direct our steps.

In previous pages you have created a bucket list of your heart's desires. You have designed a map to consider as you prayerfully focus and seek God for His wisdom and guidance.

There is now clarity in your steps and a vision to go forth. You have a plan, a purpose, and a map to direct your steps (the Bible). Foremost, the compass (God) to direct your course.

It really isn't so much about the process, as the becoming within. You have grown in leaps and bounds with each step you have taken forward and each change you have made. Congratulations!!!

LOVE NEVER FAILS

1 Corinthians 13:8 (AMP) Love never fails (never fades out or becomes obsolete or comes to an end.) As for prophecy (the gift of interpreting the divine will and purpose), it will be fulfilled and pass away; as for tongues, they will be destroyed and cease; as for knowledge, it will pass away (it will lose its value and be superseded by truth).

Recently during lunch with a friend, the discussion of eternity and death became a part of the conversation. As we continued to discuss eternity and God, I soon discovered she had both a fear of God and of eternity. This fear had come because of having been exposed to an individual that had an extremely religious spirit. God's Word was used as a tool to beat her up verbally. It left her with a fear of God.

I was raised in a similar situation. I totally understood the concerns and thoughts of my friend. I too had experienced similar verbal assaults that caused me not to want anything to do with God. It was years before I understood and overcome wrong beliefs, and these vicious verbal attacks. You too may have endured something similar.

God is a holy God and we are to revere and fear Him; He also is a merciful and loving God. So many times, people are driven away from God because of the concept He desires to destroy you. "You are not good enough, and you will burn in hell." This just isn't true. He desires obedience to His Word, but He created us for a relationship. As strange as it may sound the story of Beauty and the Beast comes to mind. The Beast is misunderstood in the Disney story and feared, such as is God misunderstood.

As I returned home, I continued to ponder this conversation further. Today I took it before the Lord God. In His presence, I asked of Him what He would desire I tell His children and all that read this book. As I waited before Him, and prayerfully listened, these were the words He gave me for each of you, "Tell them I love them. My love never fails".

James 4:7(NAS) Submit therefore to God. Resist the devil, and He will flee from you.

1. Let no fear hinder you. Allow no doubt to enter your mind. Whoever waivers will not receive. Be single minded.
2. Praise builds faith and God inhabits the praises of His people. Loving God will bring God to your side.

As with any relationship, you must spend intimate time together to grow. The primary purpose of your being created is to have a relationship with God. It is not for Him to destroy you, but for you to spend all eternity with Him. As always, this is yet another lie from the devil to create distance from you and truly knowing God.

In departing this conversation, I remind you again of His Words today. "Tell them I love them. My love never fails".

ETERNITY

King James Bible Dictionary definitions: Witness 1. To be a witness that is testify, literally or figuratively

Strong's (Def G3140) Concordance Bible Usage: Greek word is marturio [35]

King James Bible Dictionary definition: Messenger

Hebrew: mal'ak

Greek: an angel a messenger who runs on foot, the bearer of dispatches, swift of foot.[36]

I come to you now as a Messenger, as a Witness to truths that I am to reveal and tell you. As I close this time together with you, I leave for your understanding for you to come to know Him as you continue your own journey.

VALIDATION AND CONFIRMATION

Recently a visiting evangelist came to my church. At the close of the service we were invited to come forward for a time of prayer. As he

---

[35] King James Bible Dictionary /Witness/ Def G3140 marturio
[36] King James Bible Dictionary / Hebrew mal'ak Messenger

approached me and placed his hands on my shoulders, he looked at me for a moment, paused and then told me that the Lord had spoken to him and told him I had visions of heaven. After a brief exchange of words he moved on to pray for others.

As I returned to my seat, a member in my church stopped me and said to me, "The Lord had told me you had been dead and returned from the dead". Both of these were words of confirmation of a truth; that of which I want to share with you.

Several times following my wreck, starting with my daughter who asked of me, "What do you remember "? Others would ask that as well as, "What did I see?" At first, I could only recall bright lights and loving hands. As time passed, it was to continue with others approaching me and repeating these questions. It almost felt like a nudge happening with each continued time it happened to me. Finally, after several months of this occurrence, I continued to grow stronger. I sat down and thought about all that had happened as I saw the spinning tires of the truck, the outline of the driver in the cab of the truck, and its side as I hit the truck. Scene after scene I relived as I sat there.

Finally, as I relived these things, there came a time of nothingness. Then suddenly in a flashback, I saw it all. I was once again standing in the most brilliant lights all around me. I was so aware of the love, and loving hands all about me. There was the incredible peace of eternity. I looked about me, when I saw off to my right at a distance maybe 20 to 30 feet the most enormous angel standing. Clearly, he was all of 10 to 12 feet tall. He was dressed in a white robe, his wings brushed the ground and he was holding in his hands a book, The Book of Life. Then I knew I had entered Eternity.

Just as suddenly, I returned to my body. I knew that I knew, Heaven is real. There is an eternity, a place called Heaven, and it is real!!! He loves you, and He is coming again soon. That is my purpose and destiny to tell one and all. Just as you now have been told, we all have a choice, and it remains between you and God.

Heavenly Father, as Your Messenger and Witness, I have shared what you have left me here to tell. I now leave this in Your hands and those You are calling to You. As I close these pages and accounts, be glorified; in Your son Jesus' name. Amen.

MOMENTS OF REFLECTION - The Poetry Guild

Would you Love Me?

Diana Lynn Rogers[37]

If I were a child of three or four,
Would you love me anymore?
If I were a beggar on the street …
Would you love me? Would you be my friend?

If I were filled with sorrow and pain,
And my face was tear strained…
Would you love me? Would you love me then?
Or would you say, "please go away
I haven't the time today.
You see I'm on my way to pray"
Would you love me? Would you love me anyway?

I sent the child to your door.
And the beggar to ask you for more.
And I was the one with the tear stained face.
Asking for your mercy and grace.

---

[37] Moments of Reflection The Poetry Guild

Will you love me? Will you love me?
What you have done to the least of
These you have done unto me.
Will you love me? Will you love me?
Will you love when I walk your way?

East of the Sunrise -The International Library of Poetry

IF I COULD[38]

Diana Lynn Rogers

If I could but paint a picture it would be
crimson red pooling at the foot of Calvary.
I would take my brush and touch my palette
and tip it in gold, with a stroke of
my brush I would paint a face full
of mercy and grace.

Etched with a trace of sorrow and pain
Crushed to produce a glorious refrain.
…If I were to paint a picture of me
You would see one who abides in mercy and grace.
Full of joy, with laughter and tears that has
Stained her face…would be looking into
Her Savior's Face.

There would be the two of us you would see,
The Holy Spirit and me. Together we walk and
talk as he guides and directs me.
If I could paint a picture you would see only Jesus who abides in me.

---

[38] International Library of Poetry

The Whirling Seas International Library of Poetry

After the Rain, Lord

Diana Lynn Rogers[39]

After the rain, Lord
Grant me a song in the night.
As I wait for the morning to come
Help me know everything will be alright.
After the sorrow, after the pain.
Once again fragrant flowers will bloom.
Gentle breezes will blow away all the gloom.
Fields of flowers will nod and sway
In the sun-drenched fields where they play.

All summer long grass will be greener,
Streams filled will run,
Trees lush foliage will cast a
Restful shade from the sun.

After the rain, Lord,
Help me find peace and rest,
Hidden away in you, like a mother
Robin on its nest.

---

[39] International Library of Poetry

The Best Poems of 1997 / Sound of Poetry
International Library of Poetry

Sands of Time[40]

Diana Lynn Rogers

Silently the sands of time are passing by,
Memories of laughter and of tears left in
The sands of yesterday years,
Echoing in this heart of mine...
Silently and swiftly passing the sands of time.

Times together...and then apart...
Always your memory lingering in my heart.
The warmth of your embrace...
Memories of you that time cannot erase.

Silently, silently the sands of time pass by.
A God, who knows the answer of my hearts cry
A God who cares, a Father who sees
The depth of love that flows through me.

Ever watching all knowing, is this Father of mine.
The keeper of my heart, the Creator of time.
Silently, silently the sands of time pass by,
Sands of time silently drifting
and passing my way...
Silently beginning and ending each day.

---

[40] International Library of Poetry

The Ancient of Days[41]

Diana Lynn Rogers

I will sing a song of triumph. I will sing a song of praise,
In the stillness of my soul is my future foretold
all glory to the Ancient of Days!
Hallelujah! Hallelujah! All glory to the Ancient of Days!

In the darkness of the days
To Him I give all praise, as I look all around
His answer cannot be found.
I will sing a song of triumph,
As I place my trust in the Ancient of days.
Hallelujah! Hallelujah! All glory to the Ancient of Days!

Though trouble is all around; His glory is to be found.
Faithful is He who threw the horse and rider in the sea!
I will sing a song of triumph; I will sing a song of praise.
Faithful is He the Ancient of Days!
Hallelujah! Hallelujah! All glory to the Ancient of Days!

What He did for them, He will do for me.
He will lead, guide and direct my ways.
His glory I will proclaim, who was and is the same.
I will sing a song of triumph I will sing a song of praise!
Hallelujah! Hallelujah! All glory to the Ancient of Days!

---

[41] Diana Lynn Rogers

EPILOGUE

Sometimes you just have to dance. Friday is past and Sunday is coming...

Morning has come, and you have discovered within it has come a time to quit staring at the grave. Sometimes life is like a balloon you look up to the one who knows and sees all. You let go, and release that which has been clutched so tightly in your hands. You watch as it slowly rises drifting to the heavenly places, you continue to watch as it slowly ascends and disappears. All is over and you know it.

Tears well up and fill your eyes, you remember faded memories; in His time God will do all He promises and has said. He will make all things beautiful in His time. Eccl.4-1(NAS) reveals to us there is, "a time to weep, and a time to laugh; a time to mourn and a time to dance."

A gentle smile caresses your lips; within your very being you know, God's got this! Across the span of time, suffering and sorrow, you have come to know as your friends. They somehow have come to feel comfortable being with you as both your friends, and companions when all walked away. Just breathe! God's got this you are going to be alright!!!

Still smiling, you glance over into the corner of your heart, forgotten and tossed aside you reach. Silently, you slip them on your feet, as old friends joy and peace envelop your feet; flooding your heart as they give you warmth. You hear a song that has filled your heart. As you look about, you realize your toe is tapping to the beat of your heart you stand up and you know; you just know you just got to dance!!! Morning has come the gift of a new day has begun and you dance; you dance before the King of Glory.

Come dance with me the battle has been won; you have made it through the storm. Let's dance!!!! God's got this!!!

A Time for Everything

Eccl. 3: 1-10(NAS) There is an appointed time for everything. And there is a time for every event under heaven--- 2 A time to give birth, and a time to die; A time to plant and a time to uproot what is planted. 3 A time to kill, and a time to heal; A time to tear down and a time to build up. 4 A time to weep, and a time to laugh; A time to mourn, and a time to dance.5 A time to throw stones, and a time to gather stones; A time to embrace, and a time to shun embracing.6 A time to search, and a time to give up as lost; A time to keep, and a time to throw away.7A time to tear apart; and a time to sew together; A time to be silent, and a time to speak.8 A time to love, and a time to hate; A time for war, and a time for peace.9 What profit is there to the worker from that in which he toils?10 I have seen the seen the tasks which God has given the sons of men with which to occupy themselves.

DAYS OF PLUNDER

Finding light in the Darkness to Overcome and Recover All

THE PROMISE Volume II

PRELUDE

In the following pages, I want to help you discover the promises of God hidden away. He has directed me to look at His Promises and seek His Kingdom first above all.

Open your heart and mind as God reveals His ways, as I share various encounters with Him as He has come close. May this help you apply the promises of God in your own life and see the keys of the promise open doors that have remained closed. May we all receive from God and His Word guidance as He breaks every chain and moves us all forward to a greater, better life than we might hope or imagine.

Heavenly Father, according to Your will and way, open eyes to see and ears to hear what the Spirit is saying to each one who reads The Promise, in Jesus' name. Amen

THE PROMISE

The familiar old rusty gate of the corridor of time slowly opens on its rusty hinges with an ease, despite the time that has passed. At the entry as I stand ready to step entering the room filled with memories of former things. I feel my heart fill with a thanksgiving and praise to God. Entering the secret chamber containing so many memories; I stand searching for yet another book. Hidden amongst the many volumes stored on the shelves of my heart. While I searched, I saw memories of days past in my childhood, former things that have long since passed away. I continued to look around; I spotted the book with the golden cover. There a distinctive sheen surrounds it as I reach to remove it from its protected shelf. Embossed on the beautiful golden cover are the words, *"Days of Plunder, Finding light in the Darkness to Overcome and Recover All, The Promise, Volume II."*

I recall having read *"But seek ye first the Kingdom of God, and His righteousness; and all these things will be added unto you."* (Matthew 6:33). His promise. The treasure house of blessings come from the Kingdom of God through His promises. The promises are the keys used to open the door to the treasures of God's grace and favor.

"Not by might, nor by power, but by my spirit," says the Lord Almighty. (Zechariah 4:6)

[42]The story of a promise unfolds with the tale of a young woman named Hannah. She was the wife of Elkanah. He had two wives. Peninnah and Peninnah had children, and Hannah had no children.

---

[42] biblegateway.com/ study of Samuel

Written in the word of the Lord, her womb was closed. (I Samuel 1:2).

Yearly, Elkanah would go to worship and sacrifice to the Lord in Shiloh, giving all a sacrificial portion; but to Hannah, whom he loved, he would give her a double portion. At about the time to pray, grieved, she wept before the Lord at the lack of a son. She vowed before the Lord she would give the baby back to Him if he would provide her with a son. Eli, the priest, mistook her prayers as being drunken, of which she denied and told of her grief and petition to him. Eli then blessed her. (I Samuel 1:11) She returned

home with her husband, Elkanah, she had relations with him, she conceived and gave birth to a son. She named him Samuel and said, *"Because I have asked him of the Lord."*

Hannah remained home with Samuel. Neither going to the House of the Lord until when her son Samuel no longer nursed and the time of offering in Shiloh arrived. She prepared an offering to the Lord, Hannah left Samuel in the care of Eli, the priest. (I Samuel 1:24-28) Annually at the time of offering to the Lord; she would return with a robe for Samuel. The offering to the Lord made, she then departed Shiloh to return home.

Great is the faithfulness of the Lord God to those who trust and believe in Him, from generation to generation. Hannah blessed by God received three more sons and two daughters. And the boy Samuel grew before the Lord.

Due to the evilness of Eli's sons, the word of the Lord came forth with His judgment, and obeying the Lord's decree, the sons died. The young man named Samuel remained near Eli. Eli's eyes were growing dim, and Samuel slept nearby.

⁴³Samuel was lying resting when the Lord called to him. Samuel replied, "Here I am" and ran to Eli's side. Eli responded, "I did not call; you go back and lie down." Samuel returned to his place of rest once more. Once more the Lord called to him, and Samuel responded and ran to Eli's side, saying, "Here I am, for you called me." But Eli said to him, "I did not call, my son, lie down again." The Lord called to him a third time. Once again, Samuel ran to Eli's side and said, "Here I am, for you called me." The third time Eli discerned the Lord was calling the boy. Eli instructed Samuel once more to lie down, but this time to respond if He should call him and say, "Speak Lord, for Your servant is listening." (I Samuel 3:10-11) The Word of the Lord continues to this day; for such a time as this.

Similar to the story of Samuel, I found myself awakened in the night. The first two nights, I didn't understand what was happening as I awakened each night. The third night before bedtime, the Lord led me to read the story of Samuel and the Lord calling to him. When nighttime came turning off the light, I drifted off to sleep, I had decided I would respond in the same way as Samuel had, should I be awakened. With this thought remaining in my mind, I drifted off into a deep sleep.

At the third watch, between three and four in the early morning hours, I again awakened from a deep sleep, I lay there a moment in the silence. Without hesitation, I spoke out in the darkness of my room saying, "Speak Lord, Your servant is listening." As I lay motionless, listening, I heard, in only my right ear, a pattering sound, began as the sound of fluttering wings. The pattering ceased, and the voices of a multitude began chanting; again, only sounding in my right ear. The voices chanted, "It was and is to come. It was and is to come. It was and is to come. The rain, the latter rain, it was and is to come." Suddenly, all fell silent. I heard a male voice speak to me, "It was and is to come; the impossible, the thing you thought God was not going to do, it was and is to come." Since then, there remains the sound of silence for approximately thirty years.

---

43 Scofield Study System Bible NASB

To this very day as I write this, I am waiting with expectation and total belief. He who began a good work is faithful to complete it; the silence has been long, and the battles with intensity have remained. Like Abraham, I remain looking for the fulfillment of His resurrection power and His promise.

In the upcoming pages, it is my hope for us to dig out the promises of God. These will enable you to apply the promises of God to your own life. The Promises are the keys to open doors which have remained closed. May we all receive from God, His words and guidance as He breaks every chain and moves us all forward into a greater, better life than we can hope or imagine.

With a journey, there are things you need to pack, and things you leave behind. Even when you believe you know the ultimate end of your destination; you don't always see the weather or change of seasons along the way. You study the maps to see what route is best. If you are a captain of the seas, you chart your course. The promises of God are much similar to the ship charting its course, to be used to direct your path with His hand guiding you.

[44]Course Correction God's Way/Your Way

Patterns/Cycles

Has your life ever felt like you have been there, done that? Maybe, "that" may have occurred perhaps more times than you care to consider or mention. Take a closer look as we examine the repeated patterns and cycles.

Sometimes, we are like the bird flying south or the salmon swimming upstream. Despite all resistance, we continue to press on, repeating

---

[44] Days of Plunder dianalynnrogers.com/course corrections

the cycle over and over again. Often, we re-pattern, negative situations, relationships, or a similar loss of something of value to us.

As you read this, pay particular attention to your own life; does your street have holes in the sidewalk? Is it time for you to make a course correction and move on to a different street?

THERE'S A HOLE IN MY SIDEWALK [45]

Portia Nelson

"I walk down the street.
There is a deep hole in the sidewalk.
I fall in.
I am lost... I am helpless.
It isn't my fault.
It takes forever to find a way out.
I walk down the same street.
There is a deep hole in the sidewalk.
I pretend I don't see it.
I fall in again.
I can't believe I am in the same place.
But it isn't my fault.
It still takes me a long time to get out.
I walk down the same street.
There is a deep hole in the sidewalk.
I see it is there.
I still fall in. It's a habit.
My eyes are open.
I know where I am.
It is my fault. I get out immediately.

---

[45] https://drchadcoren.com/drchadcoren/Dr._Chad_Corens_Blog__Bucks_County_Therapist,_Mental_Health_&_Addiction/Entries/2010/10/1_THERES_A_HOLE_IN_MY_SIDEWALK-a_poem_by_Portia_Nelson.html

I walk down the same street.
There is a deep hole in the sidewalk.
I walk around it.
I walk down another street.

Portia Nelson- THERE'S A HOLE IN MY SIDEWALK Psychologist Chad M Coran PsyD, CAADC, "Nelson's poem is an incredibly powerful metaphor describing the change process that often occurs with addiction & recovery.

It begins with the denial of a problematic behavior followed by the growing awareness that continuing to engage in it will lead to the same negative result over and over again.

Admission this is an unhealthy pattern then allows for triumph over it by making important changes to prevent it from happening again." [46]Health begins when we can recognize and understand what created the pain. With recognition of the event or occurrence, we are then able to start the process of change. The discovery reveals how to overcome the very thing which created our behavior, both during childhood and as an adult.

Strength comes in proportion to your level of belief your guide (God) will do exactly what He has promised. (Hebrew 11:1) Healing manifestations can occur, one day at a time, slowly as you patiently walk through; or other times, it occurs suddenly and unexpectantly after much time and trials, to be released to bring forth new life. It all remains in God's hands to determine the outcome of our way. In others, the answer may come forth in eternity with Him. It is His to decide the answers and solutions.

Habakkuk wrote he would watch and wait at his door, watching and waiting to see what God would speak. (Habakkuk 2:1)

---

[46] Psychologist Chad M. Coran PYSD, CAADC

Similar repeatable patterns with a familiarity are not coincidental events; but by God directing your circumstances. Repeated patterns reveal situations not easily noticed in your circumstances. Insight in a setting allows you the revelation to understand while guiding you to see the bigger picture.

He is directing you when peace is present. Stop the moment your peace departs.

When the door remains closed to move through the circumstances, this is another means of guidance.

The meaning of abiding/appropriating[47] is to take for one's use, without the owner's permission; to lay claim.

The promises of God compared to the word appropriate; as you take hold of and apply them to your own life. You look at the Word of God and its many promises. Does it fit your situation? Does it apply to the needs of your circumstances? How does it fit?

Are circumstances or coincidental happenings no more or less than something unusual re-occurring? Is the hand of God moving in the background of your life? Look closely, what are you seeing and noticing? How might it apply to the present circumstances you are praying and seeking answers and solutions for as you wait?

With skillful hands, He led them. (Psalms 78:72).

Many times, you will notice a circumstance repeats itself (as discussed above). They may appear as a coincidence, but God is revealing the way we should walk.

---

[47] Dictionary.com

Sin Patterns

Where your treasure is, there your heart also will be. (Matthew 6:21)

I read an account of a monkey whose hand was to become trapped inside of a coconut. He wanted what was inside the coconut but refused to let go of it to free himself. Have you too held on, refusing to let go of bad habits, wrong relationships, familiar things. The situation is not necessarily sinful, but you may need to let go, to enable your next step.

Sinful patterns:

1. Thinking is involved. First, you wonder, you may consider the correctness of the situation or your reasonings of what to do.
2. Next, it becomes an act/action creating a behavior pattern until we are entrenched.
3. Deception permeates the entire process.
4. Sin's demands keep increasing with loss of benefits. Short term experience is one of emptiness, pain in a place of comfort, loss rather than gain.
5. Habitual sin splits the mind and emotion — less time for responsibilities, more time for the craving.
6. Care and concerns diminish. Over time guilt entrapment leads to self-destruction.

Ultimately, much like the writings of Portia Nelson, "There's A Hole In My Sidewalk," there comes the recognition doing the same thing brings the same results. You know it is time to walk away and bring an end to the situation.

Everywhere the sole of your foot treads I give it to you, just as I spoke to Moses. (Joshua 1:3)

How often have we walked across the land and measured off, in Christ's name, the territory given to us? *For all the land you see, I will give to you and your descendants forever. (Genesis 13:15)*

Sin is similar to the behavior of a Narcissistic pattern, drawing you in and kicking you out, while using the disguise of love as its sole intent is to destroy you. While sin is ever wooing you and convincing you, it is filled with love. Sin will tell you just listen to me. It will criticize you saying, you are really messed up. It will say, if you would just do it my way, it will be wonderful and filled with love. Sin's temptation is trying to convince you how perfect things will be enticing you to yield.

It destroys your self-esteem, self-worth, self-love till it convinces you. Then you question your own reality. It will Love Bomb you, Gaslight you and taunt your very being. When you look at a Narcissistic behavior pattern and the evil one's ways you will quickly recognize a sin pattern prevails and one of the countless way's hell is intent upon destroying you.

Promises! Promises! A World Filled With Promises!

The world points to the stars in the sky, promising you the very thing your heart desires, the bait placed and set before you, the lure is so tempting. You are methodically set up with one crumb at a time leading you into a trap.

The deception was created by an illusion; just as the package promised fulfillment of the expectation desired. The promised gift was beautifully disguised and wrapped delightful to your eyes. Excitedly, with hopeful anticipation you wait for its arrival, you even pray.

You receive a note; it remains unexplainably delayed; it needs additional postage. You dig around and find the funds. The promise date of its arrival is given.

Once again, you are disappointed, but you continue to set up your tree, you decorate it, and the lights are aglow. The doorbell rings; the package arrives tattered, but it still needs more postage. "What! You already paid for it once before!" You go and grab the money, paying the additional fees. It isn't quite the way you expected it to look, but at least it has arrived. Prominently positioned under the tree for you to see, you now wait for the perfect time.

With an exccitment, you unwrap the package. So what if you got it for yourself? It is your gift, you chose it, especially for you, right? You know it is going to be all your heart desires. You begin excitedly unwrapping the package. The paper and tissue are flying; you are so excited. Wait a minute! Suddenly you realize the box is empty, only filled with the empty promise. Now you know the truth, it was all a lie.

How do you respond to the realization? You are hurt, disappointed, and angry as you now realize you have been played. You feel like lashing out. Do you blame others, or do you look deep within yourself and you now know you were deceived?

There is no lower level in the garden than a snake's belly. Eve discovered she had become deceived by a false promise. Not one of us is exempt from the ploys and strategies of the enemy. The Word warns us to take heed lest you fall (I Corinthians: 10:12).

Eve chose not to follow the instruction of God. The moment she reached out, picked the apple and took the bite. She found herself both in sin and rebellion. You may have bought the lie and temptation to do things on your own or your way. The children in the wilderness forgot the goodness of God and gave in to their cravings. In the wasteland, they put God to the test. He gave them what they asked for but sent a wasting disease upon them.

v.12 Then they believed His words; They sang His praise v.13 They quickly forgot His works; They did not wait for His counsel, v.14 But craved intensely in the wilderness, And tempted God in the desert. v.15 So He gave them their request, but sent wasting disease among them. (Psalm 106:12-15)

Matthew Henry Commentary[48]: (Psalm 106:6-12) "Here begins a confession of sin; for we must acknowledge that the Lord has done right, and we have done wickedly. We are encouraged to hope that though justly corrected, yet we shall not be utterly forsaken. God's afflicted people own themselves guilty before him. God is distrusted because his favors are not remembered. If he did not save us for his own name's sake, and to the praise of his power and grace, we should all perish."

Take a moment and look at your situations and circumstances. Examine each issue thoroughly, noticing what patterns have occurred, or problem appears in a variety of ways. Note this may be God working in the background to expose the enemy's methods. Do not move without God in these events. Do you have peace? Is there a word of scripture that continues to speak to you? You are being led. Are there people, perhaps randomly saying the same thing? Are you hearing it repeatedly or showing up in a variety of ways? Pay very close attention; God is working in the background, alerting you, guiding you.

The Parrot

[49]There was a man who was lonely and thought, perhaps, that buying a pet would help his loneliness. At the pet store, he looked at many animals and found himself drawn to one in particular. The sign over the cage said. "Talking Parrot: Guaranteed to talk!" Surely this will solve my problem," thought the man, "For here is an animal that can even talk!"

---

[48] Matthew Henry Commentary: https://biblehub.com/ Psalm 106:12-15 https://www.christianity.com/bible/commentary.php?com=mhc&b=19&c=106

[49] http://blog.adw.org/2015/01/a-parable-on-thedevil-and-false-promises-of-the-world-lies-of-the-/

"That'll be $250.00," said the Merchant.

One week later the man returned saying, "This Parrot still isn't talking!"

"You mean to say," said the Merchant, "He didn't climb the Ladder and talk?"

"Ladder? You didn't tell me about a ladder!"

"Oh, sorry." Said the Merchant, "That'll be $10."

One week later the man returned saying, "This Parrot still isn't talking!"

"You mean to say," said the Merchant, "He didn't climb the Ladder and look in the mirror and talk?"

"Mirror? "You didn't tell me about a mirror!"

"Oh, sorry." said the Merchant," That'll be $10."

One week later the man returned saying, "This Parrot still isn't talking!"

"You mean to say," said the Merchant, "He didn't climb the Ladder and look in the mirror and peck the bell and talk?"

"Bell?" "You didn't tell me about a bell!"

"Oh, sorry." said the Merchant, "That'll be $10."

One week later the man returned saying, "This Parrot still isn't talking!"

"You mean to say," said the Merchant, "He didn't climb the Ladder and look in the mirror and peck the bell, Jump on the swing and talk?"

"Swing?" "You didn't tell me about a swing!"

"Oh, sorry." said the Merchant," That'll be $10."

One week later, the man came to the shop, and the Merchant asked, "How's the Parrot?"

"He's dead!" Said the man.

"Dead?!" said the Merchant... Did he ever talk before he died?" "Yes! He finally talked," said the man.

"Well, what did he say?" ask the Merchant.

He said, "Don't they sell any birdseed at that store?"

The lesson to learn in the parrot's story is the ways of the world and those of the tempter's ways always are filled with promises. If the results are lacking, the demand changes to something requiring you to pay, give or do just a little more. Then the answer will come for the promise. Often it goes from the free to the upgrade. One more drink, one more roll of the dice, just one more and then you'll make it. Happiness is just one more thing, or the next person away. The temptation dangles in your face, waiting for your response to the desire to set the hook.

The sad truth is the world cannot quench your thirst; it can only draw you deeper into the things to destroy you. One selection at a time, always looks so fulfilling. Many do not recognize the real thirst is for God. You repeatedly will go back and try, try, try, with the hope this time it will be different.

Things of the world aid us in our life but are all only temporary and allow us to perform our primary duties. When it fails, and it will, then you declare bigger and better will fix the lie you bought. Only God can fill you to thirst no more, like the woman at the well. (John 4:13-14).

Timing is hand-picked for you by the devil, and he will take advantage of you at every turn. When you are lonely, just like the man at the pet store with the Parrot he tried to fill his loneliness. Things it entices us to draw us into the world and its systems or provoke us to "Just do it!" While this leads us into our self-efforts and not using God's way or provisions to provide.

Pit to the Pinnacle

There is another story, as we study together; you will see the process of how the tempter does his business. The presentation of the tempter the devil's attacks has limitations how they may come to you. They are through your Finances, Health, Relationships, Vocations; equally important are your values and the journey you are on all leading you to your eternal homes.

The story shared in the accounts of Jesus in Matthew 4:1-15. I believe this account is one which will open your eyes to the many ways of attacks. With discovery there becomes a different perspective of the mind.

Let us begin by unpacking a few of the relevant details given.

1 Then Jesus was led up by the Spirit into the wilderness to be tempted by the devil. 2 And after He fasted forty days and forty nights, He then became hungry. And the tempter came and said to Him, "If you are the Son of God, command that these stones become bread." 3. But He answered and said, "It is written, 'Man shall not live, on bread alone, but on every word that proceeds out of the mouth of God'." (Matthew 4:1-4)

Note the timing was relevant; led by the Spirit into the wilderness Jesus was left alone. He was directed to go there. He was hungry; he had not eaten for forty days. Jesus dieted like an athlete ready to compete; fasting before a competition. He gave every appearance of having been abandoned.

The Holy Spirit led him and then isolated in the wilderness after just being proclaimed the Son of God. Isolation does not keep you insulated from the tempter's attacks. There is no conquest without a battle.

The meaning of the word succor[50] is to be in a place of assistance and support in times of hardship and distress. The temptation itself would at first glance seem to be harmless. For all given appearances, Jesus was in a place of difficulty, tired, hungry, abandoned, and isolated. It is a deadly time for one when we are brought low. It is the perfect opportunity for the tempter to move with a deftness of his crafty plans.

1. The tempter's goal was to cause Jesus to sin against God. To cause Him to despair of God's goodness.
2. To presume upon His Father's powers.
3. The effort intended to alienate Him from His Father. The scheme was for Jesus to side with Satan separating Him from God.

II. Through poverty and physical needs, the temptations were to create distrust in God's care and love. These areas of lack were on an outward appearance to overthrow the relationship with God by cutting off His dependence upon God through self-efforts.

---

[50] Dictionary.com

III. The temptation of unbelief was a subtle question based on the outward appearance of the Sonship of God to question the authenticity.

With Adam and Eve, it created disbelief, "did God say that?" Questioning what God said.

Perhaps you have a dream, a vision, or a promise God has given to you personally. The tempter will send a trusted friend possibly saying, "'Are you sure God said that?' 'you surely misunderstood?'" The subtle voice of the tempter is a guise to manipulate you to agree with disbelief in an alliance. The questioning done is through the subtle questions in variations, then voiding the promise.

He will pose as light; in a friend, a family member, a Pastor, or anything to prevent you following the way of God. He will use anyone, especially those closest to you, where your guard is down. He will do whatever it takes to remove the dependence. He will try to get you to feel self-sufficient and that you don't need God. The more credible the temptation, the more appeal of good, the more dangerous it is.

IV. Temptations come through a variety of sources and ways; always intended to cause you to question. Temptations are done with hidden disguises. Each targeted for you to harm yourself. He is not selective how this is to happen. The concealed temptations are as follows:

1. To put on trial or to question God's motives and care.
2. To cause you to distrust Father's care or limiting Him.
3. Continually with the intent of setting you up for the tempter to control you.

Jesus honored the Word and scripture of Moses, when He stated, "It is written." Pay attention, there are those who are the devil's children, and they may well know what is written. The devils and demons all believe and tremble at the Word: adeptly using it to appear as truth with a twist or a turn to deceive you.

When the tempter found Jesus so confident of His Father's care that, He presumed and assumed, His power and protection in the provision of His food. The tempter then moved to another strategy to tempt Jesus.

(Matthew 4:5-7) 5 Then the devil took Him into the holy city and had Him stand on the pinnacle of the temple, 6 and said to Him, "If you are the Son of God, throw yourself down; for it is written, 'He will command His angels concerning You'; and 'on their hands, they will bear You up, So that You will not strike Your foot against a stone.'" (Matthew 4:5-7)

7 Jesus said to him, "On the other hand. It is written, 'You shall not put the Lord your God to the test.'"

Mirror, Mirror on the Wall, Who is the Fairest of All?

How the tempter delights to drag you into his snares and traps. Similar to the Magician, always with the sleight of hand and hidden in his ways to create illusions, is Satan's strategies. Masterfully, he tempts to bring you into your defeat. Invariably created by your willingness and hand to destroy you and your relationship with God.

v. 8 Again, the devil took Him to a very high mountain and showed Him all the kingdoms of the world and their glory;

v.9 and he said to Him, "All these things I will give You if You fall and worship me."

v.10 Then Jesus said to him, "Go, Satan! For it is written, 'You shall worship the Lord Your God and serve Him only.'" v.11 Then the devil left Him; and behold, angels came and began to minister to Him. (Matthew 4:8-11)

In the first temptation, the attack, on first glance, appeared reasonable because of being hungry; it would meet the need for food. Observe how he was taking advantage of the outward need. The other tactic was to question Jesus' Sonship (recall, He gave confirmation) questioning the lack of provision as God's Son and why He had not been given food. The subtle suggestion was He had been left to starve when even the beast of the field received care. (Psalm 50:10-12) Or was God just a tight-fisted God?

The second temptation, he took Jesus to a place where all the world's admiration a place considered one of the seven wonders of the world. High places are slippery places where the advancements of the world make a man a fair game for the devil. He delights in allowing one to be raised to bring down low to destroy you. He will enable you to be filled with pride to bring you to nothingness. Those in prominent places gain great reputations. They have a greater need to walk in humility; lest they think too highly of themselves. They who stand high must stay concerned to stand fast.

The tempter schemed to cause Jesus to take the authority for granted, to assume that God gave Him authority. Hence, the tempter tried to draw Him to step forth in presumption, which would be the temptation of pride.

The goal of the temptation is yet another effort to cut Jesus off from His relationship with His Father, which also is an ongoing attempt for each one of us. Self-efforts cause you to not be in alignment, cutting off the dependence and communion with God. The temptation is creating a wedge, causing you to question the truth of the Word then. Like the stacking of cards cleverly, this then creates a question of His care. It implies that He is holding out on your need, begrudging your having it fulfilled. All are false accusations and from the father of lies. God, your Father, desires your very best in every situation. He also sees when there can be a harm to you to fill the need or has something far better for you when you wait and trust Him for His best.

Next came the challenge of His Sonship, telling Him to prove the relationship. The more reasonable, justifiable, the need or situation or the higher appearance of good to be done is, the more dangerous it becomes. At the point of distress when your supply has been cut off, prayerfully come to God. Be thankful for what He has provided. At different points during my healing from a head-on collision, I have experienced challenges, just as you have been confronted with difficulties. With the multiple injuries creating an inability to obtain work, often financial crisis would arise.

One time, in particular, my funds were exhausted; I was running out of my groceries and without money. It was close to Christmas when a friend, whom I always shared a lunch at holiday time, called for our annual luncheon. I had to explain I couldn't make it; I didn't have the means for lunch or gas to drive the distance. She insisted that she would pay and help with the gas, so we met for our holiday luncheon. With the completion of lunch and a delightful time together, we walked out to the cars. We were parked close by to one another; she asked for me to come over to her car. When she opened the back door, were several bags of canned goods and various dry goods. She had cleaned her pantry and asked if I could use them. Thankfully, I accepted the supplies.

Returning home, I soon received a call from my daughter. She was cleaning out her freezer to receive new beef. Could I use the things in her freezer she needed to empty it for the meat she was receiving?

Later in the evening, my neighbor, another friend of mine, showed up at my door with bread, milk, butter, and eggs. She had noticed my supplies were running low. But God . . . each of my needs were met as I prayed and sought His help, never asking, but seeking Him. He saw my every need and supplied it.

I want to interject, this thought; no matter where you are or what is happening in your life, God is willing and able to provide for you. The greater the need, the greater the opportunity for His hand to move; trust Him. I am not telling you it is easy to wait, or that it won't take every ounce of courage you have to trust Him, but as you learn to rely more and more upon Him, you will see Him in more significant ways. Never be deceived; the trusting may be difficult, the trial long but He is Jehovah-Jireh; some way or other He will provide.

Just as Jesus said, "It is written." So, we must appropriate the promises of God. It is better to trust God in our neediness than have the products of our sin plentifully.

The devil next took Jesus to the city of Jerusalem called the Holy City. How subtle was it arranged that Adam was in the holy garden to be tempted, and Jesus in the sacred city? Pinnacles are places of temptation where one can be prideful, thinking highly of oneself. Remember, the devil is always looking to bring failure. The devil couldn't cast Jesus down.

The hidden temptation is to prove yourself as valuable, better than, or higher in position. When drawn into temptation, the harm done us is of our own doing. Every man is tempted when drawn away by his lust and not forced but enticed. Let us not harm ourselves; then no one else can hurt us.

Faith Barriers

I. Snares and Traps -Unbelief vs. Wisdom

Love believes all things (Corinthian 13:7). When the tempter demanded Jesus to prove Himself, the mindset was of that of unbelief. Unbelief hugely needs to protect itself from being fooled; it only reigns where fear has lived for a long time.

Faith works through love; it isn't wisdom to continue to ask for God to show Himself, that you might believe. *(I John 4:18)* Unbelief operates off of the opinions of others, all the while praising oneself for not falling into the extremes that others have stumbled. The religious spirit will draw you into self-worship, attempting to cause you not to recognize it is the trap is that of an unbelieving mindset.

Unbelief has the outward appearance of a conservative approach to life; but works to lessen God, Himself, to the mind and control of people. The love of God frees you from the tendency to protect yourself.

The troubling question that so often is asked, "Did God really...?" The real question, tucked subtly away, is a question that requires close self-examination. Do I love God more than the fear of loss of money...last meal... loss of a relationship more than the last whatever; you fill in the blank. The love of God many times requires risk as you step in faith.

The next question that follows that above is when you have risked, will you still trust God, and still believe when the situation fails, or the answer is delayed? Will you continue to trust and obey believing Him when the check doesn't come, or the pain continues, and the suffering doesn't end? Will you still trust Him and believe when there appears to be no answer, only that of silence and the question, "where is your God now?"

Do you immediately try to change the situation, reacting in anger or self-efforts to try to correct what seems to be an error; or do you lean into God, knowing according to His promise in *Romans 8:28 all things work together for good, according to His plans and purposes...* just not yours?

Is it possible that Jesus was waiting, like with Lazarus, for a greater miracle. Perhaps for the time Lazarus was to come out of the tomb in grave clothes raised from the dead? There is a second possibility; perhaps Jesus was there, as with Mary and Martha, waiting to be recognized, for His will to be done; for a higher purpose and His glory

Keeper of the Vine

v.1 I am the true vine, and My Father is the vinedresser. v.2 Every branch in Me that does not bear fruit, He takes away; and every branch that bears fruit, He prunes it so that it will bear more fruit. v.3 You are already clean because of the word which I have spoken to you. (John 15:1-3)

Stages of Obedience

Fear of consequences evolves into love and devotion. This changes as you grow through the Word and knowledge of Jesus.

When I first came back to the Lord as an adult, I discovered through revelation knowledge there was a third person, the Holy Spirit. He was called the Comforter. The Paraclete[51] in the Greek definition meaning Holy Spirit, an advocate or counselor. As a child, even though I attended church regularly along with Bible schools, I was naïve of the fact there was this person called the Holy Spirit.

You too may be naïve as I was or don't know the One, I am talking about, the Holy Spirit. Because of this, I am going to share my discoveries of my most Beloved Friend, who is very much a reality and one of the most incredibly meek and gentle of persons.

In the days to come, following my discovery, I started in desperately hot pursuit to come to know and find who this One indeed was, called the Holy Spirit! To this day, it is a continued quest to know Him in greater and deeper ways. It is a thirst nothing, but God can fill. It is alarming to realize, I, like myself, along with many others, either don't know or are fearful of the Holy Spirit.

I had a friend who was a believer, and yet she was terrified of the thought of the Holy Spirit. How very sad to never know or learn

---

[51] Dictionary/paraclete

who the Holy Spirit truly is, and all the ways He leads you. He is continually guiding, directing, and protecting you in countless ways. I have been very blessed and privileged in coming to know the Holy Spirit. While I sought out who He was, gained the truth, and grew in knowledge of Him. I have grown to know the reality of the Holy Spirit and His indwelling presence. He has revealed Himself in many ways and truths.

I desire to ask you to consider and stop putting God in the box of your limited understandings and beliefs. Hosea 4:6 states, *"my people are destroyed for lack of knowledge."* As I share with you and write the unique and supernatural encounters I have experienced, I challenge you to open your heart and mind. Cast aside any of your limiting beliefs. I am asking you to ask yourself this question, "What if I am wrong and I need to know Him?" Check this out (John 14:15-26). Jesus tells us when He leaves; He will leave us one, the Helper, to abide with us and in us. The understanding is only for those who love God and keep His commandments; not those in the world. He also promises not to leave us as orphans.

I am blessed and privileged, through many varied encounters, to know that I know, the reality of His indwelling presence. For a moment, I would like to invite you into the inner corridors of my heart as I share truths from a few of those experiences.

The first encounter I had; I didn't recognize what was happening. I was standing in the entry of my home and talking to my date as we said our goodnights. The Holy Spirit spoke within my heart and said, "I love you," and I in my mind I responded, "I love you too," more or less brushing it aside as I continued the conversation. After my date left, I only then realized what had happened; I was being spoken to by the Holy Spirit!

Time passed, and I continued to knock, seek, and ask. Ever seeking to know Him in greater ways, a second encounter occurred. Having read an article about meditating on the name of Jesus. The article's comments intrigued me, so I decided I would check it out. I sat down on a late afternoon in the living room. As instructed, I began to consider and ponder on the name of Jesus; at times speaking it out and at other times falling silent reflecting on His name alone. I pondered from who He was to all the many things I knew of Him. While I was sitting there, I spoke out, "Jesus, I love you, what a beautiful name, Jesus." With a suddenness within my soul, from the heart, came a very gentle meek voice that began singing, "Amen, Amen, Amen." Rising to a crescendo as it was repeated and continued again to be sung. As the words began, they rose within my soul from my heart to my ear, then fell silent. In the days following, the beautiful song and the voice echoed in my heart.

Even as I write this remembrance of the incredible encounter, my heart sings with joy and delight…Jesus, what a beautiful name it is; do you know Him, or do you merely talk about who He is as though He isn't present? Are you like Mary and Martha at the tomb? Is Jesus standing now beside you, waiting to be recognized like He was then as He stood outside the tomb? Could this be you; is your heart longing to know Him more deeply?

Several weeks passed silently by I was sent for a window design appointment. At the conclusion of the appointment, as my client and I sat and visited briefly, the conversation turned to her recent travels to Europe with her choir. While there, the choir had the opportunity to sing in the Sistine Chapel in the Vatican city where the monks sang in approximately 1500 to 1600 AD.

I told her of my recent experience and sang her the words I heard. She looked at me and then asked, "'Do you know what you just sang?' My response was 'No, I never heard of it before.'" She then told me the song I sang was the very song the monks sang in the Sistine Chapel; it was the Gregorian Chant! Jesus!!! What a beautiful name it is; Jesus Christ, my Lord!

The Call to Obedience

Complete obedience is a choice to follow God, regardless of consequences. Often this means our friends may walk away or choose a different path when we are suffering, or embarrassment is a certainty. It is more important to obey than to follow your comfort or personal agendas. You may look ignorant or foolish, as though you are blind and being taken advantage of in all your ignorance. These circumstances are when we commit the consequences to God and cling to His promises.

Two hallmark scriptures I cling to in the hard, strange places are Hebrews 13:5, and even though I may look foolish, Romans 8:28 *all things work to our good.* The placement of restrictions on our submission is tempting, especially when you are in a hard place. It is difficult when the results are unclear, or we're scared; perhaps it is going to cost you personally. Even so, are you willing to let Jesus be Lord of all your life? Are you willing to let go of control and stop setting limits? Your only criteria should be to ask, "What does God want me to do?"

The answer may cost you or cause you suffering, but obedience is always the right answer.

Make sure your character is free from the love of money, being content with what you have; for He Himself has said, "I will never desert you, nor will I ever forsake you," so that we confidently say, "The Lord is my helper, I will not be afraid. What will man do to me?" (Hebrews 13:5-6)

And we know that God causes all things to work together for good to those who love God, to those who are called according to His purposes. (Romans 8:28)

DIANA LYNN ROGERS

ME LOVE COOKIES! From the Tales of a Cookie Monster

[52]I delight in the varied ways God teaches us of His love and ways. Often, He reveals Himself in His Word, or even a little blue fuzzy character called, "Cookie Monster"![53] Much like our fuzzy blue friend, Cookie Monster; you may find yourself struggling with desires. A hunger for a cookie that appears to fulfill your appetite.

Allow me to introduce you to my furry little sidekick,[54] Molly. She loves to watch her cartoons, one of which is "Daniel The Tiger" and the other is "Cookie Monster."

When Molly's cartoons come on, she stops whatever she is playing with or doing. She then runs and retrieves a treat from her favorite treat bowl, then proceeds to plop down to sit watching her cartoons, munching away at her favorite cookie. She will give an occasional bark here or there, running to the TV to begin jumping up and down in excitement with the cartoons as she watches them.

This particular morning, I was working in the kitchen, and she sat watching cartoons and munching away with the occasional bark. I popped into the room to check on her. As I stood listening to Cookie Monster, I was just in time to hear Cookie Monster say, "Ommnom-nom-nom! Me, love cookies!" As I chuckled and listened to the storyline, it caught my attention.

Cookie Monster loved his girlfriend, but he just wanted to eat his cookies now. She adamantly told him he could not eat his cookies before they were married. She persistently told him he was to wait.

---

[52] https://www.dianalynnrogers.com/me-love-cookies-from-the-life-of-a-monsters-tale...
[53] Cookie Monster/ Fandom/Wikipedia powered by Wikia
[54] https://www.dianalynnrogers.com/me-love-cookies-from-the-life-of-a-monsters-tale...

Oh, my goodness! How he carried on, "Me, love cookies!" he moaned over and over as he struggled with being told no cookies. Much like Cookie Monster, you may find yourself struggling with desires, his primary craving is cookies, but he can and often does consume anything and everything.

Has God ever told you to wait? Many times, we are tempted to take matters into our own hands despite God's promises for perfect provisions. Desires can blind us; you either want what you don't have or are dissatisfied with what you do have. Often you may wrestle with denying yourself of that one "cookie."

Luke 9:23 instructs you to deny yourself and daily follow Jesus. The tempter most often paints a beautiful picture of how amazing and lovely life will be if you will just change your circumstances. You then begin to buy into the lie of self-gratification, and your personal satisfaction overtakes. Then you may find yourself planning and decision making. In the midst of the lie, you may forget that God is your completer, or, for that matter, forget to consult His guidance and wisdom.

As you continue, you are becoming blind. Gradually, your personal satisfaction becomes the priority, and you discover yourself living beyond the will of God; in independence, choosing to please yourself. You will begin to push against the constraints to obey. You have just entered the pathway of self-destruction, much like that of Eve.

If you will, notice Cookie Monster's focus was entirely upon himself, "Me love it, me want it." This little fuzzy blue character is very much like where you may find yourself in a place of, "I," "my," and "me." Unfortunately, when you try to do things your way and leave God out of your situation, daily not seeking His help, you are on a pathway of self-destruction. Then, when it is too late, your discovery will reveal you have positioned yourself in a very self-inflicted place of compromise.

Cookie Monster has the correct answer as his desires begin to draw him along… His song goes like this, "Me want it, Me want to grab it, but Me wait!" #Self-control.

[55]"When me lose control, When me have no doubt, Me have strategies, That can calm me down, Me can talk to self, Me can stand up straight, Me can take deep breaths, Me can self-regulate, Me wait, Me want it, but Me wait."

How often like Cookie Monster, do you find yourself drawn by a desire to the "cookie on the plate," as you too want to grab it. But you know that self-control is the answer and to wait, is to learn, to wait for God knows best. There is always a subtle temptation to try just a bite, but much like Cookie Monster, "Me want to grab it, Me want to eat it, But now Me know self-control is something Me must try… oh boy oh boy, Me must try."

Yet those who wait for the Lord will gain their strength; they will mount up with wings like eagles, they will run and not get tired, they will walk and not become weary. (Isaiah 40:31)

Self-control is a fruit of the Spirit. As you learn to grow, the dominant desire becomes greater to walk in obedience and less to walk in the ways of the world or your desires. Patience.

Have you ever noticed that you may have begun the day as a beautiful day, only to have it stolen away? You start your day; all is going well. So, you are moving through your day, and it is a great day, but then things begin to go wrong.

There was just such a day I want to share with you. I had a design appointment, I was on time, but traffic hadn't been flowing there was one delay after another. I gathered my samples and grabbed my briefcase as I slid out of the car. I quickly closed the door and started

---

[55] https://lybio.net

to cross the street, heading to my client's house. As I began to walk away, feeling more than a little frustrated, I said to the Lord, "Oh Lord, give me patience." Have you ever been there?

I walked to the door, juggling my samples. I rang the doorbell and began my appointment. I ended up going back to the car several more times for samples; the lady couldn't make up her mind. Finally, the fabrics were selected, and I began to measure her windows. As I bent to measure, my name badge fell off, plunk, it fell onto the floor! Not thinking anything about it, I began once again to measure, sure enough, plunk, it fell off on the floor again! A little agitated, I put it back on again, only to have it fall off yet again!

Then I realized and started to laugh at myself; didn't I ask God to give me patience as I stepped out of my car? Many times, we ask for things, not comprehending God was answering our request. I got what I asked Him for; this was a test for patience. Often you are put in places to be tested, some of which you don't ask for; then times like this one that you receive your request in the form of a test. The Bible states, *"And not only so, but we glory in tribulations, knowing that tribulations worketh about patience."* (Romans 5:3-4 KJV)

Matthew Henry Commentary[56] states that tribulation isn't going to hurt you; to have patience is a needed thing. Tribulation is much like the iron that is hardened by fire; it proves and improves you that patience brings forth more patience and ultimately gives you joy.

It is a consolation of God to give you songs in the night as you pass your test. Tribulations are trials; they continually come forth in varied ways. Job's tribulations brought forth patience, and that brought forth grace and approval from God, that brings forth your hope as you trust in God. But the fruit of the Spirit is love, joy, peace, patience, kindness, goodness, faithfulness, gentleness, self-control; against such thing; there is no law. (Galatians 5:22-23)

---

[56] Matthew Henry Commentary https://Bible Hub.com

Peace

Peace I leave with you; My peace I give to you; not as the world gives, do I give to you. Do not let your heart be troubled, nor let it be fearful. (John 14:27).

Often peace doesn't come immediately to you but rather is a process. As you learn to abide in God, your peace comes forth.

Outside my window, as I look about, I see the leaves are budding on the trees; the flowers are beginning to burst forth. The sunshine is spilling forth, caressing the tender new growth of spring flowers and leaves.

Peace comes just as God designed for it to come forth. It comes after the cold of winter and its trials. with the outpouring of the warmth from the sun, it starts to caress the flowers as they are sleeping and awakens them to come forth. Then comes the rain, sometimes it is caught unaware of the storms but ever changing until it becomes a gentle rain with all fear gone. A calm fills the atmosphere and brings forth a rest that all is well.

Jesus promised to leave His peace, just as He gave Himself to this world. You learn to grow and trust in Him as you open your heart. Peace is a gift to you and a promise. Peace isn't an absence of difficulties, nor an end to strife or disagreements. The gift of Jesus' guidance and the Holy Spirit means you may have peace amid the storms of life among the struggles of the fallen world. The promise that God is with us and never leaves you abandon brings forth hope and great peace. Your walk-through life and all of its trials, knowing you never walk alone, is a gift that only God can give.

Just as the seasons change, it is a sign and a promise from God that He is with you. The stars in the heaven, the sun that shines, the moonlight casting its nighttime shadow are promises of God, and as in Hebrew 13:5 He promises never to leave or forsake thee.

Endurance

[57]Transition: 1. The process or a period of changing from one state to another. As the butterfly was dangling, hidden under the branch, attached to a leaf, it struggled. It came into this world a single egg, and it grew. It remembered the days of being an ugly caterpillar during the larval stage after it had hatched. As it grew, it recalled the many times of shedding away of the old outer garment (skin) to meet its every growth and the time of its wings forming inside of its (chrysalis) cocoon. During the time of development, as it prepares to leave behind the familiar, it must struggle its way into the world just as we do. The process to strengthen itself and cause the blood to flow during this stage is like our growth process in the Kingdom of God.

Then came the day at long last it emerged with its wings wet and folded. It now had to wait to fly as its wings had to dry and become strengthened. The time arrived for its wings to flutter, to mount up and fly.

In the chrysalis's process stage, the caterpillar dissolves itself to a fluid state by God's design to reform and be created into the butterfly.

Faithfulness/Faith

Anything we value of importance; is continued with commitment. We must love Christ above and more than we love all else, or we do not love Him at all. We are to give willingly all worldly possessions, forsake all earthly friends, and obey Him above all others, including our desires.

God so loved the world, that He gave His only begotten Son, that whosoever believeth in Him should not perish, but have everlasting life. (John 3:16)

God works in the seed principles of your life. The growth of a nation begins with the seed placed in a mother's womb, as the beginning of

---

[57] https://www.dianalynnrogers.com/wings-to-fly/

Abraham's seed produced a nation. Life begins the instant it is fertilized or germinated in the Kingdom of God; whether it be a flower, a tree, fruit, or an infant in the mother's womb.

The faithfulness is shown of God from Genesis through Revelation. In Genesis, He spoke the earth and heavens into existence; every star which was named. The moon and stars came forth, and all creation began.

The faithfulness of God and His Word and promises are in the story of Abraham. You will see as you read the life of Abraham, the promise spoken by God to him. Sarah wasn't in the same spiritual place as Abraham, and she laughed at God in unbelief.

Only the person who walks with God can take the leading of God. He will lead you with evidence that is real every day to you. Your part is to trust, lean, and rely upon Him. He is not a man that He will lie, but we know He is God. Daily His plan is unfolding, and He is faithful.

When the time of His promise to Abraham came forth; it is essential to notice that all evidence of the natural laws didn't apply. They were both in their old age and beyond the physical abilities of conception. It was the power of the Spirit that brought forth a son. Only then was the law of faith in God activated. *"Is there anything too difficult for the Lord?"* (Genesis 18:14)

The law of faith in God manifested in what He had promised. Could a child be born, but by natural law? Allow us to look at another birth; the promise of God, that He said to Mary. She activated her faith when she spoke saying, *"Behold, I am a handmaiden of the Lord, be it unto me according to Thy word."* (Luke 1:38) Jesus was brought forth in the same way; the natural law was superseded by the law of faith.

There are two forms of righteousness; one is according to the law; the second righteousness sees God and obeys Him in everything. He is a rewarder of him who diligently seeks Him. God is a reality, and in Him, there are no lies.

In the Bible, we see the reality of God; He calls forth the dead and calls those things which are not to be as though they were, with no limitation of possibility.

The hidden condition of God requires us to believe. Satan will try to plant one of many ways to interfere with your perception and truths of God.

Being righteous by law or by believing faith determines your way. Believing faith is to act upon what God says. The way to come into the promises of God is open to all who believe. What you believe is the challenge.

Faith is the hand that moves the key to the promises of God to receive from His storehouse.

When you believe, God changes your weaknesses to strength, character, and power. One of the greatest acts of believing faith is your salvation. Believing faith challenges, you to believe the Word of God; that Jesus died on the cross and rose again. Just as important, when you believe, you receive the gift of salvation and eternal life. As you believe and receive the former leaves and you become a new creature in Jesus. Just as the caterpillar leaves its former life to become a butterfly shedding away its cocoon; you leave your former life to change into the likeness of Christ Jesus.

Mary, Mary, how does your garden grow?

Joy

The Greek word for Joy is chara [58]

The Fruit of the Spirit is a biblical term that sums up nine attributes of a person living in accord with the Holy Spirit, according to Galatians

---

[58] Wikipedia/ chara

chapter five. The fruit of the Spirit is love, joy, peace, patience, kindness, goodness, faithfulness, gentleness, and self-control. Each fruit gift has its individual uniqueness. Often joy is described as a collection of all the fruits.

One summer, my daughter, who was a member in 4-H, chose one of her projects to be gardening. For her project, she selected to grow flowers. I remember her determined little face as she kneeled and prepared her flower bed. She relentlessly turned the soil with her hand trowel, uprooting every visible weed. She dug her hole in the soil and plop! the seed dropped in and was covered by the soil. One by one, she planted!

Before she had planted, she read her gardening manual. She made a check list of all the things needed for her flowers to grow. She made sure she had plenty of sunlight and shade. Diligently, she watched over them, keeping all of her flowers watered. she checked and charted each flower's growth. First came the fragile little seed sprout coming out of the soil. As it grew stronger, the stem began to show and the leaves to come forth daily she cared for her little flower bed. Then one day, her bud became a full-grown beautiful flower.

With anticipation and excitement in the fall, she submitted her Zinnia at the fair. She showed the beautiful Zinnia her little seed had become. The flower placed as Grand Champion receiving a purple ribbon, it was so beautiful. With pride, she displayed her ribbon for all to see.

God uses the seed principle as well in His Kingdom plans. As you receive your salvation, the gift of the Holy Spirit, similar to the seed becomes planted in the soil of your heart hidden away from eyes to see. You, too, are provided all needed to grow and become the beautiful flower for the world to see. There is a rare fragrance and beauty as you grow in likeness to Jesus. Joy is the fruits of the Spirit, coming to full bloom in you.

When I went through the painful loss of being separated from my family and all that mattered to me, I went from a wife and mother to being alone and abandoned. During this period of my life, I had returned to the Lord. I was broken, so fragmented emotionally I was grieving myself to death.

During the long nights, I would fall asleep early in exhaustion. I would awaken and from midnight to daybreak; I would read the Bible. Countless nights I would awaken at dawn, embracing my Bible to me on the sofa.

It was summer, comfortable enough to have the windows open, the screen door locked, and the front door open. I began yet another night, much as I had done, opening my Bible and reading on and on. It was nearing three in the early morning; I was reading the Song of Solomon, which I often did. I had been crying as I read my Bible the pages were open; my eyes were tear-filled when I realized I smelled something.

I closed my Bible, walked over to the open door, and sniffed about. Nothing was there; then to each of the windows, but the odor had disappeared. I re-opened my Bible and continued to read; there came the scent again. Once again, I sniffed the air, unable to find where this fragrance was coming from, could it be outside, the windows and doors were open. The third time I seated myself and opened my Bible, then I knew Jesus was in the room; the fragrance of a rose I was smelling, it was that of the Rose of Sharon.

I Am the rose of Sharon, The lily of the valleys. (Song of Solomon 2:1)

These words are written along the edge of the tattered faded pages of my Bible, "I am an ordinary person, yet loved and cared for by the Lord." A testimony of so many days of struggles to survive as the Holy Spirit sustained me. He loves and cares for each of us, the one who feels unworthy, the castaway, the broken, the lost one; everyone is precious in His sight.

The Seed Principle of the Kingdom of God

[59]There is a principle of scripture learning that says all truth is parallel, which means to understand spiritual truth, look at the natural.

Jesus used many natural examples; Luke 8:4-15, He teaches from various kinds of soil. When a farmer plants a bean seed or a pumpkin seed, he expects that to grow into either a bean or a pumpkin. We expect the seeds planted to produce a result of the harvest. He believes by faith; those little seeds will yield the crop he desires.

The same principle creates new people. When a man and woman have sex, a "seed" becomes planted to create a new person. The embryo formed from the seed becomes a baby, to continue to grow into a full-grown adult. The characteristic, talents endowments, and appearances of both parents are formed in the fertilized egg but to be revealed in the grown egg at maturity. As it grows into adulthood, both time and experiences of life will create the person each will become.

Each of these is processes of becoming; much like the butterfly and the seed in the ground. All are fundamental principles of the Kingdom of God.

Life is a gift the finished form of a seed when it is completed. It has all that it will ever be or become contained within the seed. The seed given to us to produce spiritual life was the Holy Spirit that was given to each of us when we received our salvation. The Holy Spirit was the promise of Jesus when he left us. (John 16:7) The Holy Spirit resides in Him, and in us are all the characteristics and attributes of God. As we abide in Him, we are to grow in His likeness.

---

[59] https:/www.covenant-kingdom.com/ THE "SEED PRINCIPLE" IS VITAL TO UNDERSTANDING SPIRITUAL GROWTH

"For you have been born again not of the seed which is perishable but imperishable, that is, through the living and enduring word of God." (I Peter 1:23).

The Gift of the Holy Spirit

The promise of the Holy Spirit following our salvation is the "seed" given when Jesus said He, Himself would pray to the Father. The Holy Spirit is an answer to His prayer, the Counselor or Helper would come to stay. (John 14:16-17)

[60]The Holy Spirit is a divine Person and comes to abide with, to lead, guide, and direct our ways as we come to know God in higher ways. Seven of the gifts of the Holy Spirit are wisdom, understanding, counsel, fortitude, knowledge, piety, and fear of the Lord.

Love

There are many words, and lessons taught and written about love. There is the story of Jesus asking Simon Peter of his love for Him. (John 21:15) There are many verses written of His love revealed throughout scripture, each speaking of God's love. The Bible is a love gift guiding us to our Heavenly Father and a means to know Him. He gave us Jesus, His only Son that we may have everlasting life and spend eternity with Him.

During this week, as I write it is the season of remembrance of the death and resurrection of Jesus. It is the week of Passover, and the ultimate act of love, when Jesus sacrificed His life at Calvary. A memorial of when His blood was shed for your sins. An appointed time to celebrate His Resurrection and the gift of your salvation for those who believe. This a time to celebrate His life, goodness, and

---

[60] https:/www.covenant-kingdom.html

love for each and all of creation. It also is a time of recognition and an acknowledgment the Holy Spirit; that Jesus had asked the Father to enable all to receive. Passover is a celebration of remembrance that He laid down His life in love for you.

Here in Texas, it is a time all creation is bursting forth. I love this time of year as the Bluebonnets and Indian Paintbrush are in bloom. It reminds me of a precious friend and her family that I would like to share.

The first days of my arrival in Texas, I stayed in a local hotel. Within just a day or two, I met a young woman, wife, and mother. She worked the front desk as a clerk. Our friendship was an immediate connection. From that time forward, we shared many hours drinking coffee and hours of fellowship, as we grew in our friendship. We talked of the Lord and the struggles she had as a former minister's wife. She spoke of her hurts, struggles, and her hunger for the Lord. She spoke of a complicated second marriage, and of the various trials she was going through; but how she loved him!

Within the first days of meeting her, she wanted me to meet her husband and children. We agreed on an evening at the end of her shift. At the time I met him, he was so mean and rude to me. I returned to my room, saying, "God only if this is of you!" As God would have it, we continued to ignore his rudeness, and we grew in our friendship. His anger was because of being hurt by a Christian mother and her friends. I, too, had been hurt many times by believers that had, in well-meaning ways, cut me to the emotional core, so I understood the reactions.

As I came to know this little family, I would after church on Sunday spend time with them. While we visited, I did my laundry with my new friend's insistence during this time. The anger subsided in her husband; the barrier came down. At long last, he decided I was a friend, not a foe. To my surprise, as I was about to do errands one day, here he came bouncing up my driveway. We chatted a few minutes, and finally, I asked what he needed. Much to my surprise, he looked at me and said, "I just came to tell you, I really do love you!" and with a hug, he was off again. God was answering our prayers.

Soon they attended church from time to time with me. Finally, as he struggled with his bowels, the diagnosis was terminal Crohn's disease and given less than a year to live.

We all continued to pray for him. Then came the Sunday as I passed by the kitchen window while visiting. When he saw me, he immediately stubbed out a joint of marijuana. I knew he had used some drugs and drank alcohol, but he had never done so in my presence. My friend had told me he had used the drugs to control his pain.

This Sunday was a very different time together. After lunch, he confessed to me what he had been doing to help his pain — also admitting that he had stopped when he saw me. This Sunday was a breakthrough Sunday! This Sunday, he asked Jesus into his heart. Within the next two weeks, he entered eternity to go home to his Father's house.

The story doesn't end there. It is God's love and will that no one should perish according to His word. Allow me to share more of this little family and God's love.

The time came when his ashes were received. It was my friend's desire to spread them. How we struggled to find that perfect spot that her husband would like. We dropped one child off at our Pastor's house, and the other insisted upon coming along. Between times of laughter and tears, the pain so great for us both to do this, we drove literally for hours searching.

We continued driving when the words entered my mind, "Beside still waters, and the cattle on a thousand hills." I turned and shared it with my friend, who agreed that it was the perfect place, but where? Within a matter of minutes, I looked over, and there were the cattle on the hillside. As I glanced over, I also saw the still waters of a pond. We exited the highway and followed the gravel road leading to this peaceful place. The car rolled to a stop as we put on Christian music to play.

I glanced back to the back seat, her little one was asleep. Slowly the car moved forward while she released the ashes. A gentle breeze began and lifted the ashes across the field, ending just as we passed by the still waters of the pond. We proceeded slowly down the road; I turned the car around. By now, the sun was setting; the day was near over. Slowly we approached the pond, and we were facing into the sunset. We slowed to a stop and looked one final time, saying our final goodbyes. Suddenly a white dove mounted up and flew into the sunset. As we slowly continued to go back to the interstate, off to my left as we rounded the bend, I stopped the car; four flowers were growing. I felt lead to get out of the car, and I picked three Indian Paintbrushes and one purple Jack in the Pulpit flower for her. As I handed them to her, she started to cry. She told me she had just asked God, "Who will give me flowers now?" Great is the faithfulness and love of God.

While I am sitting here writing this; I was listening to Pandora. The song that just began playing was "Beyond the Sunset." How very faithful is our loving Father, even to this moment in time.

There is one final story I would like to share with you of this little family. In recent months, my friend passed away from cancer. I was brought back to Texas if no other purpose than to spend time with her. To pray together and make certain her heart was prepared to go home.

In the last hours of her life, during the night hours possibly, within forty-eight hours of her passing, I was given a vision of her. She was in a field of flowers, as she walked across the hillside of flowers, she looked back at me. Only now do I recognize why it felt so familiar to me. She was in the same field where her husband's ashes were released. She had been restored to when I first met her. Gone were the ravaged marks of her battle with cancer, both in her face and body; she was healed and restored.

Unfailing love, how great is the Lord's love for you. Even when a sparrow falls to the ground, he attends the funeral of the sparrow, how He loves and cares for you.

Gentleness

The servant of the Lord must be gentle. (II Timothy 2:24). What truly is gentleness?

[61]Gentleness also is translated as "meekness." It does not mean weakness. Instead, it involves humility and thankfulness toward God and a polite, restrained behavior toward others. The opposite is anger or desire for revenge.

Gentleness doesn't mean to ignore wrongs and sinfulness. To be gentle is to confront the sin in a spirit of truth, allowing sin to be pointed out with a gentle, mild, loving encouragement, and to speak with the clarity of holiness. It takes a strong person to be gentle.

[62]"The Village Blacksmith" is a poem by Henry Wadsworth Longfellow originally published in 1840. The poem is about a blacksmith and balance in his daily life. The blacksmith serves as a role model who balances his job, family, and his community. One of the most striking examples of gentleness portrayed is in the following verse:

"The Smith, a mighty man is he,
With large and sinewy hands;

---

[61] "The Fruit of the Holy Spirit- What is gentleness?" gotquestions.org
[62] The Village Blacksmith, Wikipedia

And the muscles of his brawny arms,
Are as strong as iron bands."
When in the church, he heard his daughter singing a hymn, and the Smith was overcome with emotions.
"And with the hard, rough hand, he wipes a tear out of his eyes."

The Smith reveals and is gentleness. It is might that is restrained by humility and grace. Reliance upon our logic, we tend not to be inclined to submit to God's leadership. With wisdom given us by the Holy Spirit, we soon learn it is far better to yield ultimately. It is a difficult task for self-will to lay all control down and surrender all to God. Walking in yielded obedience to His ways you find that you are a vessel submitted, and it is producing for you the strength and power to accomplish God's plans and purposes.

8 "For My thoughts are not your thoughts, Nor are your ways My ways," declares the Lord. 9 "For as the heavens are higher than the earth, So are My ways higher than your ways And My thoughts than your thoughts." (Isaiah 55:8-9)

In the previous section, I cited an example of a wounded soul. When filled with the Spirit's fruit of gentleness, it is essential that the one confronted is done so in a loving, gentle way. God does not intend for us to argue and build resentment in others. It is of far greater importance for the person's salvation than of your pride.

John the Baptist said, "He must increase, but I must decrease." (John 3:30)

Words Matter

From the beginning, when God spoke creation into existence; to your life, words are powerful. From your birth as is written in the *Song of Solomon 8:5, Beneath the apple tree I awakened you: There your mother was in labor with you, There she was in labor and gave you birth.*

From the time the great I AM having given life by His very words.... Let there be, and it was so; until to this time, words have mattered.

In the battle of purity of the mouth, is fought in the mouth. What is in your heart comes out of your mouth, from the abundance of your heart, your mouth speaks. Evil and foul words spoken, show the condition of your own heart, exposing the darkness that is displeasing to God. Your love for God is demonstrated in obedience, honor, and respect of His Word. You would not stomp on your wedding ring if you were angry. Why ever would you stomp on the heart of God with unfiltered words? It isn't just a dirty word, or my trying to force change; it grieves the Holy Spirit when you speak evil, and it is called sin.

Sin does not have to require the word to be a disgusting word necessarily. The intent of the heart of what is spoken from your mouth that is what God sees and hears. He weighs and judges your spoken words, hears your every thought, and sees your every motive. Words intended for evil are judged, just as loving words are similarly judged.

Wisdom is to look at the root of the words used; what is the motive, and where does it lead? Vulgarity and four-letter words used with sexual intent are words being used to bring scorn, disdain, or hate to the one the words are being directed to or about. The unclean sexual words spoken are in reality the rape of another's spirit. These forms of words express selfish, uncaring, and abusive intent. They derive from the same spirit as does rape. What the one speaking such vulgarity doesn't realize, it is exposing the condition of the heart and soul of the person speaking.

Remember, you are heart, mind, body, and spirit. You are unable to disconnect from one, separating yourself; it is your entire body that is involved. You can't remove your heart and remain alive. It is parallel to any sinful behavior like lying, stealing, or over-eating. What the results of an action manifests, is where the intent of the heart is based. Just as your choices matter and have consequences, so do your words matter tremendously.

Let no unwholesome word proceed from your mouth, but only such a word as is good for edification according to the need of the moment, so that it will give grace to those who hear. (Ephesians 4:29)

Recently I listened to a mentor as he shared from his heart the importance of words. He had realized that some words spoken in truth were still unkind. However, words released in anger, purposefully hurt, or inflict pain upon others. He went on to say how we are to walk in love and to forgive those who hurt or offend us by their words.

Words spoken in anger are corrupt and rotten fruit. The very essence of the foul communications fills the air with pollution, wounding the spirit of the person being bombarded by them. It is like a rotten apple in a bowl of fruit; if the remainder of the fruit stays in the container, the entire bowl will eventually become rotten. Our minds and spirits record and remember the words. Wrong words, significantly impact your soul, polluting your very being. We are warned to come apart from those who use such communication, lest it harm us.

Many consider the Bible as a book of don't rules; but have you ever stopped to think they are for your protection, to heal you, deliver and keep you safe in the world around you? Have you considered that maybe it is more like that of a parent saying to you, 'Don't cross the street before you look.'? Or perhaps, 'Watch out, you are about to get hurt; don't do that!' Has your mother ever told you to wear your coat or eat your food? The Words of God are much like that of your mother to shield and protect you. Words matter! It is critical to listen and obey God's Word, particularly in the world, with all the violence and anger about you.

You are told to watch over, to *"guard your heart,"* for from out of it flow the issues of life. (Proverbs 4:23)

What is the picture you are painting in your world today? Are you emitting smog by your words? Are you releasing a fragrance of love or that of hate-filled words with roots of violence to others? Do you need to ask forgiveness for the words you have spoken? Take time to search your heart. Ask yourself if you need to wash your heart, and soul in the Word, to change your words and heart to one of love?

East of the Sunrise- The International Library of Sunrise

IF I COULD [63]
Diana Lynn Rogers

If I could paint a picture, it would be
crimson red pooling at the foot of Calvary.
I would take my brush and touch my palette
And tip in gold, with a stroke of
my brush, I would paint a face full
of mercy and grace.
Etched with a trace of sorrow and pain
Crushed to produce a glorious refrain,
… If I were to paint a picture of me
You would see one who abides in mercy and grace,
Full of joy, with laughter and tears that have
Stained my face would be one looking into her Savior's face.
There would be the two of us you would see,
The Holy Spirit and me. Together we walk and
Talk as He guides and directs me
If I could paint a picture, you would see only Jesus
who abides in me.

---

[63] DIANA LYNN ROGERS, IF I COULD, pg. 46, East of The Sunrise, International Library of Poetry, (Watermark Press) Ownings Mill, MD

DIVINE ORDER

Thy Will Be Done [64]
Diana Lynn Rogers

Thy will be done in every way.
Direct my steps O Lord, I pray.
Lest I stumble or fall astray.
Thy will be done; I choose to obey.

To submit to divine order requires us to walk in obedience to the Word of God. The divine order isn't jumping hurdles and strict disciple that brings condemnation. It is not about a performance test when in school, when there was a grade given. God is not a taskmaster but a loving Father. The devil would love for you to think of God as a taskmaster.

[65]Jesus is our ultimate example:

1. Jesus went about doing good and healing all who were oppressed by the devil, for God was with Him. (Acts 10:38)
2. He called people to be His disciples; to establish the Kingdom of God on earth. (Mark 1:16-20)
3. Jesus taught and brought truth. (Mark 1:21-22)
4. He cast out demons where He found them. (Mark 1: 23-27)
5. He brought healing, where there had been sickness and disease. (Mark 1:28-33).
6. Jesus prayed and stayed connected to the Father (Mark 1:34-35)

---

[64] Thy Will Be Done Diana Lynn Rogers
[65] Faith Tabernacle: ft11.com/What is Divine Order

Divine Order is this verse: *I can of Myself, do nothing. As I hear, I judge; and My judgment is righteous because I do not seek My own will but the will of the Father who sent Me. (John 5-19, 30)*

1. It is not what you do; it's what God can do through you. It's freedom from all bondage even that of trying to prove yourself worthy, none of us is worthy. It is instead a process of sanctification through God's ways.
2. It is your coming into a rest. (Matthew 11:28-30)
3. It is your cooperation in yielding as He works through. (Philippians 2:13)
4. It is trusting God to give you discernment, to lead, guide, direct, protect, and provide you with wisdom. (Proverbs 3:5) (Psalms 138:8).

In the tabernacle of God, instructions of divine order were given. Often the holiness of God is ignored in this generation. The casual treatment of the Body of Christ sweeps aside the holiness of God, placing their comfort in higher priority. To ignore what the House of God represents is not respecting the honor and holiness of who He is.

We as a church cry out for His presence, but we do not show Him the honor and respect of who He is; the great I AM. I am blessed in being taught the necessity and need of that truth.

In a small church I attended, I experienced an encounter with God. The encounter happened not only in the service of being touched and healed, but in a visit with the Assistant Pastor. One afternoon when picking up some needed materials, a second encounter occurred. As he walked me to the door, the fullness of God manifested. God's presence was so powerful. The Assistant Pastor and I both felt the power of His presence. It became so powerful we struggled to keep from falling to our faces in God's presence.

I am confident that the manifestation occurred as a direct result of honor. All that attended that church were taught to show the reverence, honor, and love for God in treating the sanctuary as a holy place. The protocol included taking all conversations into the lobby area. If you are not taught to do this, you won't know the significance of this training.

Jesus gave us the divine order of obedience to pattern ourselves in our daily walks. The Tabernacle in Moses' times and throughout the Bible gives us the principles of our conduct and behavior in the Holy of Holies. Our posture in His presence is to be one of reverence and a holy acknowledgment of reverential fear or awe of who He is.

[66]**Only when divine order becomes the church order will the presence of God manifest in power in its midst. The blockage occurs in our own lack of honor and respect for who He is, "Holy, Holy, is the Lord God Almighty"!!**

One may think this writing is about the law, but it is rather about the heart of man revealed. Who are you more concerned with offending the man or God?

Divine Order and Protocol

David followed the Philistine's by placing the Ark on an ox cart and one man carrying it died because of being out of divine order. When one of the men reached out to touch the Ark of the Covenant to stabilize it, he died. It was dishonoring to God.

Later, when David moved, it was placed on the shoulders of the men and carried in divine order to arrive safely. (Exodus 25:22)

In the tabernacle of the Holy of Holies, there were patterns given to how the Priest was to enter; and the process of how they were to burn

---

[66] Smith Wigglesworth; Who's in the driver's seat?

the sacrifices unto God. Instructions were given even to the priests to have bells on the bottom of their robe. The bells were attached to alert those waiting outside to remove the priest, by dragging his body out should he not do all pleasing unto God. He would assuredly die, because of not fulfilling the protocol as given of divine order.

Each article in the Holy of Holies, God instructed, from the way it was to be constructed to include the tabernacle was divine placement. Each piece also was given specific guidance to its construction. All of God's children had a reverential (awe) fear of the Lord and honored God, acknowledging in worship who He is, and was, and is to come.

The patterns and protocol established today appear reduced to having a casual simplicity. There is very little recognition as to whose house that this belongs and what the holiness of His tabernacle requires. Many places of worship bear the resemblance of a stadium or theater, which then raises the question of whose House has this become? We seek His presence, but do we truly honor and fear his holiness appropriately? What is your house reflective of? Do you honor and seek His ways, or do you have a do-it-yourself mentality, pleasing of your ideas and self.

Often, because it is found in the old testament, it is tossed aside; but it is written, *"Jesus Christ is the same yesterday, today and forever." (Hebrews 13:8)*

How then can it be, that we do not revere and fear the Living God? He does not change; we are instructed to this day to fear God. Fear of God[67] refers to a specific sense of respect, awe, and submission to a deity. Love has boundaries with God and man. Search your own heart, does it need to line-up with the Word? Are you genuinely obeying this while you are becoming "all in" entirely?

I had the honor and privilege to be in the presence of an African King who is a believer. He shared a story of an encounter which occurred

---

[67] Fear of God Wikipedia-wiki-Fear-of-God

in his palace. The incident he shared occurred late one night, as he was getting into bed and about to turn off the lights to retire. In the middle of his bedroom stood gazing at him a man who had entered his palace and bedroom. He had walked past the entry gates of the outer courts, with guards. He walked through the entry door and by the guards of the palace. He even passed by other guards stationed in the inner court areas of the palace.

The King got out of bed and asked if he might discuss with him his needs, as he walked him safely back out of his palace and courtyards. As they walked and talked, the King listened to the intruder's concerns; the King noticed a very peculiar situation. As he passed through the many areas without exception, all the guards were at their assigned post; and one and all asleep.

When he roused the guards and returned to his room, he sought the Lord why that had happened. For those who may not be aware of it, all the guards could have been beheaded, losing their lives at the instruction of the King.

It very important for all to recognize who do you honestly say is in control of your life, the King, or you? The answer that the Lord had informed the King was that He wanted him to recognize who the King's defender was; not a man but God Himself.

Who's God and Who Isn't God!

Often you may sit in the swirling winds of life. Life's storms have overcome you as the destructive winds prevail. You are licking your wounds, from the tempest storms of life that you have both encountered and endured. As you sit in the sweltering sun, viewing your crippling open wounds, each one having been exposed for all to see. Your friends surround about you commenting on the various injuries, noticed by one and all. Your wounds perhaps are emotional or physical, but all know of your bandaged heart and the incredible pains you have suffered.

Much like Job, have you received on occasions pious lectures? Sermons of various kinds; with judgments and presumptions, all with well-meaning guidance of course; you do understand, right? My advice is watershed them and look to God. Listen for His gentle instructions as peace guides you along. God remains in control.

Just as Job reminds us, who's God and who's not; all tend to underestimate God's wisdom, foreknowledge, power, patience, faithfulness, timing, holiness, sovereignty, and goodness.

Shift your paradigm from the sufferer to the friend that is suffering. Transform your thoughts from the broken to the Healer of the Broken, as you come to know God's ways; look through the eyes of His perspective. Change your thoughts from a victim to a deliverer. Move from "Overcome" to more than a Conqueror, mighty and victorious through Christ who strengthens you. The transformation requires a shift in your paradigm and thoughts, as you become like Him, in your weakness, lies His might and powers. You are being taught to step from glory to glory, as you grow in likeness to Christ Jesus.

I can do all things through Him who strengthens me. (Philippians 4:13).

Honor

When in the presence of a King, there are protocols to be used you do not casually shake hands, but you bow. You don't come as you are, but rather you are required to dress to a particular style or risk being exiled, imprisoned, or beheaded. It is entirely different behavior than that of a common man.

[68]Honor definition: to give honor, homage, reverence, deference, respect and esteem shown to another. Honor may apply to the recognition of one's right to great respect or any expression of such recognition.

[69]Disrespect is the opposite of respect; it is failing to acknowledge another's worth, withholding the honor that should be given, or actively demeaning someone.

Waters of Transition

To everything, there is a season and a time to every purpose under the heaven. (Ecclesiastes 3:1)

The waters of the Jordan are lapping at the shorelines. The time has arrived to cross over to the other side. The edge of the waters was a source of life for Israel, but a barrier for their many enemies. It was to become a change of leadership from Moses, to that of Joshua leading; Moses was not to cross over. It was also a changing of seasons for Israel, crossing over into the promises of God.

The Jordan River is symbolically a place of transition of the dead (former things) to bring forth new life, and a giving of a new purpose. Ironically the 156-mile-long river that flows from the north to the south flows into the Dead Sea. One of the most significant events, from the one hundred and eighty-five times, its mentioned throughout the Bible, was the baptism of Jesus and the beginning of His ministry. It was the same location where He was led into the wilderness by the Holy Spirit and tested. The occurrence that, set in motion the time of Christ's crucifixion.

---

[68] Merriam-Webster Dictionary.com/dictionary/honor
[69] https://www.gotquestions.org/Bible-disrespect.html

Jesus was immersed in water by John the Baptist in the Jordan River. There was a representation of dying to the old self and yielding to the Spirit. It was an exchange of life and death in the waters when He was baptized.

John baptized Jesus in the same river area that the children of Israel crossed into the promised land. Jesus' life brought death to the former life; to bring a new life by His resurrection power.

Notably, there are patterns and biblical foundations put in place by God. There are seasons ordained by God. The Universe moves in cycles and patterns, just as the ebb and flow of the tide, the sun, moon, stars, all with a design of the flow of creation. There are times of darkness and times of light; all determined by God at the beginning of the Universe.

[70] Each event was directed and deftly guided by God. Each one occurred on the Jordan River, none by chance, but each selected and arranged with a purpose by God. We all have God appointed times, places, and destinies, pre-ordained at the forming of the earth. You are not a random accident, nor your choice of preference who you are. Without an option, all creations genetic identity was and is pre-determined by God; it is not yours to select; it is in the DNA seed, hand-picked by God. False teaching is believing anything other than the Truth of His Word. Despite all the countless controversial conversations, it remains His choice, not ours.

As we see the signs of time in the natural, there are signs of time in our lives, both physically and spiritually. There are times, as written in Ecclesiastes, for all things.

---

[70] Rabbi Curt Laundry/International House of Prayer

Spiritual Laws of Transition

[71]Breakdowns can create a breakthrough. Things fall apart so they can fall together.

[72]The unique thing about transitions is that all changes begin with endings. It is a separation and dying off of certain parts of your life and identity that no longer work for you. Ends may include relationships, lifestyles, work, meanings, values, desires, mental attitudes, or a false sense of mortality. It is much like that of a surfer trying to balance on their board. There, in fact, may be an element of fear of unstable situations, understandably so. You may desire to grasp hold of the familiar, your old ways, returning to familiarity of life and spiritual decay. You may face the sense of loss of empowerment and individual successes.

You now have arrived confused; you have found yourself, thrown into the chaos, turmoil, and a sense of disorientation of change. Often there is a sense of desperation with the throes of change. You have a choice to succumb to the fear or to try to replace the seeming losses with that of finding a deeper understanding of life. The distress of the darkness and the diseases of life's tolls advance you into a place of change. As the surfer has struggled to keep his balance, so have you. The change is all right; you did nothing wrong. The changes have created an open window, and your time has come to move forward into a new season; Let go of the former and ride the waves of change. Now is an appointed time for you to grow, to find a new start and better life. This is not the end, but a new beginning, breathe. Changes are a time to discover deeper meanings and enter into inner peace and serenity; a time of becoming healed and whole.

---

[71] Unknown
[72] The Six Stages of A Successful Life Transition by Elliott Dacher www.transition.com

Now is the time to remove old fears, limitations, illusions, and fantasy. Change is a time of a new, final, and complete healing a time to receive the call to a more expansive life.

[73]Six primary events occur during this time of transition:

1. The call of change to a more purposeful, more meaningful life.
2. Change has called you to depart from the former that was binding you and the familiar.
3. There is an in-between time, a period of rest.
4. There are lessons to glean from both the release of the old and the entry into the new preparations.
5. The return to a life now transformed through the passaging of the various changes.
6. A time of discovery of the gold of all the treasures you have gained, both in spiritual and natural elements. Within, there is a sense of joy, peace, and wholeness.

Spiritual transition is the testing by stretching in circumstances and relationships. God calls us to move forward into the new season. He has invited you to transition, to partner with Him to share our love with others in every place of society. The invitation will expose you to giants, hostility, rejection, and skepticism as you pursue your destiny.

[74] A Perspective will be necessary from all you have learned in the places of growth. There are four aspects provided in His Word.

And we know that God causes all things to work together for good to those who love God, to those who are called according to His Purpose. (Romans 8:28).

1. The leadership of God is always to the good.

---

[73] dianalynnrogers.com /Transition
[74] International House of Prayer.

2. He will complete His workmanship, and you are His workmanship.
3. The work will transform you into more of the image of Jesus (Psalms 17:15)
4. God is for you, not against you. The only person who can take you out is you!

Transition trail markers

[75] Transition bears the mark because a new season of fruitfulness is on its way. It may be a part of your going through to pass through these times:

You may experience a low time in life; an emptiness, a sense of barrenness even to the point of feeling hopeless. The cutting back is only an indicator you are in a time in the wilderness. (Jeremiah 29:11)

God is at work in your heart; it brings hurts forward, leaving you with a sense of vulnerability. God is calling you to a place of intimacy. Your mind-sets are tested and challenged. You can't take that thinking into the new season. You must foster a mindset of faith. Rest in your identity as a son or daughter of God.

You may find yourself with a sense of displacement or not fitting in to the new normal. Your attitudes and faithfulness are in a period of testing. There will be spiritual warfare which will surround you; the enemy is trying to rob you of your destiny. It may tempt you to take shortcuts to bring this to an end; that is not God's best. Surround yourself with Godly people and time with the Holy Spirit to strengthen yourself. The Holy Spirit is working in the background.

---

[75] www.enlivenblog Helen Calder

PREPARATION FOR THE NEW SEASON

When a mother is preparing for birth, there is a period of development and growth. The Word describes it as a time of travail when you are birthing a new season. The Holy Spirit will draw you by longings of your heart. Give God your imagination to create and design your new season and a fresh anointing.

There will be a need for additional studies to accommodate what lies ahead. In I Kings 18, the promotion of Elijah, God had arranged before his arrival. He had time for rest; there was a supply of supernatural food, a time to heal, and food given for the next season of instruction to be fruitful. You, too, may find yourself in a season of grieving, rest and replenishment where your need is the greatest physically and emotionally.

You are at a pivotal point where God is leading you into a new encounter. There He will provide you with guidance to move forward to walk into your new season.

There are benefits in the transition by shedding and releasing no longer needed things to move into a new season. At the middle of this, you may feel a sense of frustration, and a grieving period for all the former things you are letting go of or have left behind. You have arrived discovering there is a time of waiting; your faith remains challenged. It is taking all your courage, and there is a desire within you to hide in the cave, rather than to stand and let the winds of doubt and puzzlement assail you. Stand firm, God has you in the palm of His hand.

Behold, I have inscribed you on the palms of My hands; Your walls are continually before Me, (Isaiah 49:16)

You will find yourself in a series of adjustment as you release the past. Before the time of Jesus' departure in Acts 1:3, He remained with His disciples for forty days. The time of His remaining was a period of adjustment for all as to what was to come.

The letting go of the former is a piece critical to the path of change. The letting go is prior to your entry into the season of new beginnings. It is important to examine and release the old that no longer can come with you. The release whether it is a relationship or a habit, action, or a hidden sin that needs to be addressed and removed from your life. You are being called to come apart. To separate from those things; they can no longer belong in the days of your life The call to come apart now summons you to travel and move on your journey of life. Examine your heart and allow God to reveal those things that need to be addressed and released.

Jacob wrestled with the angels; many refer to it as wrestling with God (Genesis 32:30) to bring forth a release into those things of the heavens. As you read the encounter, you discover God blessed Him. Remember, the primary key is always that of obedience and yielding to the ways of the Lord.

As a punishment, there was a period in ancient history where under the law, the one who was the assailant was to carry the deceased victim's body, strapped or chained to his own body following judgement. The body of the corpse would become rotten. Decay would set into the attacker's body, and he would die from the diseases the corpse brought as his body decomposed.

Sins and weights of the former life cause the same effects in our spiritual body. Holding on to the past will ultimately cause the dream or a vision to die, aborting your destiny and calling to become all that God has planned and purposed for you.

'For I know the plans that I have for you,' declares the Lord, 'plans for welfare and not for calamity to give you a future and a hope.' (Jeremiah 29:11).

DAYS OF PLUNDER

Elijah rested for forty days and nights, fed by the angels of the Lord, he set forth. Elijah came to a cave and hid there. Seen hidden by God he was instructed to go forth and stand outside of the cave. (I Kings 19:8-11).

A strong wind assailed the mountain breaking the rocks into pieces, after the wind, an earthquake, then a fire; but the Lord was in none of these, what followed was a sound of a gentle breeze blowing. (I Kings 19:11-13).

When Elijah stepped outside of the cave, a voice came to him; then, God gave him an instruction. (I Kings 19:13-18).

In each of these transitions, there was a time of waiting for forty days. Each period was to rest and renew strength, instructions were given following the rest. Are you able to identify yourself in this process and pattern? Observe the surrounding events that have been changing in this period of transition. They are most likely subtle, but none-the-less there are movement and changes quietly occurring around you. You are now beginning to understand and identify the pattern and process of the Lord's leading you in the chaos's background and pain of your situation.

Old patterns are still with you, which is why you sometimes struggle with sin. The only way to rid yourself of the familiar is to have zero tolerance. In my walk with God, at the earliest part of my journey, I struggled with many sins; one was smoking cigarettes. I had a minister's wife earlier verbally assault me, telling me I could not be a Christian and smoke. The assault was by a religious spirit, the result of it caused me to walk away. I wasn't ready to hear any of it, which was what the demons desired.

When I returned to the Lord after having lost all that mattered to me; I knew I would not allow this to happen to me twice. I asked God when He was ready, not a man, He would guide me, and I would then obey, but until then I would remain as I was. He had many other far deeper concerns and issues to work out of my soul than a bad habit.

The day arrived when it was time for me to make a change and let go of the old habit. I struggled and tried to do it at first on my own. Until the time came, I was sitting in the Design Studio and a friend who I had met from another store called, and we talked for a while. Then the subject of a little book came up when she told me of it, I asked if she would mail it to me, and I would return it at the next regional meeting.

After many attempts to read it, I decided I would not answer the door, the phone, or allow any interruptions. I wanted to read it and obey God. As I began reading, there was a scripture that leaped off the pages and stuck in my soul.

Like a dog that returns to his vomit is a fool that returns to his folly. (Proverbs 26:1)

Without a doubt, I knew it was time to end this fool's game and madness; it was a time to stop! After reading the little book, I thought about it for a few minutes; then I said to God, "I have five cigarettes in this pack left; if you make me so sick, I never want to touch them again, I will quit now!" With my having stated this I lit the first one and began to smoke it. I started to sense a choking sensation and coughed. By the second one, I was not so good; I was coughing, and hacking before the third one was finished, I was near vomiting. Never underestimate the love and strength of God in your situation, no matter what your giant is which needs conquered God can and will. Ask, and with asking to expect an answer. From that day forward, I never smoked again. I went throughout the house and my car, emptying all the butts and ashtrays; I immediately destroyed all in a fire, I left nothing to tempt me. Later, a boyfriend stopped by my house. He offered me a cigarette, and I told him no, I had quit. That didn't stop the enemy from taunting me. He then said, "You know you want one, don't you?"

The purpose in my telling you about this incident is to impart revelation of the God we serve and the countless ways and people the enemy will use. Also, you should be aware of the many attacks when you are delivered. Never, and I do mean; never touch the temptation again. Never!!! Someone in the family who I know of was released and then returned to smoke just one, and the battle was horrid to get free. Never turn back to that which God liberates you.

Remember this; the enemy wants to keep you entrapped with anything he can to destroy you, your walk, or your testimony. There is no limit of his attacks on those weaknesses we all possess. There is a scripture I would like for you always to remember. Post it where you can recall it when you are under attack by religious spirits. The attack is not of the Lord but hell and the demons working through the individual. We are to walk by His grace. When He says "so" you are to walk it out in obedience to Him, not a man.

Therefore, there is now no condemnation for those who are in Christ Jesus, (Romans 8:1)

What does Jesus say? Be honest and truthful the soul you save may be your own! Confrontation of our feelings or facing the facts of God. Emotions may be uncertain as that of the sea; God's truths are precise and reliable.

[76]Matthew Henry said, "We can depend on God to fulfill His promise, even when all roads leading to it remain closed. For no matter how many promises God has made, they are, 'Yes' in Christ. And so, through Him, the "Amen", so be it through us to the glory of God". (II Corinthian's 1:20).

---

[76] Matthew Henry Commentary

Fruit Inspection

[77]The lemon tree is very pretty, but the fruit of the poor lemon is impossible to eat!

[78]Good works does not make a good man, but a good man does good works. Martin Luther.

In every season of our life, it challenges us to recognize what is surrounding our life. Previously we discussed the Fruits of the Spirit as written in Galatians 5:22-23; the authentic fruit-bearing begins in the heart. The hidden motives, standards, loyalties, attitudes, and ambitions, all are a part of the heart issues we have discussed.

43 For there is no good tree which produces bad fruit, nor, on the other hand, a bad tree which produces good fruit.

44 For each tree is known by its own fruit. For men do not gather figs from thorns, nor do they pick grapes from a briar bush.

45 The good man out of the good treasure of his heart brings forth what is good, and the evil man out of the evil treasure brings forth what is evil; for his mouth speaks from that which fills his heart. (Luke 6:43-45).

My Father is glorified by this, that you bear much fruit, and so prove to be My disciples. (John 15:8)

[79]In this chapter, there are four degrees of fruit-bearing illustrated concerning fruit.

No fruit (v2 "does not bear fruit verse"); the Fruit of Repentance (Romans 1:13)

---

[77] Song lyrics Lemon Tree By Peter Paul and Mary
[78] Martin Luther
[79] Scofield Study System NASB pg. 1483 commentary

"Fruit" (v2); Abiding

"more fruit" (v2); Fruit of The Spirit (Galatians 5:22-23)

"much fruit" (v5,8); Fruit of Righteousness (Romans 6:21-22; Phil. 1:1)

In the fall, the apple orchards become loaded with fruit. At harvest time, the fruit inspection occurs at the time of picking. The fruit appearance is a luscious red tempting you to eat, but with the first bite, you discover it is rotten on the inside.

We have discovered the Fruits of the Spirit are a part of the inward workings of the Holy Spirit. Beginning now as trained fruit inspectors we scrutinize the fruit to determine just what is good fruit.

"Do not judge so that you will not be judged." (Matthew *7:1-6)* To judge is to discern, to decide, to make a choice or decision about something. Before we determine, the fruits of others, let us first look at our fruit yields. What fruits are we bearing in our spirit and life.?

An arborist examination begins with looking at the tree. Is the tree leaning? How is the soil mounding at the base of the roots? Is it rooted in sandy soil; is there little if any nutrition? When removed, will the tree reveal its inside one of a rotten heart? Will only the outer bark be holding it up?

No matter how healthy the outside of the rotten heart looks, it cannot produce good fruit. If it does not secure the fruit to the tree, no matter how it tries, it will fall off of the tree, roll away and dry; it has no water to supply its fruit.

When it is fruit found on the ground, soon you will see fruit bugs, wasps, and worms enter the fruit, consuming and destroying the lovely fruit it once was.

Our souls will also become rotten if we do not remain abiding and attached to the vine. Attachment to the vine is where we gain the food supply and nourishment necessary for one and all to produce healthy fruit.

I am the vine; you are the branches; he who abides in Me and I in him, he bears much fruit, for apart from Me you can do nothing. (John 15:5)

BREAKING THROUGH

I remember when it was time for the arrival of my duaghter; I looked like the great pumpkin. I had my bags packed; we all were ready and alerted to her imminent arrival. I knew she was there with every kick and movement. Regularly, my physician affirmed all was well; then we waited and waited some more.

I recall I checked and rechecked, and with assurance, all was ready for her arrival. I checked to see all her little gowns, blankets, and supplies had been packed. Her diaper bag was all stocked and ready; then I waited! I was counting the hours and minutes until I was looking into the precious little face of my firstborn.

It is much the same when we are expecting and ready to receive the arrival of His promise. Never forget God is God; His ways are not our ways. He alone determines the timing and day. There is a tendency to become weary of that time of waiting, especially right before the arrival. God is always on time, never give up!

In Genesis 17, there was a man called Abraham, and there was another baby promised. It was thirteen years that had passed between Genesis 16 and 17 since he and his wife Sarah had been given by God, the promise of a son.

As he sat outside his tent, staring off into the heavens, he recalled the many trials and times of attempting self-efforts to fulfill the promise

God had given him. He recalled, when the answer didn't arrive at the expected time, how they tried to manipulate the timing of the promise with a son, Ishmael. God in His mercy remained faithful to His promise and Words to Abraham. He considered the times he had repented after examining his heart, the changes, and removal of those issues that were wrong but God, ever mercifully, kept His Word, and the promise remained intact. But God!

Abraham sat pondering all these events and many ways, napping outside of his tent in the mid-day heat. Upon awakening, there appeared three men standing opposite of him. *(Genesis 18:1)*, *"Now, the Lord appeared to Abraham."* When he saw the three men, Abraham hurried from his tent door to meet them, bowing himself to the ground. He then said, *"My Lord, if now I have found favor in Your sight, please do not pass Your servant by"* .... (Genesis 18:3) Abraham hastened and desired to prepare a meal and served these guests. While they rested, he continued to fix and spread a feast before them.

After having eaten, they inquired of Sarah's location. Then He said. *"I will surely return to you at this time next year; and behold, Sarah, your wife, will have a son." (Genesis 18:10)* Sarah, Abraham's wife, was listening at the tent door. They both were advanced in age, well past childbearing age. Sarah then laughed to herself, saying, *"Shall I indeed have pleasure, my lord being old also?" (Genesis 18:12}*

The Lord said to Abraham, "Why did Sarah laugh, saying, 'Shall I indeed bear a child, when I am so old'?" (Genesis 18:13)

"Is anything too difficult for the Lord?" At the appointed time I will return to you, at this time next year, and Sarah will have a son." (Genesis 18:14)

Sarah denied it, however, saying, "I did not laugh"; for she was afraid. And He said, "No, but you did laugh." (Genesis 18:15)

Through the encounter with God, there are a few things revealed. The sacrifice was made to the Lord in the feast prepared. The question of doubt from Sarah did not stop the spoken promise of God. God not only knew where she was but that her unbelief was exposed both in her comment and the child was to be named Isaac a name meaning "he laughed." Peek ahead in (Genesis 21:1-7), "*Sarah said, "God has made laughter for me*, unlike her husband, Abraham, who had faith and believed God's promise.

The significance of Sarah's laughter was not only to point out her unbelief and doubt but earlier, in Genesis 17:19 God told Abraham that *laughter for me; everyone who hears will laugh with me."*

The Lord said to Abraham, "Why did Sarah laugh saying, 'Shall I indeed bear a child, when I am so old'?" (Genesis 18:13)

"Is anything too difficult for the Lord?" At the appointed time I will return to you, at this time next year, and Sarah will have a son." (Genesis 18:14)

Sarah denied it, however, saying, "I did not laugh"; for she was afraid. And He said, "No, but you did laugh." (Genesis 18:15)

Are your circumstances laughable? What have you hoped for; that which is seemingly so impossible now, it's ridiculous? Or, are you so ready to give birth to the impossibility that your soul and heart long for, are there tears falling as you read this?

Don't you dare consider the offer from hell to "just give up"! You have fought this battle time and time again. You know there is nothing too difficult for God, and He is a Keeper of His Promise. You are about to receive the greatest gift of your life from God, never underestimate the love and power of God in your situation, no matter what your giant is that needs conquered God can and will. Ask, and with asking to expect an answer to His promise for you! It was determined and chosen, handpicked expressly for you while you were still in your mother's womb. It has taken you a lifetime of preparation to be ready to receive His promise and your destiny. Don't quit!

GOD'S TIMING

But when these things begin to take place, straighten up and lift up your heads, because your redemption draws near. (Luke 21:28)

[80]*Sarah became pregnant and bore a son to Abraham at the very same time God had promised him. NIV* (Genesis 21:2)

1. God's timing is precise. (Psalms 33:11) We must wait.
2. At the appointed time next year, Sarah will have a son (Genesis 18:14) God will cause us to forget waiting with His laughter.
3. The One you wait for will not disappoint you. *"but your grief will be turned to joy" (John 16:20)*

You will not be disappointed at the time of delivery when the baby's head is crowning (showing) you are but a push away. I recall, watching as the mother would be so intensely pushing with all her might. While the mother-to-be was straining, she would listen for the first cry of her newborn. When the baby is so near its arrival, suddenly there is a final gasp, push, and the baby cries as it bursts forth into this world. The baby then is lifted and wrapped and placed in the mother's arms. This is how very close you are. Breathe and push!

When God brings laughter to your house, the song, "[81]I Can Only Imagine" rises in my spirit. I can only imagine when that moment in time comes. What will it be? Will we laugh, will we cry from the presence of God? Will we be surrounded by His glory. I can only imagine while trusting God. We wait, each one of us, for the hope,

---
[80] https://www.biblegateway.com
[81] I can only Imagine, Bart Millard/ Mercy Me

the promise, the answer for our next steps. For the very thing, you dare to dream as impossible; with God, all things are possible to those who believe.

BELIEF

Some of the most significant issues in our walk of faith is, what do you believe?

1. Will you wait and believe, no matter how long the time or distance between what God has said to you?
2. Will you hold on until the promise comes forth?
3. Will you step daily in faith to what you know is God's way?
4. Will you trust God to get you to the answers?
5. Will you try to fill the gap with your works and hope it is from God? Do you wait for clarity or plunge into the question?
6. Will you resist the temptation to let go? Will you try to create the answer in self-efforts, filling in the gaps?
7. We all will wrestle from time to time, with the imitations and distractions the enemy will drop in front of us to tempt us to falter our very steps and way.

PROMISES

[82]The unconditional promises and their fulfillment rests solely with God. God promised in Genesis 9:1, the earth would never be flooded again as in the times of Noah. Another illustration of God's conditional promise is your salvation that you confess with your mouth and believe in your heart. (Romans 10:10)

---

[82] In touch.org / Dr. Charles Stanley

The confessions of your sins are founded on His Word and cleansing in (I John 1:9). The first is, no matter how evil the world becomes, another flood will never occur, such as in the times of Noah. The second is God's willingness to act under certain conditions. It requires our cooperation; it is an "if then" condition.

The Main Thing is to Keep God the Main Thing!!!

Full commitment and love for God are displayed in your obedience and your choice to yield and surrender your will to His plans, purposes, and ways. More times than not, it will cut down the middle of your projects, your ideas, desires, and choices.

Those things God has revealed in His Word, such as those things that are in Divine Order, you are without excuse if you fail to follow.

The desperate desire to obey God the moving of the Ark of the Covenant by David had becomes clear 1 Chronicle 13:12. The fear was overwhelming, as a result of the earlier study, in the loss of life, when the Ark was touched while wrongly carrying it.

Frustration can cause you to give up your desire to the status quo of the church and ways of the world. It also can be an instrument to drive you deeper into God's way, causing you to find Divine Order. The desperation can push you to pay the price for the Open Heaven and will of God.

When you enter into the Open Heaven, the grace and mercies of God abound, and you will cease striving. God delights in your sacrifices and extreme praise and worship. The suddenly of success will flourish, and blessings will come down entering your life.

[83]**Great faith is not the faith that always walks in the light and knows no darkness, but the faith that perseveres in spite of God's seeming silences. That faith will most certainly get its rewards.**

Wilderness to the Promise Land

In the book of Zephaniah, there was a converting grace, given to Jerusalem, who had gone from being a holy city to that of a nation of harlotry. With the return of the people back to God, and the removal of judgment of God, it brought with it an end to the distresses, troubles. It also ended the calamities and the noise of war. There was a work of reformation and cleansing that took place.

[84]Converting grace refines the language. The Jews after captivity needed a reformation of the dialect. The mingling of the language of the Canaanites with that of the Ashdod, half of the children spoke the language of Ashdod or of the other people. They did not know how to speak the language of Judah. (Nehemiah 13:24)

In one and all, there is a continued divine order and cleansing taking place as we grow in the Lord. One subject of grave importance is an undefiled language as a choice and bears an impact on your prayer life. It carries an eternal value. The converting grace of refining the language is not by conversion from all that is profaneness, filthiness, and falsehood, but a deliberate choice to turn away. It is deliberation and choosing your words. The goal is to strive to become one of a pure language by choice of your words, the cleansing of unclean lips. (James 3:9-12)

There is a very significant reason behind a pure language; many who love God have yet to understand or be given enlightenment to the

---

[83] Unknown
[84] Converting Grace/ Understanding Ministry of Reconcilation

importance of that. You may have been taught or reasoned it is just a bad language. What is coming out of your mouth is that which fills your heart. The purification of your mouth is a heart issue. It is essential to be changed and cleansed to bring forth a pure language; a fragrance pleasing to God. Your words truly matter. What is the aroma rising to God from your lips?

The good man out of the good of his heart brings forth what is good; and the evil man out of the evil treasure brings forth what is evil, for his mouth speaks from that which fills his heart. (Luke 6:45)

In worship to God, early in the Bible, there was the use of sacrifice and incense made for prayer. Prayer is our spiritual offering to the Lord. In olden times they were to give only the best sacrifice according to the law and to burn incense. We are to enter God's presence with that same measure of reverence and fear of the Lord to this day. Many have concluded it is a "come as you are," with little deference or regard to the very fact that God is a Holy God.

Heart purity is a rarity discussed in the hustle and bustle of our society today. However, it has yet to be changed; God is the same today, yesterday as He will remain forever. Our prayers will go up as either a sweet sacrifice unto a Holy Father or one of a noxious odor and foul fragrance before the Lord. Selah! Think about that! It is a matter of your own choice how you will reperesent yourself before the Living God. Will you have clean hands, a pure heart, and clean lips? It is all your own decision to consider and settle. The decisions and choices you make will ultimately determine your eternal destiny.

COVENANT

A covenant is an agreement, a solemn and binding agreement. An agreement between God and His people, a sacred agreement between a person or a group of people. God sets specific conditions, and He promises to bless us as we obey those conditions. When we choose not to follow, sometimes we suffer a penalty or consequences as at of disobedience. (Jeremiah 31:31-34)

[85]The Creation Covenant

In the book of Genesis, God spoke creation into existence. He created man, and later woman; Adam and Eve were both created in the image of God, and they were told to reign and ruled the entire world as Priest-Kings. As God's son and daughter, they were said to live and dwell in the Garden of Eden as long as they lived in righteousness and obedience to God. The instruction given to them was to not eat of the tree of knowledge of good and evil. If they ate of the tree, they would be cursed and banished from the Garden of Eden.

Noahic Covenant

The sin of Adam and Eve continued to corrupt and permeate the world until God swept the entire human race out, leaving only Noah and his family. As we read Genesis, he was of the lineage of Adam. We further read; *"Noah found favor in the eyes of the Lord. Noah was a righteous man, blameless in his time; Noah walked with God." (Genesis 6: 7-8).*

Because of the grief of God, the judgment of the Lord was coming upon the land and people. Before the destruction, God gave Noah a command to build an ark with specific instructions; then to gather all the animals two by two. Then the rain came, and the world was flooded, consuming all and leaving only those in the shelter of the Ark.

---

[85] www.http://crossway.org/articles/why-we-Must-understand=the-covenants-to-understand-the-bible Thomas R Schreiner

God always has a remnant of people. In writing this, I also totally see those in obedience always are kept in the shelter of His hand. What a great hope to know when we obey God, no matter the world about us, we are always safe in His care.

Noah was the new Adam, reviving the Salvation covenant. Salvation though would not come through Noah, as Adam sinned in the Garden of Eden and evil persisted.

[86]The Noahic Covenant reaffirms the conditions of life.

The accountability of man for protecting the sanctity of human life is by organized rule, even to capital punishment

No new curse is placed upon the ground, nor is a man to fear another universal flood.

The order of nature is confirmed.

The meat of animals was included and added to man's diet, if not previously included.

A prophetic declaration made descendants of Canaan, one of Ham's sons were to be a servant to their brother.

[87]A prophetic declaration made that Shem will have a unique relation to the Lord. All divine revelation is through Semitic men, and Christ after the flesh descends from Shem.

The promise to Noah the rainbow was to become as a sign to every generation. (Genesis 9:1-19)

---

[86] Holy Bible Scofield Study System/ The Noahic Covenant 9:16 pg. 18
[87] Scofield Bible NASB/Chapter 9 studies

After Noah, the world again slid into sin with the Tower of Babel, the signature of sin. Then the Lord set forth the Abrahamic covenant. The land promised Abraham was Canaan, then to the offspring, Isaac, and blessing to the ends of the earth. Abraham was a type of the new Adam and Canaan the new Eden. All where God dealt with His people.

The act of obedience fulfilled the promises in Genesis 15. God pledged He would keep His promise, but He would do it through the offspring of Isaac.

The Covenant of Abraham

v.1 Now the Lord said to Abram, Go forth from your country, and from your relatives. And from your father's house to the land which I will show you; v.2 And I will make you a great nation. And I will bless you. And make your name great, and you will be a great blessing; v.3 And, I will bless those who bless you, and the one who curses you I will curse. And in you, all the families of the earth will be blessed. (Genesis 12:1-3 NASB)

God promised Abraham, "And I will make you a great nation." Within that same promise was given that of a son and a covenant for future generations. Then Abram began his journey to the far country in obedience to God's instruction and Word.

Many encounters were to take place along the way, from the time of the Word of the Lord. There were times of failure, forsaking the place of blessings, such as when he lied to help shield himself, telling Pharaoh that Sarah was his sister.

Abram settled in the land of Canaan and Lot moved his tents as far as Sodom. After the division of the region and Lot's departure, the Lord again spoke to Abram and gave him the covenant land of the promise. After the time of separation from Lot, coupled with the events of Sodom and Gomorrah, Lot's wife was turned to a pillar of salt when she looked back, God's grace for Abraham and his family all superseded the promise of a son.

With the promise of a son, there came about more failures and self-efforts with the birth of Ishmael. Finally, the birth of Isaac came forth by the promises of God and his mercies.

The promises of God were all fulfilled with the birth of Isaac.

Indeed, I will greatly bless you, and I will greatly multiply your seed as the stars of the heavens and as the sand which is on the seashore, and your seed shall possess the gate of their enemies. (Genesis 22:17).

Covenant With Israel

Freed from Egypt by God's grace, the Israelites were led by Moses into the wilderness. Israel, Abraham, and Jesus, were all led into the wilderness. They all lived in the land of Canaan, the New Eden. God ruled and dwelt among His holy people.

The importance of the covenant with Israel is the boundaries written within the Ten Commandments, along with the blessings God promised. He set forth the condition and stipulations of the benefits when they followed; the consequences if they were to become violated. It showed the suffering of sin and disobedience. Rebellion and sin are unpleasing and grievous in the eyes of God, even to the point of being rejected and sent into exile.

The Covenant With David

The promise of victory over Satan was promised to come through the descendant of the offspring of Abraham. As promised in Genesis 3:15, 12:1-3; additional stipulation stated he would come through a

King, who was a descendant and offspring from Abraham. Jesus was the one who would conquer both sin and death.

The promise of the land and universal blessings remain secured through the legacy of David. The king was a new Adam in a new area. Again, there were conditional and unconditional promises. If the king sinned, he would face God's judgment. With the progression of time, it again became apparent that things were wrong. The expelling of both Israel and Judah from the land is documented to be in approximately 722 and 586 BC.

[88]The Davidic Covenant foundation base is on the 89th Psalm.

"I have made a covenant with My chosen; I have sworn to David My Servant; 4 I will establish your seed forever and build up your throne to all generations." (Psalm 89:3-4)

1. The covenant comes forth through the lovingkindness of the Lord and rests upon His Oath. (Psalm 89:1-4)
2. The power and goodness in connection with the promise. (Psalm 89: 5-18)
3. The Lord responds (Psalm 89:19-37) in two parts:
    a) Confirms the covenant (Psalm 89:19-29)
    b) Warns of disobedience and punishment
4. Plea of the remnant (Isaiah 1:9, Romans 11:5)

THE NEW COVENANT

Israel left the nation in a horrific mess; it would appear that Satan had overcome Israel, and they were with a broken promise. There was an unconditional promise in Genesis 3:15 the Lord guaranteed a victory would come through a child of Abraham and a son of David. Still, there remained a sin problem with Israel; they failed to keep the

---

[88] Scofield Study System/Scofield /The Davidic Covenant/893

covenant and experienced the curses of the covenant. (Jeremiah 31: 31-34)

The new covenant was fulfilled in Jesus Christ, who is the true son of Abraham, the true Son of God, true Israel, true David, The Son of Man, and the Servant of the Lord. The new covenant promises forgiveness of sins which was fullfilled in the blood of Jesus Himself. He pours out His Spirit on His people and enables them to do God's will.

Keys To The Covenant

Covenant = God + Man

1. Within the contents of each covenant, God had a plan for His people.
2. The covenant had a design with a plan which was created to overcome sin and Satan.
3. The Covenant came with promises on God's behalf and conditions fulfilled with consequences, blessings, or curses.
4. In the New Covenant, the Holy Spirit is given to enable us to do God's will.
5. A specific land/region has been given to man.
6. The base of God's character, love, grace, and desire for a relationship is within each covenant with His people.

[89]A Christian is and remains a Christian because of the bond between the person and God. "What comes into your mind when you think of God is the most important thing about you." A. W. Tozer

---

[89] https://www.covenantandcontroversy.com/hear-the-story/ A. W. Tozer

Covenant Building 101

With the experience of sales, marketing management, and construction understanding; I would like to invite you to read along with me as we review the covenant of God. Things revealed of His ways in these studies.

Foremost, remember it is all started by the love of God and founded on His loving kindness, a desire for a relationship with His people.

Within us, there is a desire and a heart longing for that of a land that is to become home to the one seeking. There is a desire for something more, and the search to discover that begins. There are many places that one has searched to find the answer with many options presented along the way.

Finally, there is bonding with the One who has shown you that ideal location, and the perfect plan is revealed. The designer skillfully is presented with the layout of a blueprint; this explains all that is to detail to complete the promise. Some conditions need to be agreed upon and understood by all parties involved.

There are a few changes based on these conditions and situations. There will be some things are conditional in the construction's preparation, others which are unconditional. The Master Builder is the only one permitted to determine whether it is a conditional, or an unconditional term of the agreement. The builder is to determine where the best placement of the home site it is to be established. It must be a location that will fit the design plans of the blueprints. He alone knows best.

There are meetings to determine the electrical, the plumbing, the position on the lot, even to planning for the drainage easements. Within the terms of the contract, there is a meeting with the designer to assure all the perfect colors and materials to be used and included.

There are certain conditions for you, the buyer, to meet, such as financing arrangements. When all the plans are settled, finances in place as were agreed upon the contract is signed, and the plan begins to build. There is an understanding by everyone of compliance with the contract.

The day of completion has arrived; all now have met and fulfilled the agreements. It is time now to receive the key to open the door of your promised home. Congratulations! You are the new owner, and the family moves into that home.

Still, some responsibilities can cause issues in your new home, which will void your warranty. Maintenance and repairs of the house are requirements committed to in the original agreement. Payments are to continue as required to be paid. Upkeep is essential to keeping the beauty of your home inside and out to exemplify the beauty of your dwelling place. Both your new home and covenant with God include defined responsibilities and obligations required of you.

Behold, I am laying in Zion a stone, a tested stone, a costly cornerstone for the foundation, firmly placed. He who believes in it will not be disturbed. (Isaiah 28:16)

UNDERSTANDING

Dear Reader, one of the fascinating things to me about the studies of the covenants is the discovery of the many parallels revealed and the application in our culture today. To realize how it has been put in place all before the foundation of the earth, for such a time as this. I encourage you to watch for the patterns and similarities hidden between the lines, as I attempt to reveal God's ways and hand that are so much higher than our ways and thoughts. As you read, I hope that you will see and realize the sovereignty of the amazing God we serve. Thank you for allowing me the privilege to share and tell you of the Living God.

The beginning of wisdom is: Acquire wisdom and with all of your acquiring, get understanding. (Proverbs 4:7)

Covenant Promises And Conditions

There are three main reasons for choosing to enter into a covenant. A covenant partnership is to provide protection, trust, and love; it includes strength, needs, and weaknesses. The covenant partner promises faithfulness, loyalty, and dependability. Often the covenant extends to seven generations.

You see this with God's promise to Abraham was that through his offspring (Christ), all nations were to be blessed.

[90][91][92]There are various kinds of covenants that give us an understanding of the type of conditions laid out. It is important to understand that a covenant is a voluntary choice.

Irreversible, sacred agreement, it is not a contract. A true covenant is agreed upon by two individuals within the pact they are to "*<u>die to self and are reborn as one</u>*."

<u>Patriarchal</u> is a voluntary covenant based on the obligations of a superior party, (father) to benefit the inferior party (son). (Deuteronomy 7:6-8) Chesed (*one of goodness, love, kindness*) foundation is a John 3:16 love that God gave all humanity. It is a love based not on feeling, but what you do. The covenant is a Patriarchal Covenant based on love.

<u>Vassal/Suzerain</u> is between unequal parties. The Suzerain is the more powerful and the less powerful is the vassal, such as a Lord/ Master or a servant/slave. (Psalms 89:3-4, Joshua 23:16)

---

[90] www.bac?torah.com/covenant
[91] https://susancanthony.com/res/dennis/covenant.html
[92] Scofield Study System NASB Oxford

A Mutual Contract is a two-sided contract between two parties voluntarily accepted. It may be such as two brothers and or a friend. A phrase that would imply would be that of "blood thicker than water." Jonathan and David are an example of that type of covenant. (1Samuel 18:3)

The meaning of that phrase is stating the blood covenant is of higher significance than that of the blood of family or that of a brother who shared the mother's womb. A true friend is an individual who is joined in a covenant bond and is lifelong. The other relationship is an acquaintance. A marriage is a covenant relationship between a man and a woman. Covenant friends are of the same gender; often, these covenant parties are referred to as "Blood brothers."

A man of too many friends comes to ruin, but there is a friend that sticks closer than a brother. (Proverbs 18:24)

In many cultures, the independent person is considered being in spiritual poverty. Real wealth to them would be a "blood brother" or covenant partner. The covenant individual has pledged to be with you, without question or doubt, regardless of inconvenience. If need be, he would gladly trade his life for yours.

James 4:4 tells us that friendship with the world is hatred or hostility toward God. It speaks of one being in two places; you can't be both in the world, and with God. It places you in a position against God and His ways.

B. Torah (books of the law) Covenant between God and Abraham. Abraham's belief in God was counted as righteous by his faith and trust in God. As the sun went down, Abram fell into a deep sleep, and in the darkness, God appeared as a smoking oven and a flaming torch which passed through the two pieces of meat. On that day, the covenant was made. (Genesis 15:7-8)

When God made the promise to Abraham, since He could swear by no one greater, He swore by Himself. (Hebrew 6:13-18)

The name of this covenant is the Abrahamic Covenant. The Abrahamic Covenant is known as the blood covenant. All blood covenants indicate life is from the blood. (Leviticus 17:11)

C. Nevi'im (Prophets) Covenant between the Israelites and God; this is a Mosaic Covenant. The blood of animals served as a covering or atonement. The life of the animal was a replacement of the sin of the people. The animal's life can never forgive sin by its life. It is a copy or shadow of that of a better covenant to come. (Hebrew 9:23) The shadows became realities through the blood shed by Christ, who fulfilled the old testament shadows with His blood. (Hebrew 9:24-28)

II. BLOOD WALK

As a part of the blood walk in the Abrahamic covenant, five animals, a heifer, a ram, a goat, a dove, and a pigeon; all except the birds were to be cut lengthwise and placed side by side to create a wall, like that of a river of blood. The partners would walk through and around the halves of the dead animals, creating a figure eight. Eight is the symbol of Infinity. Another matter of interest to the blood walk is that the cutting of animals sacrificially is still being done to this day in Africa.

In the Abrahamic covenant, the smoking furnace (God's justice) and the blazing torch (God's mercy) passed through the pieces. God alone was the sworn one, as Abraham himself was in a deep sleep. It was within the description of the blood covenant; the sacrifice occurred.

Following the blood walk, the walk was an exchange of vows made by both, each swearing unto God. In the covenant vow, the phrase "so help me God" was used. The partners of a covenant would speak, each calling down a curse of death should this be broken. Within the exchanging, both swore unto God that should either break the covenant, that person and his family, all members of the family should die.

The Mingling of Blood Cutting

[93]In the Bible and many cultures, blood symbolizes life. The giving of blood and taking of blood represents that of life-giving and taking. Just as blood gives life when given by a blood transfusion, the donor's life-giving blood pushes back death for the recipient. The covenant is the taking in of blood of the other and gaining the other's life. In that way, two become one "flesh and Blood." In the Bible, Jesus' blood was given to bring life to all of mankind by the shedding of His blood. By receiving His life (blood), two become one.

There were a variety of means of blood mingling, from cutting and dipping the left ring finger into wine or droplets placed in the wine. Partners often would cut the palm of both hands and mingle the blood, which is where the handshake originated. With the cutting of wrists, they would wrap their arms and mix the blood at the wrist. The mixing of blood is the origin of swearing and raising the right-hand swearing, "so help me God."

The left ring finger is believed connected to the heart. The ritual often was to cut deep enough to draw blood, and then a powder was poured into the cut to create a scar. A ring was then placed upon the finger when healed, hence came the origin of the wedding ring.

The Torah covenant requires covenant parties to be circumcised. (Genesis 17:10-11) The B'rit Hadassah (covenant) is a circumcision of the heart. The cutting away of the flesh (world), yields a new sensitive heart, one of submission. It is done, not by a knife, but the cutting away by the sword of God (His Word) used to attest to Rauch

---

[93] http://www.gotquestions.org/blood-covenant

Hakodesh; Spirit of the Holy One. Mashiach Himself, Y'Shua, bears scars of the cross. (John 20:25-27)

III. Two Witnesses

The witness or seal of the covenant with Christ is the Holy Spirit. In any covenant, there were two witnesses, one of each party, each standing on the opposite side of the other. An interesting note is that it is similar to the bride's maid and the best man's positioning in a wedding, each serving as witnesses to the families of both the bride and groom by being placed on opposite sides of an aisle.

IV. Exchanging of Names

The changing of names, and the merging of names, it is to acknowledge that of a new covenant and authority. Often, there may be included many names, carrying with it the past covenant names.

- Torah The name was changed from Abram to Abraham; and Sarai to Sarah. (Genesis 17:5,15) Jacob exchanged to Israel. (Genesis 32:27-28)
- B'rit Chadashah (new covenant) The Father's name given to the Son, Jesus was given the power of authority. In today's world, your name is replaced to be called Christian, and the power of authority comes through the name of Jesus. In Mark 16:17,18, the authority was given, as it is for you today, in the authority of Jesus name.

In the Covenant with God, in relationship with Y'Shua (Jesus) you will be given a new name and a white stone, *"and I will give him a white stone, and a new name written on the stone which no one knows but he who receives it."* (Revelation 2:17)

IV. Exchanging of Gifts/Authority

- **Authority** an illustration would be a rank in the military, where authority by a ranking party is over the lesser parties. A giving of a crown to an heir, or a title, represents empowerment and authority.
- **Torah** Joseph's coat of many colors revealed Israel's intent to give Joseph the inheritance.

Ketuvim Jonathan exchanged his robe for David's tunic. The robe and tunic represent the authority and identity of the person. David put on the royal robe of Jonathon. Jonathon put on the cloak of a shepherd. The belt from which the sword hung represented strength. Each vowed their power available to the other. The weapons were for the protection of the other. All assets have converged and considered as two become one.

- **B'rit Chadashah** New Testament covenant with the Holy One. *"You shall be clothed in righteousness" (Isaiah 61:10)*. They both are promised God's armor for warfare.

[94]The New Testament covenant is called the B'rit Chadashah meaning in Hebrew "New Covenant" (the word B'rit means "covenant" and Chadashah means "new").

IV. Covenant Feast

The final step of a covenant is the covenant feast. The covenant parties will share a piece of bread and a cup of wine. The bread represents the body that the meaning is, "I will die and let you eat my flesh before I allow you to starve." And the wine represents life. The symbolism of this means you are the blood of my life and mine is yours. Both parties and families were to enter into this part of the

---

[94] https//www.hebrewW.4christians.com/scriptures

covenant, as it is most often a lineage of seven generations to be included.

In a marriage, the sharing of the bread and wine with interlocked arms is a part of the covenant feast. It is called Seedat Mitzvah, meaning covenant meal.

In the B'rit messianic interpretation of Y'Shua, the Messiah, He is represented by an afikomen (hidden loaf), and the third cup is a cup of redemption. Both are parts of the Passover Seder, a meal performed by multiple generations of Jewish families. The meal is a sharing of their deliverance of the children of Israel, as written in Exodus (Matthew 26:26-28).

Our Covenant With Jesus

Jesus has invited all humans to enter both a relationship and covenant with Him. The Bible directs us in the requirements and promises, should we choose to enter into a covenant with Him. The foundation of the new covenant is on His death on the cross; it promises the forgiveness of your sins and the restoration of your relationship with Him (Luke 22:20).

The first promise given to Israel was of blessings and fruitfulness in a Promised land where there would be a peaceful existence. (Ezekiel 36:28). That promise is given to us of new territory that we will live, with the fulfillment of the New Covenant. We will live on earth and in heaven, for all of eternity.

Jesus Christ, Himself was provided as the sacrificial animal, the Passover Lamb (1 Corinthians 5:7). The bloody path you are to walk through is the veil of His flesh (Hebrews 10:20). The veil was torn from top to bottom in the temple at the time of Christ's crucifixion (Mark 15:38).

The vow we are to make is the oath to die to independent living and to become one with Him (Galatians 2:20). There are blessings in walking in the will of God and curses to those who choose the path of disobedience. However, Jesus remains faithful to the covenant promises regardless of our choices (Hebrew 10:16-17).

The word communion is by definition the sharing of the bread and wine in a Christian Service, [95]Eucharist, Holy Communion. The elements are administered and received, "the priest gave him Holy Communion." It also is a recognition of a relationship and acceptance between Christian churches or denominations with the receiving of the sacraments. It also is an acknowledgment of one another's ministry or that of a central authority. All the elements in both the Old and New Testament are in the act of Communion.

Entry Into the Promise Land

It has been many years of wandering in the wilderness for the children of Israel and a forty-year wait to enter the Promised Land. Near the end of their desert life, Moses was led by God to appoint his successor. Joshua now was the new leader; he had served in the tabernacle (Exodus 33:11). He and Caleb was there among the twelve spies sent out that brought back the favorable report. (Number 14:6-9,30).

The Word of the Lord came to Joshua telling of His servant Moses' death, and to rise and cross over the Jordan. They were to enter the land the sons of Israel now had been given to them. Just as was promised, every place the sole of their foot was to tread, was given to the people as was spoken to Moses. (Joshua 1:1-4).

With the instructions of the Lord to be strong and courageous, the promise of the land as was given to their fathers; they were to receive. The people were admonished to meditate day and night on the book

---

[95] www.meriam-webster.com/dictionary/communion

of the law and not allow it to depart from their mouths. To be careful to obey the law as written that all would go well with them and they would prosper and have success. (Joshua 1:9).

Joshua then commanded the officers to pass through the camp and command the people to make provisions, that in three days, they were to cross over the Jordan to the land given them to possess. (Joshua 1:10-11).

SOMETHING OLD, SOMETHING NEW, SOMETHING BORROWED, SOMETHING BLUE

Preparation in the battlefield. [96]

1. You have to look at all things as new. The lessons learned on the battlefield are instructions to learn a skill in the new season. *"Behold, I will do a new thing"* (Isaiah 43:19) It is a time to leave the former behind and experience the new.
2. Your spiritual development in the previous season has brought you to a dependency on God. The lesson learned by self-efforts are to surrender and yield to His ways, unless you miss the connection and learning of the new.
3. Jabez's prayer: *Now Jabez called on the God of Israel, saying, "Oh, that You would bless me indeed and enlarge my border, and that Your hand might be with me, and that You would keep me from harm that it may not pain me!" and God granted him what he had requested.* (I Chronicles 4:10).
4. Jabez's prayer was a prayer to make a covenant with the God of Israel. Jabez was an honorable man who had a committed relationship with God that produced spiritual fruits of greatness. It gave him a deep closeness for prayer. One way to gain honor in the Kingdom of God is through prayer.

---

[96] http://bolzministries /lessons-from-the-battlefield

5. It was a prayer of blessings and possession of the land. Jabez called on the God of Israel when he was undertaking some great dangerous service. In particular, the conquest of the land of Canaan. When he prayed, "enlarge my territory," it was to drive out the wicked and ask for blessings.
6. Jabez's prayer was one of protection and strength; it wasn't self-centered, but for his people. When God answered, all knew it was God with them, and He was well pleased. His prayer was to drive out those wicked and cursed. [97]His request, "the hand of the Lord," is a biblical request for God's presence and power.
7. Jabez's request petitioned for his safety and purity. It was a prayer to shield him from evil and that he would not cause pain. Jabez's name was given to him by his mother; it was a name associated with pain or sorrow, and this laid heavily upon Jabez.
8. It was a prayer for freedom from sorrow if the disaster was to befall him, that he would not sin.
9. Observe, the prayer was a prayer of significance, but God was pleased with the magnitude. A lesson to learn, God is willing both to hear and answer the petitions of His children.

Occupy God's Promise

Entry into your promise is an answer to prayer; it is your deepest heart's desire. It is a Word which was given to you by God. The promise was given to you without conditions rather based upon God and God alone performing and providing the answer.

The land promised is similar to the children of Israel's; everywhere the sole of your foot touches is yours to possess. The seed provided was concealed in the soil, then came to fullness. Just as the farmer plants a seed so has your seed been planted. From the seed to the

---

[97] www.https//biblehub.com/MatthewHenryCommentaries/I Chronicles 4

farmer that becomes bread for your meals; it becomes something that you can give away to others. The bread produced allows you to be a generous giver in every way. You are giving of the bread with praise and thanksgiving for the faithfulness of God in your new land.

Territory Expanded

Your territory of influence has expanded, and with the expanding, your sphere of influence has increased. Your favor will also multiply as your borders become expanded.

Enlarge the places of your tent; Stretch out the curtains of your dwellings, spare not; lengthen your cords and strengthen your pegs. (Isaiah 54:2).

Rest is Required to Enter

There is a time of rest that is required and has come upon you in your land. You are instructed to rest, replenishing your faith, and hope for your vision. It is a day of rest for all, for you to the animals in the fields.

But the seventh day is a day of rest, a day of Sabbath unto the Lord your God. (Deuteronomy 5:14).

In your new land, there is a promise of rest from warfare. You are more mature so drama, relational conflicts, politics, etc. won't slow you down or cost you time. (I Kings 5:4).

Let's Roll!

Early in the morning, Joshua and all the Israelites set out from Shittim, and went to the Jordan, where they camped. Before crossing, there was a quietness in the camp, and a hush fell as the children of Israel went to bed that night. While resting, all reflected upon their beds of the laws that God has given to them as they rested their weary bodies.

They were instructed to destroy all foreign gods, to smash the altars and pillars, to not act like those that dwelled in the land. They were told to destroy all with fire. They were to seek for the Lord of the place that was to be His dwelling place. The instructions included where they were to sacrifice. Where they were to eat and celebrate His blessings. (Deuteronomy 12:1-10).

They were told by God it was a temporary place they had yet to arrive at the area of rest. It was their inheritance that He was giving to them. The Lord God told of the promise of rest on all sides from their enemies; they would live in security. (Deuteronomy 12:8-10)

Being in a place of preparation to move can cause you to become complacent, it is easy to fall into the compromise of accepting less than God's best and promises. When you become too comfortable with the familiarity of your situation, it will make it hard to move. Just as the washing of the Word consecrated the children of Israel, so must you have prepared yourself. To attempt to move into the promises of God, and the land He has given you, it is critical that you are properly cleaned and prepared. The results of a lack of preparation are that you become powerless. You will bring a disgrace, if not outwardly, then certainly inwardly in the eyes of God.

THE THREE CORD AGREEMENT/PRAYER

We are all called to prayer just as Jesus, Himself prays so are we to do so as well. Jesus said, *"I can do nothing of Myself, but what I see my Father doing I also do."* In preparation of your entering the promises and Promised Land, there is one essential thing; to learn to pray. Prayer is key to the access of the promises. (John 5:17-24)

Grab your Bible, open it as I am sharing with you an experience today that only recently happened. Those who know me also know that often, as I write, I first receive the lesson experience, or I am walking through the situation for the privilege to share with others and give encouragement to others.

My attempt in transparency for you is to reveal the way of the Lord; to touch, heal, and bring forth enlightenment and encouragement. I want to bring hope to you that God is not only able but willing to touch you. Your promise may not be like my own. You may not have an actual promise, but a heart's desire; nor is your need the same as what mine may be. It isn't the size or the need that is of importance, but that the Lord God sees and tends His children's every need and desire. In Genesis 18:14 NASB, it is written, *"Is anything too difficult for the Lord?"*

This past week has been a week physically pain filled. I had a negative report following a diagnostic mammogram — the diagnosis brought with it a sonogram biopsy. The procedure is painful, and the report returned was cancer. Let's push pause.

First, this is man's report; we have to acknowledge it, but even that isn't the last word on the situation. How we respond is of vital importance before the actual arrival of the answer to the problem amid the pain. The Lord had given me a song in my heart. He told me," Rejoice! My steps are ordered, by God, He would sustain me."

Previously, I wrote of the need to pay attention to the little things. How important it is to notice patterns and what is, happening about you. Allow me to share what brought me to hear God in this.

A few weeks prior, I had my annual checkup and physical. I refuse any additional x-rays because of a situation so much radiation exposure resulting from the head-on wreck; that I share in my book,

"Days of Plunder."[98] My doctor, who is not a pushy doctor, became very adamant that I needed to do the mammogram. At first, I refused the request and reminded him of my concern of ex-rays as a result of a situation that had happened earlier to me. While we continued to discuss the test, I realized it was unusual for his behavior, and recognized God was leading him and directing my steps.

Fear isn't an option for the child of God, but a decision based on who and what you are believing. Often fear is more destructive than what is happening. God admonished Joshua not to be anxious or dismayed, that He was with Him. (Joshua 1:19) I particularly like (Isaiah 41:10), *"So do not fear, for I am with you; do not be dismayed, for I am your God. I will strengthen you and help you; I will uphold you with my righteous right hand."*

Fear is a tool the enemy uses, along with worry and anxiety. It can overwhelm and engulf you with darkness that can control your every decision. Fear is the door to allow the enemy into your life. Child of God close the door to this destructive thinking, it is not of God.

Fast forwarding let us move forward to Sunday and the prayer group, I attend on Sunday mornings. It is a group of Intercessors which gather to pray, before the church services, bringing various needs requested to pray over in unity.

Prior to this participation, you may recall, in my book, *Days of Plunder*[99], I wrote about how on horrible days in the Rehab Hospital, I had learned to grow and focus on the Lord. One of the many things, following conscious awareness from my wreck, was the presence of God with me. Another tool I used in my greatest pain was to count my blessings, causing me to adjust my focus from the pain onto God.

---

[98] Days of Plunder Finding Light in the Darkness to Overcome and Recover All. / Diana Lynn Rogers
[99] Days of Plunder/ dianalynnrogers.com

To this day, it is a practice I have established in my daily walk with God.

Sunday, when I arrived at church, I began by praising God. I started by acknowledging His faithfulness in allowing me to discover cancer in an early stage. It was with the simple act of listening and following His nudge. Sunday morning, the leader of the group had obeyed God and brought with him a prayer shawl. The shawl was a rare event seldom used. I had not seen it before used in the Upper Room prayers. However, he told me that God had directed for it to be placed and cover me. The group that morning was unexpectedly small. This morning the group had been hand-picked by God, some had been and left, others detained or unable to come. There were four of us, and the presence of the Holy Spirit was in our midst. I was seated in the center of the group. The placement of the Prayer shawl covered my head and shoulders; my forehead was anointed with oil; as the Lord had instructed the leader. Each individually prayed, touching, and agreeing upon those requests that had been discussed and requested with understanding. Petitions included my health to my personal and financial needs; all three were in one accord at the close of their prayers; I too prayed in agreement with faith and thanksgiving at the end of the prayer.

The Lord was not yet through with His instructions. He impressed the leader as he began to refold the prayer shawl to have me grasp the cords attached in each corner of the shawl. Uniquely enough, I only saw three cords; I held the three cords in my hand. I momentarily thought that odd but again obeyed the instruction given. The leader then explained to the group the cords symbolized the cords on the priest, hem and the hem of the garment of Jesus.

Suddenly, I could discern to the purpose of the three-cords. Previously, I was touched and healed as I continually said to the Lord, "I don't know what is wrong with me, but if I could touch the hem of your garment you would heal me," in the months following I was touched and healed. He touched me!

I now know that I know, God, was binding the covenant agreement with us with the three-cord agreement. Just as He was with Daniel, God is with me in this. His will shall prevail, and it is agreed upon by God, and it shall come to pass as we agreed upon it. God is now in a covenant based on the three-cord agreement... He has heard, and His answer has come forth! His answer is Yes and Amen.

A final observation I want to point out is the grave importance of following God's instructions and leadings. Prayer is not a name it assumption and claiming, but an act of request and trust in God to answer. Moses didn't enter the Promised Land as a result of not following the way of the Lord. Selah.

A Review of the Three-Cord Agreement

And if one prevails against him, two shall withstand; and a threefold cord is not quickly broken. (Ecclesiastics 4:12).

[100]There are specific directions required to fulfill the agreement. Wisdom is to repent of any known sin, unclean action, or thoughts in your life. The prayer of agreement in Matthew 18:19-20 is the Three-Cord Agreement.

Truly I say to you, whatever you bind on earth shall have been bound in heaven; and whatever is loose on earth shall be loosed in heaven. (Matthew 18-18).

Little faith or a need for answered prayers, the Prayer of Agreement takes you beyond your level of faith to obtain anything according to the will of God. It may be a loss of a job, a need, healing, whatever your situation and request may be. It is a joining together in one accord unity to agree upon an answer quickly.

---

[100] https://victorythruchristchurch.org/Christian-healing/prayer/prayer of agreement

Again, I say to you, that if two of you agree on earth about anything that they may ask, it shall be done for them by My Father who is in heaven. 20 For where two or three have gathered in My name, I am there in the midst. (Matthew 18:19)

In the prayer of agreement, it is crucial to recognize that not always are all in one accord agreement, and it is better not to pray the prayer if you are not in agreement. The key word in "agree" is to be selective with whom you pray and agree in prayer with regarding your prayer request. The Three Cord Agreement is a unique form of a covenant that brings Jesus in the midst of the ones praying. Jesus hears you loud and clear your prayer request. He is taking it straight to the Heavenly Father without delay.

Pray only with those of like desires; those whose passion is to see God's Word manifest. All are to have a heartfelt faith and believe for what the other wants. Note, not always do family or others have the same heart of faith to respect or believe. Often throughout the scriptures, you will read that the man of God cleared the room as a result of a lack of faith. Those with unbelief will deter the strength of prayer power, better to pray alone than invite them into the petition.

When we pray, we are loosening the desire or binding the hindrance of our petition. Make certain all are in aligned agreement with your exact need and that the request reflects that precisely.

Heavenly Father, please heal me of drug addiction, (name the actual drugs name). Be as specific as you can be in your petition. What do you want? Exactly that state.

Overview of the Three Cord Agreement

1. Two or more in an agreement can have anything they ask (desired or requested) according to the will of God. (I John 5-13-15)

2. Ask in Jesus' name, and our Heavenly Father hears.

Pray only with those absolutely in one accord agreement — the degree of unity brings power to the prayer.

Be specific in the petition; how much, many, and purpose why you want it.

3. Pray the prayer with clarity. State the entire petition requested. Be honest about the situation. God already knows.
4. One heart accord brings forth only those with your best interest in the agreement.
5. Agreement combined with unity is the principle of the Prayer of Faith.

Now faith is the assurance of things hoped for, the conviction of things not seen. (Hebrew 11:1).

The final tips to consider are always asking forgiveness of sins, repenting, and trusting God has forgiven you. A heart of peace is a scriptural answer to prayer.

Upon completion of the prayer request, thank and praise God for answering as often as possible. Surround yourself with praise and worship music. God inhabits the praises of His children.

This is the confidence which we have before Him, that, if we ask anything according to His will, He hears us. (I John 5:14-15).

Lord's Prayer

[101]Christ's instruction about prayer: (Matthew 6:9-10) (Luke11:2)

---

[101] Scofield Study System Bible NASB/Matthew 69-10/ pg1316

v.9 "Pray then in this way 'Our Father who is in heaven, Hallowed be Your name. v.10 Your kingdom come. Your will be done, on earth as it is in heaven. v.11 Give us this day our daily bread. v.12 And forgive us our debts, as we also have forgiven our debtors. v.13 And do not lead us into temptation but deliver us from evil. For Yours is the kingdom and the power and the glory forever. Amen.'"

1. The prayer of Jesus, as prayed to His *Father*, is a prayer based on a relationship with the Father.
2. *Hallowed* is a sacred holy acknowledgment to the absolute holiness of God.
3. The prayer is a petition; *Your Kingdom come* requesting heaven be first and to bring heaven down to earth.
4. God's will to bring heaven to earth is to operate through us.
5. A true prayer accepts the decision in advance. Whether you know or unknown to grant or withhold.
6. Give us this day our daily bread; one will find it is proper to include concerns in prayer within their present conditions.
7. *Forgive us our trespasses;* unforgiving is a sin which will create a blockage, hindering the flow. Sin will create a broken fellowship with the Father. (Matthew 6:12-15).
8. Jesus gave us a definite instruction to pray in His name. (John 15:23-24).
9. Although we are not instructed in this the Lord's Prayer to give thanksgiving throughout the Word, we are told to give thanks and with gratitude make our petitions known. When should we ever not be grateful for His help and many blessings to our petitions and requests? (Philippians 4:6-7)

So, I say ask, and it will be given to you; seek, and you will find; knock, and it shall be opened to you. v10. For everyone who asks, receives; and he who seeks, finds; and to him who knocks, it will be opened. (Luke 11:9-10)

Based on the conditions of these promises and instructions, we may come confidently to the throne of God knowing that our Father has heard and will answer. When it agrees with His will and purposes established in His Word. He is not a tight-fisted Father but instead gives instructions to follow for answered prayers. He is a good Father who loves us all.

I love the Word of God in Luke 11:11-13; it reveals the heart of the father. When his son asks for a fish, will he give him a snake; or an egg, will he give him a scorpion? If our earthly father knows how to give good gifts, how much greater will our Heavenly Father's gifts? He gave us the gift of the Holy Spirit to those of us who asked.

Our Father's Heart

[102] ***The heart of the soldier....*** he stands both dedicated and committed to watching over those in his care. He is a father to his troops. He watches and observes each need closely. He stands guard as a shepherd, tending his flock as he watches and protects their every step. While tending to their needs, he provides shields and protects them from their enemies' evil ways. He relentlessly monitors the equipment, supplies and evil forces about them.

He leads them into fields and rugged, treacherous ways, always searching unless one goes astray. He knows continually where they are and when one is missing, always alert. He brings them to a safe place and the safety of the camp.

He loves them with the passion and heart of a father. He calls them to a better and nobler life than they have previously known, not of an ordinary kind. He is both willing and has laid down his life, dedicated to always keeping them in his ever-watchful keep. Greater love has no one than the soldier who will lay down his own life for his friends. The truth of his love is in the sacrifices he makes for the sake of others. Even

---

[102] https://www.dianalynnrogers.com/the-heart-of-a-soldier/

in the most difficult of circumstances, he is giving for the benefit of others, forgiving when one fails and encouraging all to try once again.

Many will be changed and transformed in his care by his examples of care. They will be changed and gain new strength as they learn to trust his faithful watch. He is their master, but also their friend. He has endured suffering, as well as disappointment and sorrow. He has laughed and cried along-side of them, as he faithfully has kept watch. His willingness to serve others has come with a high cost personally to him.

Rituals and traditions have played a significant role as it has brought self-discipline, order and is of the utmost importance that these are but a foundation of his life; but not to consume him. It is of great importance that his troops are to yield in absolute surrender, with a commitment and obedience as they follow him. They must learn to trust him as he leads and protects them through every battle, snare, and trap of the enemy.

Surrounded by personal setbacks and tragedies, in hardships and disappointments, many blame him for the situations they find themselves. Tragically they do not see the disasters of this world cannot be attributed to his lack of care, but by the foolishness of man and the relentless attacks of the enemy's plans.

He is but a soldier with love for his troops . . . In the troublesome times, when bitterness and prejudice abound, it is hard to remember that love triumphs. He is not so unlike the love of his Heavenly Father who cares for us, who shields and protects us continually with a heart of love…he is but a soldier, walking in the shadow of His Heavenly Father.

Lord, I thank you for the soldiers that lay their life down that we may live and have the abundant life, those who are committed and stand faithfully at their post. God be with every one of those who are serving us to keep our shores safe and our highways and byways protected. Today we give thanks for one and all of them. In Jesus' name. Amen.

In remembrance of those who have gone before us. Those who have served and fought the good fight. Those who are serving our Lord and to those who continue to fight, the battle of good and evil till the day of the return of the Lord, we are grateful.

Father's Love, Part I

[103] In the Pre-Father's Day service, the sanctuary had filled with regular attendees, friends, and fathers. The Pastor's teaching was a two-part series carried over from the prior week. In both Sunday's lessons, he spoke from his heart. It was such a poignant message I would be remiss not to allow you, the opportunity to be told of it and share the Father and son relationship. As I write this, I encourage you to consider your father and then our Heavenly Father's love revealed in this story.

As the message unfolded, he shared how he had visited his father in a nursing home. His father had been the former pastor; now he was the senior pastor. He spoke of the fact that his father had Alzheimer's. He shared how when he visited the nursing home, his father was standing at the nurse's desk. There was a struggle for his father to recall the medication. He was trying to ask the nurse if he had received it yet.

When the Pastor came up beside him, his father didn't recognize him and told him to get in line. How difficult to know that this man, his father, who not only had grown a very sizable church but also went to college to get a doctorate to enable himself to open a Christian School, didn't recognize him, his son. Without saying, the Pastor's heart broke when this happened.

He said to him, "Don't you remember me?" and spoke his name to his dad. Still, his father struggled with recognition.

---

[103] oaks. church /message-library /fathers-love/Pastor Scott Wilson

Finally, recognition came, and they hugged each other, and he was able to connect with him for a while. In his message, he pointed out three essential things we all need.

The importance of relationships.

1. The significance of his identity when recognized and acknowledged by his father.
2. The importance of the need for affection and the exchange of love in the hug and words received.
3. The affirmation that came when he called him by name and told him he had missed him.

Often life leaves us lacking. With the discovery of the loss, you may find yourself in life parentless, without family or with the need for recognition. There remains a great need for love and affirmation in all of us. As a reminder, remember, God sees you. You are never out of his sight and hearing.

Those who feel that to show affection is a weakness allow me to share a second story. Following the loss of my marriage, my daughter moved away to school and to stay with her grandmother.

After my marriage had ended, what was best for my son's stability arose, forcing a decision. I remained jobless when school started. My jobless state forced the decision to allow my son to stay in his childhood home and school. That devastated me.

In early winter, I attended school for several weeks training for my new job. I was still in a state of deep emotional grieving from all the losses and abandonment. Until the time came the Lord touched and healed me of a broken heart.

Following my healing, I transferred to Indianapolis to work in a design studio. I found myself unable to attend the sister church. The church was on the far south side, and I was on the west side of the city. During this period, I tried to visit my former church as often as possible, but scheduling made it impossible. I became very isolated in my continuing grief. The opportunity finally arrived when I visited the sister church. I was standing alone, not knowing anyone, when the pastor's wife came over to speak to me and hugged me. I suddenly began crying from the human touch I so desperately needed. Never underestimate the value of a hug or the love you show a stranger; you may be God's touch to help them survive the pain. The human touch and affection are necessary for the survival of life's crises and times of abandonment.

Father's Love, Part II

[104]On Father's Day, there were visitors, and the usual church crowd filled with fathers and their families. At the beginning of the message again, the Pastor opened by sharing his father's condition and their visit. However, this week, he wanted to share about his childhood with his father and family. Daily, he and his brothers were driven to school by his father without exception. The ride to the school was designated as a time for review and learning. A previously learned scripture they quoted, and the boys practiced the learning of a new scripture.

He told of the several routines in his childhood. One in particular stood out, that I desire for you to read. It was a nightly routine. They all dressed for bed and brushed their teeth following their family prayers. Each boy would go to their rooms and prepare for lights out. They would individually call out to their dad they were ready for him. Each was given time with him to pray, while saying goodnight.

One by one, he visited each room. His father nightly told each of them a story. It was always the same people in the story, a little boy and his father. He would discuss with his sons the events of the day

---

[104] https://oaks.church/message library/fathers-love/Scott Wilson

tailored to each son's day, with the same story of a little boy and his father. They would discuss the ride to school and the day's events as he shared the story. When the story ended, as the lights were about to be turned off, he would discuss the love and pride the father had for his son in the story. He would reach down, always placing a kiss on their foreheads, hugging each of them. Then he left the son with the words, "I love you." Remember, always to tell those you love, that you do love them; you never know.

Near the end of the message, he shared another visit with his father. And this time the roll reversed as he tucked his father in and told him a story and hugged and kissed him on the forehead, saying, "goodnight," and how he loved him. Check out the Father's Day message online at the https://oaks.church /message library to hear more of this story. Listen to the story love of the father and his son. And if our earthly father knows how to give good gifts, how much greater does our Heavenly Father love us?

Disappointments

What happens when you are faced with a disappointment, a loss, a tragedy? When all shaken has been shaken in your life. Then what? Do you become bitter, angry, retaliatory, or do you recognize it is the way of the Lord?

It Is The Lord

Diana Lynn Rogers

We went through the fire and through water, but thou brought us out into a wealthy place. (Psalms 66:12).
[105]It is the Lord who passed my way in all the pain and sorrows.

---

[105] dianalynnrogers.com/It-is-the-lord

It is the Lord who gave me the strength to walk each step of the way.
It is the Lord in whom I take my stand. The grain has been sifted, the corn has died.
"It is the way of the Lord," said I. It is all part of the Master's Plan.
In the darkness, I have walked through this land.
The starless night, the perils along the way.
Struggling, unable to understand for a moment, much less for a day!
It is the way of the Lord, teaching me to lean on Him and trusting His mighty hand.
Hardships come, and hardships go, shadows turn to light.
It is not ours to know or understand. It is the way of the Lord.
Be still and know your name is written in the palm of His hand!

Often God's way and your ways are two entirely different paths. Frequently, God takes you through the river of difficulty, and the fire. Job 13:15 (KJV) states, *"Though He slay me, yet I will trust in Him: but I will maintain mine own ways before Him."*

You must come to a place where you see your situation as it is. When you lower your hopes and expectations, it is also possible to close yourself off from what God has planned for you.

The choice is yours to learn from the mistake and become more resilient in following God. This has the potential to reduce the number of self-efforts that will lead you into wrong pathways. You will develop endurance and spiritual muscles while learning the way of the Lord. God uses repetition to bring forth changes, similar to an athlete in training.

A frequent strategy hell attempts to use is to isolate you from others. Do not allow that to happen. Surround yourself with those who love you, those who are for you to help you gather strength. If you don't have trusted friends, ask God to send you one. We all need somebody, but not just anybody. Don't try on your own to fill the gaps, but allow God to lead you, and lean on Him.

When you spend quality time with God, you will grow deeper. Remember, the present situation is not the end but a transition to a new beginning. Change can be painful. I remember as a child when my legs were growing, and my legs hurt; it was painful. Often so is our spiritual growth. Inch by inch, you have grown to become who you are. If you are an athlete, "No pain, no gain" often is said when pain comes. Therefore, it is easier to keep pressing on. The difficulty lies in not understanding the purpose or why God has taken you on this pathway. Ask Him to teach you and help you gain all He has purposed in allowing this valley of disappointment.

The King's Kingdom

But seek ye first the Kingdom of God, and His righteousness; and all these things shall be added unto you. (Matthew 6:33 KJV)

What is the Kingdom of God? What does that mean? How do I know what that really means for my life? How do I enter the kingdom of God? How do I get there from here, you might ask? All of which are good questions. [106]The kingdom of heaven is the dwelling place both in earth and heaven. It is in the universal sphere as well as the earthly sphere, the two have many things in common; although they are interchangeable terms in some context.

[107]The kingdom of heaven, like the Kingdom God, it is realized in the rule of God in the present age and will also be fulfilled in the millennial kingdom. It continues forever in the eternal state (compare Daniel 4:3).

When we seek the kingdom of God, those things become a priority over the things the world has to offer. Primarily, with our salvation,

---

[106] Holy Bible Scofield Study System NASB pg.1309, pg.1317
[107] Holy Bible Scofield Study System NASB pg.1317

we are given an inheritance of the kingdom of God. The Kingdom of God is of greater value than the things of this world.

Great emphasis in Jesus' teachings is placed on the kingdom of God. Jesus said, *"And as you go, preach saying, 'the kingdom of heaven is at hand'"*. (Matthew 10:7) He came to bring heaven to earth. God's power is the kingdom of God. (Matthew 6:9-10).

We earlier studied the instructions given to us in the Lord's Prayer of how to pray. In this segment of teaching, we will examine how to bring God's kingdom into our daily prayers with supernatural power.

You may have been taught a variety of teachings. Training of man's ways and beliefs often are taught instead of God's ways. Jesus taught with power, yet, He walked on earth as a son of man, and Son of God. (Matthew 10:7-8) His prayer is a model for us to follow. His life is our role model as we walk through the kingdom of God here on earth. In the Lord's Prayer we are told to pray this way, "*Your kingdom come. Your will be done, on earth as it is in heaven.*" He also stated, *"as you go, preach, saying, 'The kingdom of heaven is at hand."* With further instruction He said to His disciples, *"Heal the sick, raise the dead, cleanse the lepers, cast out demons. Freely you received, freely give."* (Matthew 10:8). Wow! How does that work for you? The answer to that question is, it works through the renewing of your mind. The change results in cleansing, purging and aligning your thoughts with God's kingdom and purposes.

These are the very things God has been teaching us to do in this book. Step by step, He has guided not just you, but me included. We all are being taught to grow deeper and change into a greater likeness and understanding of His ways. With each page you have turned, greater insights and understandings of God have been revealed.

Keys to supernatural empowerment of God's kingdom, starts within your own life. You, throughout the pages of this book have often been challenged to examine your mind, heart, behavior, thoughts, and mouth. You have been shown how to discover the acceptable and unacceptable ways of your walk with God. I, personally, have sought the Lord for His daily bread, that I may share with you as we grow to know Him in a deeper and closer relationship. At the onset of my relationship with God, I asked of Him, "What was the lesson I was to learn?" He declared clearly the words, "To know Him." May you also come to know Him in greater ways as we grow together.

You are nearing the water's edge. You are now trained to step into the Promises of God. The power of God is essential for you in the coming days to enable you to pursue, overtake. and recover all of the plunder.

Forgiveness and Repentance are heart issues that absolutely must occur for you to be fully empowered. [108]Repentance is a turning back from an action with a sincere regret and great remorse. Each person who turns to God in genuine repentance and faith will be saved. It is a heart change to turn away from a lifestyle or sin.

Forgiveness is needed to continue forward with God. You are to forgive others as you have been forgiven. It is important to realize and remember, unforgiveness leaves you emotionally attached to the situation, issue or person. Forgiveness is for you and allows God to work in the situation of all the parties involved. You have just freed yourself of the evil intended. Without repentance, you are locked into a fleshly mindset.

Renewal of the mind is not about going to heaven but how much of heaven you desire here on earth. A renewing of your mind involves the words floating around within your mind. Your mental monologue contains self-focused and self-defeating chatter.

Ask God to shield your mind, your thought patterns dictate the outcome of your days. (Romans 12:2) Change thoughts change your life. The importance of examining your thoughts exposes many

---

[108] Dictionary.com/repentence

wrong attitudes and actions you may do. The Bible states, *"As a man thinketh, in his heart so he is."* (Proverbs 23-7). To guard your thoughts also places a guard on your heart. Recognize the voice who is speaking in your mind. Are your thoughts heavy and weighing you down or lifting you up? Do your thoughts bring lightness and peace or a sense of turmoil? Are they negative and oppressive expose the enemy's chatter? Open the scriptures and find a Word to direct your thoughts and renew your mind.

Submission brings permission to bring heaven down to earth, to gain entry to our assigned mission for the kingdom of God here on earth. There is not one person who doesn't stand in awe when a supernatural healing is made known. Whether it is a limb to grow, blind eyes to see or a manifestation of the presence of God, all long to see God in their midst.

Few are willing to walk in the discipline to see the manifestation of God's Presence.

The reality of the kingdom of God must change to reveal heaven on earth as it is in heaven. The anointing is not given through self-efforts or any act of the flesh or self-anything. It all comes with a cost. God's power is a flowing of His power coming through you to the earth. This is a requirement of surrendering your will and ways to Him in a yielded obedience.

A Vessel of Honor For His Glory

Therefore, if anyone cleanses himself from these things, he will be a vessel for honor. sanctified, useful to the Master, prepared for every good work. (II Timothy 2:21)

Staking Claims

There wasn't a cloud in the sky, nor had a drop of rain fallen to the ground in years. Only the dust devil's whirlwind was seen as Elijah shuffled his feet forward. The brook had long since dried up and the raven no longer came; it had long ago departed, leaving Elijah forced to move forward.

The promise of God continued with Elijah. Elijah strained, searching the horizon for the presence of a cloud. He was listening for the sound of rain. Seven times, he prayed. Repeatedly he sent his servant to see if the word of God was seen visibly. He continued to persist in prayer. He gazed with an expectancy, waiting for God's answer.

Abraham and Sarah waited for years for the inheritance and descendants. God had spoken of this in Genesis 17:15-27, and again in Genesis 26:4 to Abraham. As many as the stars in the heavens…

This week I crossed over to the other side of the attack of cancer. I endured a second surgery to remove the final margin that had not cleared.

Personal Promise Given.

In each of these examples, there was a personal promise given to one specific person. To Elijah it was for the abundance of rain. Abraham was promised a son, besides the inheritance of the land. For me, the promise of the impossible is to come. Each one has a specific hope, promise which is of great importance. There is a certain answer you are seeking and waiting for to take place.

[109]There are six things Elijah did, as he prayed seven times, waiting to hear God's answer.

---

[109] A Man of Heroism and Humility Elijah /Charles R Swindoll Nashville, Tennessee Thomas Nelson

1. He had a belief and confidence in God to trust Him to do as He said. His trust continued, even when there was not a cloud to show the abundance of rain. Elijah heeded the voice of God in his spirit when He made known the sound of rain. (I Kings 18:41)

For myself, during this battle with cancer, the "voice" that sustained me and gave me confidence was a specific word. The cords on the prayer shawl's corners symbolized "touching the hem of His garment". These words brought forth a confirmation and remembrance of God healing me before. The Word by God, given to me, was a reminder of His power of healing. It allowed me the courage and confidence to know that God had accepted our prayer petition and answered.

2. Elijah went to the sea to be alone with God. This enabled him to remove distractions. Just as Elijah, it is of vital importance for you to remove distractions.

In my personal battle, I focused on studying God's word. I studied and worked on the lessons I am sharing with you. Continuously I have listened for His guidance. I listened to worship music, surrounding myself with God's presence in praise continually.

3. Elijah spent time in prayer and thanksgiving, humbling himself. *Humble yourselves therefore under the mighty hand of God, that He may exalt you at the proper time. (James 4:10)*
4. Elijah was specific. "*Go now, to the seas.*" Look for a sign of rain.
5. Elijah remained persistent as he prayed seven times. Don't quit, never give up! Your answer may be the last door, but it will come forth. God is a keeper of His promise and a rewarder of those who diligently seek Him. (Hebrew 11:6)
6. Elijah searched the skies for a cloud. Expect an answer to come forth.

In this battle, I found the word God gave in Acts 12:5 *"when the church prayed"*. If you will recall, Peter was in prison, while the church prayed for him in their assembly. Even though the first surgery verified that my lymph nodes had no cancer, the margins were still not cancer free around the tumor. Because of the margin that showed it had evidence of cancer, the second surgery became necessary.

When you receive a negative report, continue to pray on, especially if you received a Word from God. Trust Him. Act in faith; God is keeping His Word. Keep your eyes of faith on Him. He will not fail. God is a way maker of deliverance and a miracle worker.

v13 Moses said to the people. "Do not fear! Stand by and see the salvation of the Lord which He will accomplish for you today; for the Egyptians whom you have seen today, you will never see them again forever." v14 "The Lord will fight for you while you keep silent". v15 Then the Lord said to Moses, "Why are you crying out to me? Tell the sons of Israel to go forward". (Exodus 14:13-15)

As the Church Prays

1. The one accord unity brings God's presence and power into the prayer.
2. Within my weakness lies God's strength.
3. The evidence of joy indicates the presence of God. It will raise you above your crisis or situation.
4. Hope doesn't just motivate positive action. Hope has healing power.

They define hope as a beacon, keeping us connected to what we are having faith for. Hope doesn't prevent me from expecting the worst. The worst is what the hopeful are prepared to endure. In the Bible, hope carries with it an expectation that a certain outcome will happen. This is far more powerful than a wish or desire. Hope gives us the expectancy of a good end based on God's word. Even when it looks like all is lost, we know that God is for us.

Now faith is the substance of things hoped for, the evidence of things not seen. (Hebrew 11:1) Hope is like the forerunner to faith. It leads the way and opens the door to faith.

In conversation with a friend, we discussed how a small child's conditioning to steal by her mother trained her. Years later, she has continuously ended up in jail because of this learned behavior. As an adult when lack occurred, based on fear and needs, she returned to the old behavior pattern. With a similar behavior pattern of repetition, you may develop a Learned Behavior while studying the Bible.

There are two laws that affect our minds. The Law of Cognition—you are what you think. *"For as a man thinks, so is he."* (Proverbs 23:7), Psychologist Archibald Hart has stated, thoughts influence every aspect of one's being.

Our confidence is in God or fear, one of which will become a dominant thought. The one habitually thought on will have a commanding influence in our minds. What we consider creates our attitudes, shapes our emotions, and governs our behavior. Interestingly, it also deeply influences our immune system and vulnerability to illness. Everything about you flows from inward to the outward and stems from your mind. God said, *"do not be conformed to this world, but be transformed by the renewing of your mind". (Roman 12:2)*

[110]The Law of Exposure implies what the mind most often meditates about and is exposed to effects the behavior. The repetition of anything that enters your mind will create what you do and become. Through constant exposure to violence, it will cause an outward behavior of violence. They call this an effects behavior.

---

[110] www.approach your actions.com /Habits of the Mind Archibald Hart

Thou wilt keep him in perfect peace whose mind is stayed on thee; because he trusteth in thee. (Isaiah 26:3) How do we develop God focus during a storm? Your focus and what you are pondering are of vital importance. Guard your mind, it's the only place that hell can slip into your thoughts.

Abundance of Rain

My second surgery was completed the previous week. On Monday, I received a call to set an office visit. With the office call came a certainty in my heart I was cancer free. Had the results not been clear, another surgery would have been scheduled. In my visit today I received official confirmation from my surgeon, the breast cancer is all removed. The next steps require my visiting with the specialists to decide a treatment plan to protect me from any further incidents of cancer. I rejoice! My steps are being ordered by God, great is His faithfulness.

Heavenly Father, I praise and thank you that you never leave or forsake us. That as a child of God, we can lay hold of Your every Word. We trust you for Your best in our times of trouble.

I lift each reader before you and speak peace into their life. It may not be cancer; it may be a loss of a different kind. You are our sustainer. Your Word brings healing and Your resurrection power to the broken, hurting, and those suffering. I now ask you to send Your Word to heal each one at their greatest need.

I thank you for touching and moving in circumstances only you alone are aware exist. Thank you for restoring life to the ones reading this right now. I speak life, health and abundance, into each one. I praise you for being the giver of life. In Jesus' name. Amen.

Land mines

Noticing what you notice allows you the ability to realize what is occurring in your life. What you see will give you valuable insight to patterns and situations hard to detect. In noticing what you notice, such as a repeated pattern or an unusual event that appears to be a reoccurrence, it will reveal hidden situations. This can expose and help you find the issue at work in your life, as you pay attention to the little things surrounding your life.

1. Where is your focus when fear, hope, sorrow, apathy, joy or discouragement happens?
2. What causes your focus to become distracted or broken, reducing your level of hope?
3. Identify the distraction and note who or what is creating the issue.

Set aside a time to spend with God.

4. Separate yourself from people or situations that create distractions.
5. Manage your time wisely. Remove time bandits from your life.

Waiting

A lesson I am learning is the value of waiting. Most everyone will agree; it is stressful and filled with pressure when in a place of waiting. It is most particularly trying when in need of an answer, or a critical decision has to be made. Perhaps you are pressed to wait in line or traffic is delaying you. I have discovered waiting is a friend cleverly disguised to teach patience, but also can be another tool to expose the enemy. I have discovered that a delay can be a divine intervention for my protection. Often you may have heard of the cliché "someone was at the wrong place at the right time" or "had I been there five minutes earlier or later" something bad may have happened. These are providential moves of God.

I now am discovering a new weapon of warfare as my patience has grown. I now have realized how to flip the flop of waiting from a negative thing to a positive friend.

Isaiah 40:31 says, when we wait upon the Lord, we will gain new strength. He said that we will mount up with wings like the eagle. We will run and not grow tired, walk and not grow weary. These things will happen because we have waited!

Not only do we gain new strength to rise above our problems, we can renew our strength in waiting. We don't have to experience the exhaustion, or the heaviness of the trouble involved as we wait.

When I considered joy and how God has used it as a weapon of warfare, I then realized, so was waiting. Change your thoughts. Transform waiting into a tool to expose the enemy's efforts to push you to move through distraction and pressure. Hit pause and wait. It is like sitting at a traffic light and the light is yellow . . . wait, don't move! As you wait, examine your situation. Let the dust settle around you and listen watchfully. Discern the positive and the negative you are sensing. Where is your peace? What are you experiencing, feeling? Do you sense a calm, peace or are you having the sense of turmoil and confusion? What is your predominant emotion?

Take the time to explore your thoughts and decisions. Write them down, identify where you sense a presence of peace. Continue to seek God prayerfully; God doesn't move in desperation or hurriedly. Center your focus on God; let His peace direct you to your answer. You will find your answer often will be a simple instruction.

When you recognize the pressure's center, you have exposed the plots of the enemy. Allow the hand of God to guide you, not your hand trying to do-it-yourself in self-efforts.

It may not be possible to implement every action. Try to place yourself in a position to step back and observe your surroundings. Realize God and you are in control, not the devil of your circumstance's outcome. You just took the remote control and hit pause. Now make your decision in peace. Just breathe. <u>*Partner with God in every decision.*</u>

Building Memorials

The prophet Samuel set-up a stone after the Lord had routed the Philistines, which caused Israel to win a victory. According to the word in Samuel 7:12 "Thus far the Lord has helped me." There was a time of repentance and seeking God on Israel's part. There was a removal and confession of the foreign gods, turning away from the rebellion and disobedience before worshiping God.

[111] The Hebrew word, Ebenezer stone, was recognized as a stone of commemoration of God's help to Israel. In the English word, it means a stone of help. Stones of remembrance, memorials and monuments are used to mark and establish historical events. Monuments continue on from one generation to another to remind of the story and history behind each one.

The children of Israel wandered in the wilderness for forty years. Because of the intervention from God by parting the Jordan River, they crossed over to enter the promised land. When they entered the land, Joshua commanded the erection of a stone memorial as a reminder of God's faithfulness.

What were the stones and where did they come from?

v.5 and Joshua said to them, "Cross again to the ark of the Lord your God into the middle of the Jordan, and each of you take up a stone on

---

[111] http//:www. Merriam-Webster.com/ebenezer

his shoulder, according to the number of the tribes of Israel. v.6 'Let this be a sign among you, so that when your children ask later, saying, What do these stones mean to you?' v.7 Then you shall say to them, 'Because the waters of the Jordan were cut off before the ark of the covenant of the Lord; when it crossed over the Jordan, the waters of the Jordan were cut off.' So, these stones shall become a memorial to the sons of Israel forever." (Joshua 4:5-7)

What type of memorials might you use to be a testament or memorial? What can you use to recall the faithfulness of God and His hand of deliverance? Perhaps it may be a plaque, a small figure or a simple stone. As I studied for this, I discovered some very interesting things. There are a variety of stones and memorials.

[112]The moss agate stone means New Beginnings. It represents being stable, persistent, and grounded. The agate stone is considered a stone of encouragement, trust and hope. They also believe it to be a stone to put an end to stress from today's lifestyle; it establishes harmony. The moss agate stone is one of many examples of stones that have a variety of meanings. They used stones in the Bible for commemoration of events.

The stone's type has a variety of purposes and spiritual meanings. Often the symbolism of a stone means endurance, stability and permanence, grounded and connected to the earth; they are strong and versatile and accessible. With the stacking of stones there is a balance that shows a sign of patience and a physical effort. The corner stone is viewed as a stone of strength.

There is one more thing I want to share with my readers, which is of a personal nature for me. I have talked about my recent brush with cancer. I mentioned I had decided not to allow the enemy to have any place in my life. I said I would mock and jeer him at every turn.

---

[112] www.http://charmsoflight.com-mossagate

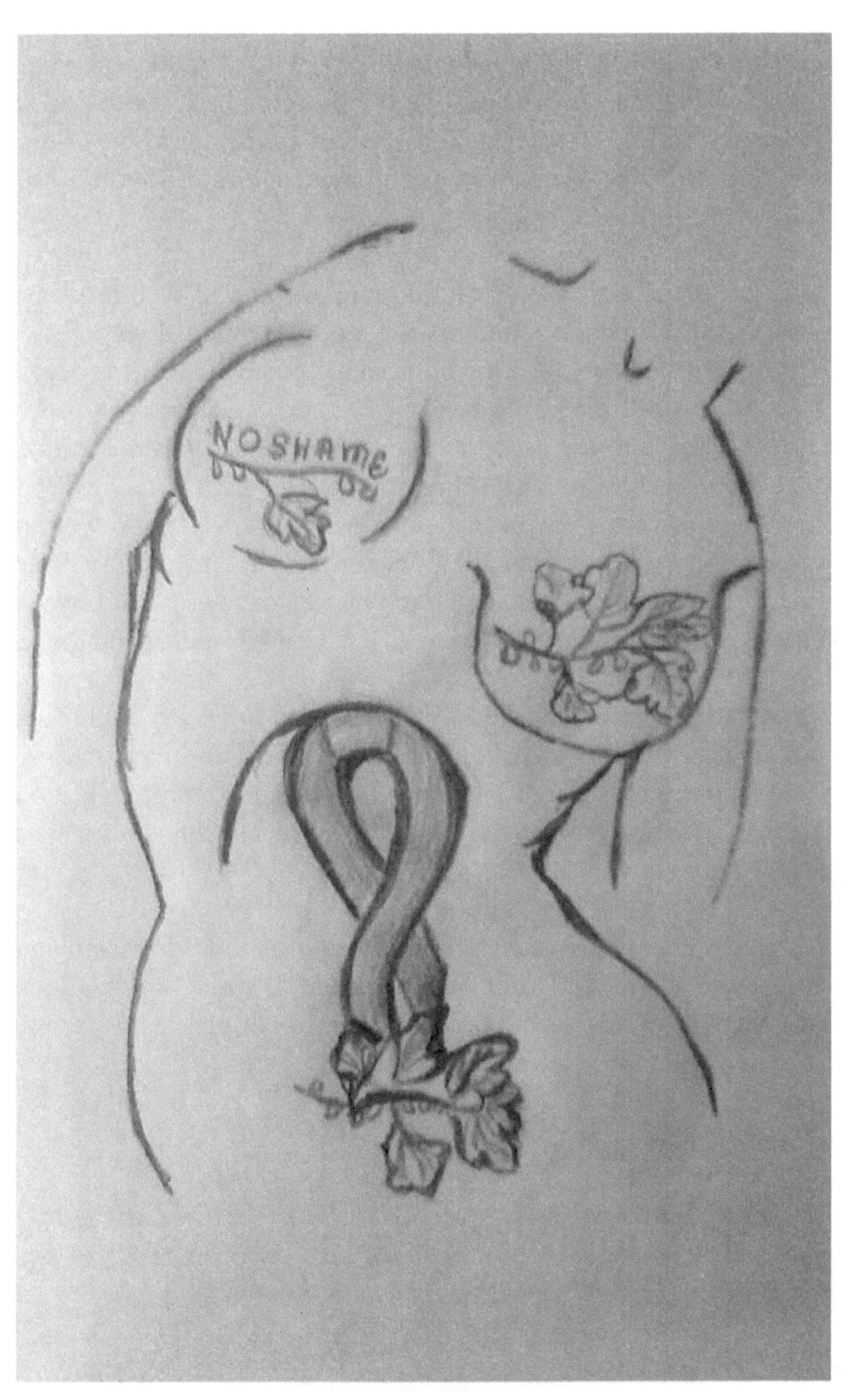

NO SHAME

There are few things in life we can control. How I think and where I place my focus are two things I can control. The choice is mine, not the devil's. The picture you see is an "in your face" to the devil. I can't control the fact that I have been targeted with cancer, but how I react, I can control.

I want to share with you my interpretation of the picture shown "NO SHAME". First my body is the temple of God. I was created in His image and He spoke my life into existence before time began. The torso reminds me it is to be respected and cared for as a vessel of honor. The fig leaf was used in the garden to cover Adam and Eve's bodies. The leaves were a covering of shame for their sin. My disfigurement of my body reminds me of the cross where Jesus' wounds and blood was shed to cover all of our sins. The leaves are a reminder I am covered in the blood of Jesus; and He healed my scars at Calvary. There is no shame in my life; I am covered by His mercy and grace.

The picture is a memorial to the fact that God has given me life and a victory over death and sin. This is my memorial and Jesus said, 'do this in remembrance of Me'. The cup I have had to drink is all about Him, He who loves me to the laying down of His life. This is what the picture represents to me.

The scar you bear most likely is not your choice, but it is part of your journey and story. Find your memorial and celebrate life. God sees and knows the scar you bear. Build a memorial; pick up a stone to remind yourself He is a healing Jesus.

Heavenly Father,

I praise and thank you for being the breath of heaven. The Giver of life. I praise and thank you for the countless ways you have sustained and kept, not only myself, but each one that is reading this now.

Allow each reader to recognize that we all have burdens, sorrows and scars to bear in this life. Be with each one in their very own private strug-

gles. It may be physical, mental or emotional that they are seeking Your help and face. Help us love one another.

Deliver us from the evil of this world. Teach us to walk in love and forgiveness as you have forgiven us. Give us our daily bread. May your kingdom in heaven come to earth. Help us walk more like you and less of ourselves.

Should there be one who is lost and needs to find their way to you Lord, send those who know you to cross their paths. In Jesus' name. Amen.

Pick up a stone and put it in your pocket as a reminder that God is faithful and in control. You never walk alone.

Double Vision

God reminded me of something this morning, as I began to write about having double vision in a situation, whether it is a criticism, a correction or as simple as a picture. My perspective of a situation, or a person, may be a different perspective from the other person's viewpoint. All should develop a double vision. All have different experiences and life filters that have changed us to see through different lenses.

None should quickly judge something evil, until we look and see the heart motive behind the situation, person or motive. A good lens filter is to look at one another first in your perspective, then filter it through Jesus' perspective. (Matthew 7:1)

We are to place filters on our hearts, minds and eyes that we, *"do not conform to the world, but rather be transformed by the renewing of our minds".* (Romans 12:2)

We all have the same assignment in God's schoolhouse. We are instructed to love one another and walk in His love and ways. We are told to forgive, that we too shall be forgiven.

The Shepherd

[113]The Shepherd gazed out across the open field as he kept watch over his sheep. One by one he called them by name. Even in the darkness, he knew exactly where each one was located. Several were born into his herd; they had spent a lifetime under his care. Many others had later come into his fold. All were provided for with the greatest care. Often when wounded, he would carry them upon his shoulders until they could stand on their own once again.

There were those sheep who had to be tended to for their many cuts, wounds and sores from all of their wandering ways.

When he entered a new field for them to graze, frequently he would go before them, leading them, shielding and protecting their every step. Snakes often pop up out of the ground as they sense the hoofs above them. The Shepherd would take his oil to oil the holes so when they tried to strike, they would fall back into the hole. Other times he would strike them dead with his staff.

Sometimes one who lingered behind would become lost and he would have to rescue them. The coyotes, wolves, bears and lions would chase them until they fell over a cliff; with his staff, he would reach down and pull them to safety.

Many times, the shepherd would spend the entire night looking for just one lost sheep. At the end of the day, one by one, he counted them as they passed under his rod to rest. They placed stones in the eastern shepherd's field in a circle to form a hedge of protection for

---

[113] Ancient-hebrew.org /Shepherd life: the care of sheep and goats

his sheep. In the center of the circle, a fire pit is made to keep the enemies from invading the flock.

The eastern shepherd never drives the sheep, as does the western shepherd. He has a relationship with his sheep. He knows each one and calls them by name. (John 10:3) His sheep all know his voice and follow him. (John 10:4)

The good shepherd is the door. Only through the door does one enter his flock. There he will protect them. The shepherd will provide for his sheep and see to his every need from the greatest to the least. (John 10:1-18)

He guards his sheep day and night from the thieves who come to steal, kill and destroy. He walks by their side to see those in front and those straggling behind. In the day's monotony, sometimes he will run ahead. He will pretend to run away from them as he plays with them. Soon they are all running to him, circling about skipping as they frolic, leaping in play.

The shepherd will walk behind them as their rear guard to see stragglers, while he protects these from hidden dangers. When crossing from one field to another, he will lead them through very narrow paths between the fields. In the middle east, most often only narrow passes connect from one field to the other. Should one sheep stray from the flock and eat in a forbidden field, the shepherd has to pay for the losses.

All of us like sheep have gone astray, each of us has turned to his own way; but the Lord has caused the iniquity of us all to fall on Him. (Isaiah 53:6)

The shepherd not only knows his sheep by name, but by touch; he senses their very absence. When He takes them through the waters to cross a forge, those who know him boldly jump full body into the water and cross the water.

Those who would falter with hesitation, get carried down the stream, finally to clamor to the water's edge. Little lambs who attempt to cross leap into the water. When they struggle, the shepherd leaps in and rescues them with his protective hands. He then carries them across to safety. The newborns he carries in his bosom as they cross to shore, bleating joyfully. He kept his eyes upon the mother sheep guarding and protecting them as they crossed the river.

When you pass through the waters, I will be with you; and through the rivers, they will not overflow you. (Isaiah 43:2)

This reminds me of a story of my son, who would wade into the water at the beach. I would wait, while I stood with a watchful eye, until I would have to grab him to keep him from bobbing up and down. Back to shore, he would turn around and run right back in, splashing and leaping. Later, when he took swim lessons, his confidence was so strong he was diving off of the high dive. When we know the Lord, we too can dive into the water with confidence, knowing God is there to catch us, as he leads us forth.

1. Can you remember times you too may have leaped in faith to have God's hand deliver you?
2. Do you recall the times you have hesitated, only to allow circumstances to sweep you away, for God to intervene?
3. Can you recall an incident where the Shepherd has protected you from certain death or injury?
4. Can you think of times in your life that he has provided and met a need where you had no way or hope to pay?
5. Has He carried you when you were so broken you weren't certain you could make it through?
6. Is there a place in your life that you feel so desperate or alone you don't know how to make it through? Do you feel so alone and abandoned you don't know where to go? Maybe it hurts so bad emotionally you can barely breathe?
7. In the life's story of a shepherd, can you see where God may hide in the shadows just waiting to carry you?

There is one more story I want to tell you about before we move on from the Shepherd of the fields and the Shepherd of the twenty-third Psalms.

There was a shepherd sitting on the hillside watching over his sheep. A young woman walking along the road passed by, when she noticed him. He was sitting with a little lamb with broken legs. She turned onto the pathway that led to where he sat.

After a brief conversation, she asked him what had happened to the little sheep; had it fallen? With an intent gaze, he looked into her eyes and said, "No, I broke its legs." In horror, the woman was shocked and asked, "Why did you do that?" Then he explained, the lamb's legs were broken so it would quit running away. Now, he explained, he carries the lamb on his shoulders wherever he goes. He feeds it by hand, and waters it as he cares for it. There would come a time it would heal, and it would not run away anymore.

You see, I was that lamb and my legs were broken. I have learned to walk very close to the Great Shepherd. Today, I am grateful that He broke my legs to teach me how greatly He loves me. If you are that little lamb and haven't come to know the Shepherd of my heart, I invite you to come to Him today. He is waiting on you to come to Him.

Heavenly Father,

Thank you, for all the love and ways you have taught me. Had life not broken me; I would never have known you and who you really are. You are a Father who loves me to even laying down His Son's life for me. I ask you for those who walk at a distance and try to stay far back, draw them close to you. To the ones who are wounded and need healing, touch them. To those who need more of you, draw them ever closer to your bosom.

Lord be with us as we walk through these lessons of life. Teach us Your ways. In Jesus' name, amen.

Valley Lessons

When I was but a little girl, it would be well past dark when the laundry chores were completed. Often it meant taking the last clothing off of the clothesline in the dark when they were dry. Once, late in the evening, we were finishing the chores. In the darkness we were taking the last of the laundry down and folding the clothes, placing them in a basket. Then there was a sudden loud pounding sound of what easily sounded like hooves beating the pavement, I became paralyzed by fear. Often a herd of cattle across the road had gotten loose to enter our yard. Out of the darkness came one of the older boys; he laughed and laughed over my horror. Later he drew pictures of me, teasing me over my fear. I never liked the darkness and liked it less then!

When you are in the valley of the shadow of death, it has a darkness all about you. You are clueless to know what to think or believe. You just know you have entered a very dark place. You may have entered it through a loss of a loved one, an illness, or a financial loss, even a loss of employment; nevertheless, you are in a very dark place. It was not of your choice; it just has happened to you.

Many times, we have seen the twenty-third psalms used at the passing of a loved one. Let's take a closer look at the Word, read what it really says.

Even though I walk through the valley of the shadow of death; I fear no evil, for you are with me; Your rod and Your staff, they comfort me. (Psalms 23:4)

The Hebrew word is *Sal-ma-wet,* it means darkness; a dark shadow. In the valley of the shadow of death, it does not mean death. Although, too often it is used for funerals. The meaning is implying a time of darkness. It is a time of uncertainty, confusion, a time to be in the dark.

Note the word *through,* meaning from side to side or end to an end. In Psalms 23:4 there is a promise, God is with you. I realized this through the rough dark times, during my recovery from my head-on-wreck. I experienced this now during the battle of cancer and recovery. I have, as should you, the confidence to know and trust that our Shepherd is ever present. In knowing this, the fear, doubt or worry brings comfort to our troubled minds. He never fails and His love is forever. Each step of our day in the dark we all are challenged to focus always on the truth of His goodness and love.

Just as the shepherd attends his flock, so does God watch over you. He promises never to leave you or forsake you. (Hebrew 13:5)

[114]Jehovah-shammah the Hebrew word means "Jehovah is there"; "*I fear no evil for you are with me*".

1. In the valley we are never alone, if you notice the Shepherd is with you; we walk by faith.

You may find yourself with an uncertainty of what to expect or what is waiting to ambush you. But God knows the what if, and how to walk through the most difficult of days. Lean upon Him, not what you think or feel, but trust Him to keep you under His wing and guide you through it all.

2. In the valley you will discover your priorities shift and change as to what is of importance to you. You are confronted in this valley with relationships and the value of each of them. You will find your list of priorities, agendas, projects all become of a far less importance than the new normal you are walking through each day.
   In each relationship, never take for granted that you have another day. Don't discount the friendship and compan-

---

[114] en.m.wikipedia.org/ Jehovah-shammah

ionship of those around you. Love one another and pour out your love to those who surround your life.
3. The importance of time shapes your every decision.

When we walk through the valley, our time with the Lord brings a rest and contentment. In the darkness, you will recognize His very Presence. He will sustain you in peace, calm and rest during this time. Life is temporary, and God's mercy, grace and love are forever.

Eventually, as you continue through to the other side, you will discover you have been led to a new pasture and fresh anointing from the Lord.

Should the sheep fear when the Shepherd is with them?

LOVE

[115]What is love? Phipps defines love as follows in these two lines:

"Love is when you choose to be your best when the other person is not at their best."

"Love is when what you want is never important. But what the other person needs and wants is paramount."

According to Phipps, love is not intended to be easy. But as you look past the romance, passion and wonder, you will recognize the depth of something far greater.

There are three distinct types or stages of love, whereas there are distinct signs of true love. True love includes respect, admiration, care and never subjecting your partner to hurt, humiliation or any form of abuse. Many believe they are in love when they really are only

---

[115] Huffpost.com Whitney Phipps' Two Definitions of True Love

infatuated, a one-sided feeling, or a close friendship exists. When one acts on romantic or sexual emotions, often disappointments and heart aches occur.

Love can be as elusive as a butterfly and just as fragile as its wings.

1. You will, in a give and take relationship, give unconditionally without an expectation in receiving something in return.
2. You discover happiness in the simplest of things. The smile of your partner, even when you are having a bad day, can still cause you to smile.
3. You may feel pain when your partner hurts you, but you aren't angry. You simply can't remain distant with them. It hurts you more to stay upset with them long.
4. You will sacrifice for their happiness or security. You will shield or protect them, even though they may not realize it.
5. You will make every attempt for the relationship with your partner to be better. You will do all you can to make them feel loved, secure, and special.
6. You will avoid hurting them, no matter what.
7. You keep your promises; your word to them matters to you.
8. When you truly love your partner, they are seen as a part of your life and your future.
9. You share your cares and concerns. You are always willing to help them in their difficulties.
10. You are proud of the other's accomplishments, even if you have failed. When you love someone, you can't be jealous. It isn't necessary to be jealous or prideful.
11. You are willing to suffer, to assure their happiness.
12. When you have plans, consider your partner's opinions before doing something on your own.

God's Love

[116]The Greek term can mean either the love for or the love by God. The Greek word theophilia means the love or favor by God, theophilo means the friend of God.

V.38 For I am convinced that neither nor death, nor life, nor angels nor principalities, nor things present, nor things to come, nor powers, v39 nor height, nor depth, not any other created thing, will be able to separate us from the love of God, which is in Christ Jesus our Lord. (Romans 8:38-39)

Most people think of love as coming from the heart, but it actually comes from the brain. The brain generates the chemical signals to make the person understand love. There are various forms and styles to express love and to understand love, but the Ancient Greeks came up with these four styles.

[117]Love Greek Style

1. Agape love is an unconditional love that sees beyond the outer surface and accepts the person for who he/she is, regardless of their flaws.
2. Philia love is an affectionate warm and tender, a platonic love. It draws you to a friendship. This type of love will draw you into an agape love.
3. Storge love is unconditional; it accepts flaws or faults and ultimately drives you to forgive. The storge love is more about a friendship love; both committed and comfortable relationship.
4. Eros is a passionate and intense love that arouses romantic feelings. Its focus is more on self than the other person.

---

[116] Theophilus (biblical)-Wikepedia
[117] https://totescute.co -four-types -of-love-Greek-style-Totes Cute

When they no longer feel good about the relationship, they will stop loving their partner.

The Love of God isn't about us, but about all the countless ways He has kept us in our lifetimes. Most all are familiar with the passage, *"God so loved the world that He gave His only begotten Son, that whosoever believes in Him shall not perish, but have eternal life." (John 3:16)*

De-stressing Stressful Situations

He tells us that in our life we will have trouble, but we also are promised we can have peace in this world. (John 16:33) I know of no one who has not found themselves in a place of stress or worries because of overwhelming difficulties. Somehow, between trusting the Lord and the countless influences of the world's encounters, our focus shifts from God to the troubles we are confronted with.

When you encounter extended, excessive and prolonged trials, it becomes distressful. It can become an overwhelming place for you. Rearrange your schedule from the most critical to the least important; delay the lesser things. Take control of those who are creating stress in your life by stepping away from them. It is alright to not allow others to pressure you or create additional tensions. Remember, God is in control and trust Him to keep you and provide your every need. Identify the things that have created the stress for you. Make a change where you are able. God is your refuge in times of trouble, pray about what you can do to create changes.

To say no when others place unfair demands upon you is entirely acceptable. Guard your health, rest, eat balanced meals, and exercise to help eliminate tension.

Job lost all in a very short span of time because of satanic attacks; his flocks, herds, and his livelihood. His employees were slain. His children died in a disaster. Then he lost his health and his body broke out in boils. All had been taken, and he sat in the dust, covered in boils.

His friends came, having heard of his calamity; even they turned upon him saying he surely had committed some evil. Never let your crisis define who you are. Job was innocent and had done no wrong. Nor does it necessarily mean you have a hidden sin in your life…it is just life.

Just as the wind blows and storms come, so can disasters hit your own life. Job had spent his life cultivating a reputation of being a man of integrity and purity. He was generous in giving. Job had spent a lifetime of seeking God's grace and ways. (Job31:1-35).

Let God define you, not your troubles. There is nothing He does not know or see. Even in Job's life, God was God. The rest of the story of Job is God replenished and restored all of his losses.

The lessons of Job remind us that God is fully in control. His sovereignty reigns over all creation. He is omnipresent in every situation; He is the Master of the winds. When we focus on His Words, more than our needs, our problems never define us. God defines our outcome, not things of this world. Remain focused on God.

In my present situation, let it not define me by the battle I face, but by the hand of God that leads me as I persevere in this trial. May all glory be given to Him; let all recall the Lord of my circumstances, and His faithfulness unto me.

May I raise up a standard and banner of faith, just as the men of God have from generation to generation. In God I place my trust…where are you placing your trust?

Shift your focus from your life's troubles to the faithfulness of your God. Let your story read, but God!

BUT GOD!!!

In the midst of this battle, I find myself in a place of praise and worship. Hallelujah! My heart sings with joy to the Living God, the great I AM. I have to be completely honest with you, I am amazed to find myself in the middle of all this, yet my heart remains full of joy and His glory. He truly is my strength, refuge, and the lifter of my head.

But You, O Lord, are a shield about me, My glory, and the One who lifts my head high. (Psalms 3:3)

There is an abiding place where all can come to find the same peace and joy. It doesn't mean that my life is easy, or that I don't have difficulties and trials. God only knows, yet what it means is the Comforter is ever present. It means that as I face five years of medication, radiation for days, and drips, all done to protect me from any further damages to my body; I can have rest and praise in my heart.

No matter what you are facing, when you recognize and acknowledge God as your helper, you may bring every burden to Him. With confidence you may know, you never walk alone. To be honest, I am not excited about all I am facing; especially after having spent the past seven years recovering from my wreck. What I can tell you is, I know with a certainty God is with me. His presence gives me joy unspeakable filled with His glory, peace and rest. My heart is filled with thanksgiving. My mouth is filled with praise. I am grateful to know no matter how dark the storm clouds appear to be, one way or another, it will always be alright God is in control. He holds my life in His hands, and in that I can celebrate the goodness of God. It is well with my soul. He has taught me to sing in the darkness, a knowing morning will come.

Heavenly Father, thank you for sustaining and keeping me. For Your peace, rest and joy. I bring before you each reader; I ask the gift of joy and peace be given to all who are in battles of every kind. Lift the burden that rests upon their shoulders from them. It is not Your will for any to be heavy laden or overly burdened with cares and woes of this world.

Today Lord, I ask you to reveal ways that have not even been thought of, a plan or a consideration, to bring an end to their very deepest concerns and cares. I cast our cares upon You for You said you care for us. You are the good Shepherd. I thank you for Your love and mercies that are new every morning.

I will take my lyre from off of the bush. I shall sing a new song unto You Lord of host, God Almighty, the great I Am. You are more than enough for every struggle and pain I shall go through. I look to you and depend upon Your sustaining grace. It is written, Your grace is sufficient for me (II Corinthian 12:9) and so it is to be, I take my stand. In Jesus' name. Amen.

David danced before the Lord, often he played music unto Him. He recalled the many times the Lord had delivered him. Many thought him foolish or was he really??? God called him a man after His own heart, and he had favor before the Lord.

Sustaining Grace

Daniel had favor with God and spent the night in the lion's den. To the amazement of the king he was waiting for his release in the morning when the king came to check on him. The story of the Hebrew children reveals there was a fourth one in the fire. It is written; *not a hair on their head was singed, or their trousers damaged, nor was the smell of fire upon them.* (Daniel 3:22-25).

Today begins the treatment of radiation. I have sought the Lord for a word to sustain me as I go through this procedure. As I pondered what scripture to stand upon, these words rose in my spirit, *"when you go through the fire you shall not be burned"*. God is with me!

v.1 But now, thus says the Lord, your Creator, O Jacob, and He who formed you, O Israel, do not fear, for I have redeemed you: I have called you by name; you are Mine!

v.2 When you pass through the waters, I will be with you; and through the rivers they will not overflow you. When you walk through the fire; you will not be scorched; Nor will the flame burn you. (Isaiah 43:1-2)

v.5 Do not fear; for I am with you... (Isaiah 43:5)

There is absolutely nothing that surprises God. He sees and knows every beat of your heart. He is in total control even when it feels like your life is totally out of control. God has you in the palm of His hand; written with your name upon it. Trust him.

There will be some who are reading this that your time to go home may be soon. I want to share an earlier experience with God which occurred. I previously mentioned my wreck and recovery, but for you dear reader, I want to tell you of one more experience that I have encountered with God.

During the hours following my wreck, I entered eternity. I recall seeing the brilliance of the bright light, it was all about me. I felt the presence of loving hands. The Angel of the Lord was standing at a distance, off to my right, holding the book of life. When I recognized where I was, I returned. I am telling you the message the Lord has given me to tell all, heaven is real, He is returning soon, and that He loves you.

To those reading this, as a messenger, the word I am to share; Fear not, low He is with you, even to the end of your time here. Peace be still, God is with you. Fear not!

v.1 Do not let your heart be troubled; believe in God, believe also in Me.

v.2 In my Father's House are many dwelling places; if it were not so, I would have told you; for I go to prepare a place for you.

v.3 If I go and prepare a place for you, I will come again and receive you to Myself, that where I am there you may be also. (John 14:1-3)

"WE MUST BE SET ASIDE AS WE ARE TO BE USED"
-FB MYERS

The past several days I began the process of the second phase of my maintenance program. During each treatment I have met some of the most beautiful and courageous Vessels of Honor. There is only one word that applies; courageous.

[118]The definition of courage permits one to face extreme dangers and difficulties without fear the courage. Bravery implies true courage with daring and intrepid boldness: bravery in a battle. Valor implies heroic courage: valor in fighting for the right.

They are courageous, each have a story to tell of the battles they are overcoming. I often exchange conversations and share as I listen to hear their hearts and stories.

A new battle strategy was given to me Sunday; when a friend whispered into my ear, it ignited a new plan. I now have adapted to make use of my radiation time. It has become a time of prayer.

The scripture Isaiah 43:1-2 I now use, besides Psalms 84:1-12. The Lord is my shield and a portion that His word says touch not His anointed. He is my Shepherd, and I come to Him for healing as we go through this valley. I cover myself with His blood to protect my heart and lungs. During this time, I ask for His strength with each encounter of radiation I am enduring.

---

[118] Dictionary.com-courage

Then I turn to prayer; I pray for those serving and helping me in this procedure. I pray for patients I have met; their battle they are struggling to overcome. I seek God for His guidance. It is a time that God alone is with me, His angels are gathered about me.

Back to my story, I was sharing about the patients. One young lady is radiant, always with a smile. She has been diagnosed with a cancer in her mouth, she has a portion of her tongue gone. She is learning how to eat and talk again. As I talked with her grandmother, she shared how her granddaughter used this to bring a smile to those treating her. She constantly smiles to make their day a little brighter.

Another patient's wife shared her story of how her husband has Myeloma. He has suffered a shattered bone in his leg from cancer. The bone has been repaired by a constructed bone, to reattach his limb, making it whole again. He now struggles with a hip that has been attacked by cancer and has fragmented.

I spoke with a young wife whose husband has prostate cancer. The strain was on her face and yet a smile was on her lips. Another patient has reoccurring brain cancer who jokes laughingly in his challenges.

The notable thing in every conversation is Jesus. The joy, peace, the rest upon these are markedly different. They are vessels of lights shining brightly in the darkness of the day as each struggle; and fights the good fight of faith. Each one's hope is in Christ alone.

There are children of God who have limbs missing from battles in combat. There are those hurting with brokenness of every kind. Personally, I have encountered many battles, physically, emotionally, relationally, financially; the one and only thing that has sustained me is Christ alone.

Life is but a fleeting passage and ever so temporary. Each of these I have written about are all trusting God for the hope to continue on their journey. All recognize they could easily be going home to their eternal rest. Just as I know that is always possible, only God knows the day and hour.

Today, I have shared about broken vessels of light, all who know Jesus as their Lord. I now turn to you and ask of you... Who do you say you are? Should God put you in a place of darkness or prepare to take you into eternity, are you ready? The truth is no one knows the date stamp He has for each life.

If you don't know for certainty, or you are unsure in any area of your life, maybe you need to get something straightened out with someone. You may have an issue with someone; the time has come to get it right. Just like the commercial that says, "Just do it!", today heaven is standing, waiting to hear your answer.

Heavenly Father,

I bring before you all that are uncertain, confused or afraid to commit to a relationship with you. Your word in John 3:16 tells of your love where you gave your Son Jesus, that all may be saved and not perish, but having everlasting life. Lord, those that are feeling the tugging of their hearts as they read this, help them come unto you. As they confess now, before you.

I am a sinner, and I ask your forgiveness. I believe Jesus Christ is your Son, that He died for my sin; that You raised Him from the dead to life. I want to trust Him and come to know Him as my Savior. I desire to follow Him as my Lord, from this day forth. Guide and teach me in your ways, that I may do your will and plans for me. In Jesus' name, I pray. Amen.

DOES NO ONE CRY?

Have you ever noticed the endless questions and curiosity of a small child? Why do ducks quack and not cry like me? Is heaven real? Does God love me? Do you love me? Do you love daddy more than me?...

On and on the questions continue. Unfortunately, as we become a little older, we are told to quit asking so many questions! A day comes we no longer ask why. Now we put on a mask you still have questions; they are just tucked away. Someone may have told you put on your big boy pants/girl panties. We hide the hurt or the deepest questions that seem to have no answers. After all, who cares?

[119]I have learned now that those who speak about one's miseries usually hurt, those who keep silent, hurt more. C. S. Lewis

Stuffing down our feelings and deepest emotions only keeps the pain inside you and leads to depression. Healing begins when we identify our questions. One of the greatest questions that occurred in my lifetime, following my divorce, while being separated from my children, was to discover I was switched at birth. The last blow came with the reality, I didn't even know who I was! There were times I would wake up in the night, crying and questioning who I was. The questions came in like a flood. Did my real parents not want me? Why??? Who was I? Thoughts of 'I don't even know who I am' would plague my mind. The only thing I knew was I didn't belong anywhere.

I had a choice to either walk through it or become frozen and numb. I could deny my discovery, but then I would not be truthful to myself. I was desperately searching for answers and truth. I walked through many days of shocked emotions. Is there anywhere we can believe or find happiness when the ones we trust aren't who we believe they are?

As I confronted and searched for my true identity, there were many dead ends. Much like Job, there were no answers in the darkness for me. Yet, there was only one answer that I knew that I knew, I could believe and trust the answer was in God alone. With the discovery, there was a sense of betrayal, an awareness of not belonging. But I knew God loved me, and I slowly shifted my thoughts to the fact that nothing nor no one could separate me from God. I was a child

---

[119] C_S_Lewis-Goodreads.com

of God, no matter what else had happened to me, I belonged with Him. He caused me to realize there were signs, but I had kept the questions buried. I had sensed the questions why, however, I ignored them. In time I have come to recognize the hidden questions as the truth was exposed.

[120]**The strong are not always vigorous, the wise not always ready. The brave not always courageous, and the joyous not always happy. Charles Spurgeon.**

When we confess our neediness to God, healing begins. It is easier to stuff down than to be transparent and allow God the opportunity to heal you. It takes effort and determination to walk into the storm and prevail to find real.

There is no hope until you confront the wounds of your soul. In the confrontation, God will, in exchange give you the grace to stand, find the truth, answers and help you to heal. The fear that you are facing in the question "what if", will end. You will find yourself coming to a settling in your soul.

SO, NOW WHAT?

There will come a reconcilement in your heart that God is sovereign, and He alone holds the answers. Life isn't always perfect, nor do you know the final outcome of the story. What you can do now is you can trust God in every circumstance, no matter how painful.

GIANTS IN THE LAND

Joshua and Caleb had wandered for forty years in the wilderness with the tribes of Israel. God had refused their entry due to the tribe's

---

[120] Twitter Charles Spurgeon@ Spurgeon.com

unfaithfulness. All the previous generation and those men twenty and older who that grumbled against God had died. Only Joshua and Caleb remained. Caleb was eighty-five years old. His age didn't matter or the fact that there were still giants on his mountain. Caleb refused to doubt. Four things you need to do.

1. Don't doubt, only believe the promise God has given you.
2. Don't let go. Jacob wrestled with God and refused to let go.
3. Determine a fixed heart and focus. Trust God.
4. Receive your rightful, inheritance just as God said.

Caleb remembered when the twelve spies went into the land and only Joshua and He believed they could pursue and overcome the giants. In the land there were dwelling the Anakim then, and to this day remain in the land of your promise.

[121]Anak means to choke or strangle the vision by a continual work in our minds from our childhood to today. There are three tactics the descendants of Anak used, that continue to be used even to this day. The three sons of Anak and their tactics are:

1. **Ahriman**; the tactic is to block or hinder God's promise, plans and purposes.
2. **Shashai;** the strategy of this giant is to whitewash or hinder. This is through embellishment of the vision, causing it to be bigger than actual.
3. **Talmai** means to accumulate. The devil wants to keep you so busy accumulating material things, so involved at work and into entertainment, we don't have time for God's plans and purposes. Demons will always be around. Acknowledge that God is with you.

Midianite giant is a spirit of strife or contention to paralyze or defeat our covenant. The strategy is to divide and conquer. It notably oper-

---

[121] Elijah list- Seven Giants in the Land/Todd Bentley www.freshfire.ca??

ates strongly in the church with disagreement. Nothing is impossible when we become of one accord in unity. *(Psalms 133:1,3)*

Philistine giant means to wallow in the dust in self-pity. David had to slay this giant; it was the first real battle. The battle today is with feelings, thoughts, selfishness. We are to put to death carnal, selfish thoughts. Faith will slip in the attack of this giant, haunting you with lies, loneliness, hopelessness, rejections.

Moabite is the giant of rebellion, resulting in a dry barren wasteland. Anyone against God dwells in this land with this giant. God brings peace, this giant brings rebellion filled with anger.

Crush the giants under your feet! God gave you power and authority through His Spirit.

Then he answered and spoke unto me, saying, "This is the word of the Lord unto Zerubbabel, saying, 'Not by might, nor by power, but by my Spirit', saith the Lord of Hosts" (Zechariah 4:6)

And when the Lord your God delivers them before you and you defeat them, then you shall utterly destroy them. You shall make no covenant with them and show no favor to them. (Deuteronomy 7:2)

If a thought has no hope in it, then it isn't of God.

Do you recognize your giant; which one do you have?

What do you need to do to overcome your giant?

To possess is to seize and take control of; to enter into control of, to grasp. We need to possess the mind of Christ to occupy and drive out the tenants of the land, to dispossess the enemy.

In today's culture the giants appear as addictions, flaws, shortcomings, temptations, blind spots, trials of anything bigger, stronger, more powerful than you. Anything we lack gives a false sense of aloneness. These can knock us down and render us senseless. Giants remind us how small we are and helpless we are without God.

Often a trial is intended to bring you to an awareness that you can't do whatever the challenge may be. Look closer, who is whispering in your ear? It always is easier to give up, but before you do realize this . . . when you give up, you give up more than a fight. You just gave Satan control of that area of your life and handed it over to reign over you.

Choosing not to fight means embracing stagnancy and accepting defeat as a lifestyle. When you decide you can't win you give up growth in overcoming.

Get up! Dust yourself off and remember, the Lord your God promised you a victory and defeat to the enemy. Go talk to God and ask Him for His help and toss the giants out. This is your land; it is worthy of the battle or God wouldn't have permitted you to enter the land. Giants will always show up to cause you to stop so they can defeat you.

Never enter a battle in your own strength, but in reliance upon God and His power.

Therefore humble yourself under the mighty hand of God, that He may exalt you at the proper time. (I Peter 5:6)

When we further read I Peter 5, you will see you are to cast your anxiety (worries, cares, woes, trouble) on Him, because He cares for you. The Word tells of how the devil goes about like a roaring lion. God gave me a dream where the devil roared and roared. The loudness was frightening, however, when I stepped out, poof! The lion disappeared; it was an illusion, a "paper tiger". Never forget, God is in control and far greater than any demon ever will be. Acknowledge that God is with you daily, you never walk alone.

HOW TO RECOGNIZE THE GIANT

When the Lord your God, brings you to the land where you are entering to possess it, and clears away many nations before you, the Hittites and the Girgashites and the Amorites and the Canaanites and the Perizzites and the Hivites and the Jebusites, seven nations greater and stronger than you... (Deuteronomy 7:1)

In the land of Canaan dwelled seven giants that the Israelites had to confront. The enemy is always trying to break your vision for the plans and purposes of God. God knows we will perish without a vision. God wants to give us a vision. Because of our mindsets we can't see the plan because we are like the children of Israel who felt they were too small, like grasshoppers, when they were confronted by the Anak descendants. (Numbers 13:33)

Yes, the giants were big, but God is bigger than your circumstances.

[122]**Canaanite Spirit** -The Canaanites dwelling place is found in the lowlands. This spirit operates from the left-handed spirit whose emphasis is on the emotions and grace motivated. Their mind is right-handed, and truth driven yet, they move in freedom and grace. They will downplay truth and judgement, as does the Hittite spirit.

The spirit of these people will be one of low morals, humiliation and shame who dwell in these places. They live in sexual impurity and depravity. Those with a low self-esteem will be found bound in addictions. They will often say, "God knows my heart." They have no self-value; many will promote homosexuality, suffering depression.

---

[122] shamah-elm.info/cananite.htm

They are found bound in every form of sexual behavior. They are slaves to adultery, fornication; in chains of confusion and darkness.

The seeds they plant are sown toward darkness, low-morals, and addictions of every form. They are found participating in promiscuous sensual dancing of every type. They are the garbage dump of the lowlands.

I study from a variety of places to prepare to write the truth and God's insights to His people; there is a particular event I studied and want to show you the revelation found in this study. This insight is one I find both eye-opening and of grave importance to every believer.

The Canaanite people are associated with cows and figures of cows.

In the Bible there is an account of Moses. He was instructed to go to Mt. Sinai to meet with God. The Israelites were told to wait upon his return at the foot of the mountain. Moses' time away was so long the children collected all of their metal and formed a golden calf. The incident is known in Hebrew as *het ha'eggel* or "the sin of the golden calf". (Exodus 32:3,4)

They created a foreign god to worship; the golden calf. Aaron built an altar to worship the lord. Then the next day they ate and drank, engaging in festivities of every manner of celebration and drunkenness. They danced before the calf in sensual dances.

Now zoom forward to history on January 23, 1998. Talk show host Oprah Winfrey made accusations in Amarillo, Texas. She basically created the term "mad cow disease". The disease is one that is gotten from infected meat. The disease causes a rapid mental deterioration, usually within a few months of eating the meat. Dementia is associated with this disease, and the people affected eventually lapse into a coma.

Returning to the golden calf incident, the judgement of the Lord was given. The Lord commanded to kill all the Hittite, Amorite, the Canaanite, Perizzite, Hivite and the Jebusite in the land that was to be their inheritance. God placed a judgement on the cows, nothing that breathes was to remain living in the cities. (Deuteronomy 20:16-17)

It is highly probable the "mad cow disease" is a throwback to the judgement of God on the cows. Because of the disobedience of the Canaanites, they opened the door to the judgement of God by worshiping foreign gods through rebellion. God changes not. Be very careful when you see a judgement of God.

The Canaanite people tend to be people pleasers. They are more likely to spend more on themselves than the Kingdom of God.

[123] **Hivite Spirit** -When reviewing the Hivite, they are descendants of Ham. Hivite means villagers. Things said about the Hivite will also apply to the Perizzite "belonging to a village". Both have a limited vision of life. The difference is those under the influence of the Hivite spirit limit their life.

The word Hivite is related to the concept of life in Hebrew. Recognize that it is not one of limitations, poverty, low self-worth by association with life. The Perizzite spirit does bear these issues. On the contrary, the Hivites love "to live it up".

Hivites are connected back to Eve when she declared, "*I have gotten a man-child with the help of the Lord*," when she conceived, and Cain was born. Cain means "possessions". These are a people who have gained some type of inheritance, it allows them the "freedom" to live as they desire. (Genesis 4:1)

---

[123] shamah-elim.info./hivites.htm

The tendency is to limit their vision by all the abundance that surrounds them. Often this is found with those who have retired, they want to travel and enjoy the good life.

Where the Girgashite people are work-alcoholics; driven by greed or covetousness, the Hivites are self-centered people. They are convinced the universe exists to serve them. The tendency is to turn God into their own servant, to give and serve their needs. They often receive only the natural grace, but not the abundance of God, much like the Israelites. There is much more to be said and studied perhaps at another time. It suffices to be said, the inheritance of the Hivite spirit often creates a self-indulgent lifestyle.

[124] **Amorite Spirit-** We move forward to the land of the Amorites, who are found in the mountains. They are a mountain people who dwell with great self-exaltation and are fame-seekers. This spirit will have the similar spirit as Adolf Hitler, Fidel Castro and similar leaders of our times. They like to dominate and control the people, asserting their authority and keeping the people under their control by whatever means is necessary. The Amorite means "to say, to utter". This spirit is the "sayers" which controls and dominates; always with the authority of what they say, "goes". The spirit will attempt to shame or humiliate the people serving beneath them.

They think higher of themselves and may consider themselves ruler over the people as an earthly king. The spiritual authority, such as a high priest, has the rightful Kingdom of God authority.

The officer operating in the Jebusite spirit was challenging Jesus' authority to speak to the high priest but telling Him to be silent. (John 18:19-23)

The Amorite king had the proper authority to exercise over the people and speak. The high priest was named by the Holy Spirit, and the

---

[124] shamah-elim.info./amorites.htm

position was created by God. There is no he or she in the Kingdom of God. (Galatians 3:28) The anointing is given to the person to either accept and use or move in the flesh. When the anointing is accepted and used, it moves and operates in the will of God. When the spirit operates in the flesh, the Amorite spirit is in control and the kingdom of the Amorite is promoted.

In scripture man is referred to spirit and woman is referenced as the soul. The expectation is for the woman to submit to the spirit. However, when she is under the anointing, the role reverses. When the woman is led by the spirit, she will know when to submit and when to become the anointed one.

The Amorite giant acts out in haughtiness, self-edifications, to accuse, judge or criticize. This giant's tendency is to be judgmental to those in leadership or persons in authority. They are known by the negative speech, complaining and grumbling. It is essential to put a watch on your tongue. Meditate on the things which are good, pure, honorable, and of good report. The will of God for you is the opposite of criticism, you are to be thankful. There is much more to be said of the operations of the spirit of the Amorites.

[125]**Perizzites** meaning is "one belonging to a village". They are associated with those of limited vision and limited opportunities to grow or dream big dreams. This is because of the environment surrounding them. They often produce spiritual poverty from generation to generation.

The spirit is operating in a low self-esteem, described as crippled, lame people. They are a people who view themselves unworthy, small in value. Their belief is that spiritually they cannot walk on their own. Walking in the scripture is described as the ability to overcome, to establish kingdom authority.

---

[125] shamah-elim.info./perizzites.htm

Perizzites meaning is one who dwells in open walls and roams with the spirit of immorality: Babylon Spirit. The goal of this spirit is to seduce, tempt away, to entice you from the call of God. Godly principles are under attack. Your conduct is attacked to persuade you to forget your purpose and destiny. It will use pornography or fantasy, while offering everything in the natural, especially emotional comfort. The spirit will try to drag the baggage of soul-ties of former relationships with you. It tries to seduce through money or pride and sexual immorality. It will attempt to convince you all you need in relationships is in the natural. The draw to compromise is also attached with the Jezebel Spirit, the sensual nature of mankind. It will attempt to draw you and separate you from Godly principles.

Do not rejoice over me, my enemy; though I fall, I will rise; though I dwell in darkness, the Lord is a light for me. (Micah 7:8)

[126]**Jebusite-** The spirit is one that dwells on the mountain top. The spirit of the Jebusite is connected with the principalities of Baal. The nations surrounding Israel had their own form of Baal, which were snares and traps to God's people.

The principalities of Baal reign over this mountain, accompanied by the Jezebel spirit. Baal means "master, owner or lord". The Baal spirit often included male prostitution. Baal worship is associated with homosexuality by the sacrificial offering of young males to Molech.

They built the high places of Baal that are in the valley of Ben Hinnom to cause the sons and their daughters to pass through the fire to Molech, which I had not commanded them, nor had it entered My mind that they should do this abomination, to cause Judah to sin. (Jeremiah 32:35)

Notice how the demonic led them to worship first Baal, then to bring them to self- destruction through their own disobedience and self-efforts.

---

[126] shamah-elim.info./jebusites.htm

I will pause in the many things that are written and said about the Jebusite spirit and take a little different insight. With this spirit I want to share and talk about the family; the heart of God. The love walk is intended to be destroyed by the Jebusite spirit. As much as the church is under attack, so is the family.

A grave social injustice is when the heart of the fathers is turned from their children and their children from their fathers. In the Word it is said in the latter days it is not just the parent's fault, but something released on the children to turn them against their parents.

I have personally experienced this attack. May I tell you; the experience will bring to the parent much grief and sorrow, even when it is out of their control. The enemy desires to destroy the family.

v.1 But realize this, that in the last days difficult times will come. For men will become lovers of self, lovers of money, boastful, arrogant, revilers, disobedient to parents, ungrateful, unholy, v.2 unloving, irreconcilable, malicious gossips, without self-control, brutal, haters of good, v.4 treacherous, reckless, conceited, lovers of pleasure rather lovers of God. (2 Timothy 3:1-4)

[127]The attack may enter your life in a varied assortment of ways. It may come through the father's absence or abuse. The father is considered the glue of the family. When he is missing, it creates a void of the love flow in the family unit. The husband's love to the wife is blocked, and then the love among the family members is hindered. When the family dissolves, the brokenness extends to the lives of those affected.

Much of the outcome of the broken family units studied behavior appears to be associated with criminals, drugs, illegal sexual activities, inability to gain employment, jail sentences and all varieties of social illness.

---

[127] sevenculturalmountains.org/apps/default.asp?articuid-39120@columnid-4335

The Jebusite spirit operates in rejection; "a place trodden down" is the meaning of this spirit's name.

The Jebusite spirit can create a tsunami in the emotions of an individual's life. Rejection can warp the developing identity of a child. A boy will often seek male identity and cross over a sexual line toward abnormality. Homosexuality is a rejection of the natural sex drive. Young girls never develop into young women and remain closed. With the father's rejection, it cause them to need nothing from a man. All of this is compounded by the stepfamily syndrome.

[128]Baal worship is linked to homosexuality resulting from the use of male prostitutes when serving Molech. The brutal and cruel inhuman sacrifice's placed children in the arms of Molech. When the Molech statue was made red hot it was used to burn the child to death. The same Baal spirit is the same spirit which operates in abortions, sacrificing the child to death. Abortions are linked to the rejection of the parents to the child. Many children have been sacrificed by the Baal spirit through the abortion of convenience.

Baal, is the principality, and the demons gain entrance through the Jebusite's spirit of rejection. The Baal spirit's motive is the destruction of the family. It is done to destroy the people of the land. In the latter days God's Kingdom will rise up; to remove this spirit.

The Jebusite spirit behavior is to trample, leading to depression, oppression, and devestation. The spirit of heaviness will often be found as these giant roams about the land. The spirit operates by using tactics of shame, condemnation, with accusations of inadequacy, while attempting to overwhelm you to give up. This giant continues to remind you of every failure or any sin you have ever committed and questions your forgiveness by God. It will attempt

---

[128] sevenculturalmountains.org/apps/default.asp?articuid-39120@columinid-4335

to use reasoning to convince you why you can't do what God says or calls you to accomplish.

The opposite of the spirit of heaviness is confidence and joyfulness. Praise silences the enemies' fiery darts. He shrinks away in God's presence.

[129]**Girgashite-** giants are dwellers of clay and marsh; it means to compromise or live in gray areas. They are neither cold nor hot, they create a mindset of complacency; "if God wants me to have it, He will provide". It causes a willingness to settle for your circumstances as God's will. The temptation is to abandon God's plan while convincing you the vision is too big. Often you will begin reasoning. Remember, we can do what God said.

The spirit moves in the natural things of the earth, which is temporal and denies the spiritual. It requires what is seen and believes only the seen! The motto would read, "seeing is believing". The spirit has total disregard for the unseen.

They are analytical, they base their decisions on only what they can see. Those controlled by the Girgashite spirit will live out their lives based on what their natural mind sees. They are not seeking the way of God to make decisions.

I know your deeds; they are neither cold nor hot; I wish that you were cold or hot. (Revelation 3:15)

[130]**Hittite** means the "*sons of terror,*" and it dwells in the land, always attempting to place fear upon you. This spirit is one which will try placing every kind of phobia, terror, and depression on you, while it operates in deceit. The attack is on your emotions, rather than what the mind can see. The Hittite spirit is behind most nightmares,

---

[129] shamah-elim.info./girgashites.htm
[130] shamah-elim.info./hitittes.com

phobias and suicide. It whispers in darkness, things of speculations. It operates on the left-hand side in the things unseen. Terror creates deep emotional despair and torments causing the desire to die; suicide is often linked to these spirit's activities.

The individual with a prophetic anointing is attacked by this spirit by its hidden false accusations. It will apply the law, questioning the Word given; "Did God really say that?" The spirit will create false rumors with accusations as it operates in the unseen left-hand side, appearing as though righteous in its behavior. It uses the law to hide its activity of darkness. It often will act as a friend rather than a foe. This is the spirit Terrorist move in. People who are spreading rumors, gossip or whisper speculations move in this spirit.

It will attempt to create insecurities or removal of self-worth, using fear of exposure from things in your past. The fear of lack challenges our trust in God. Fear acts as a barrier, it creates a sense of being stuck. It will try to get you to hide in your past.

You may read the account of this spirit in Judges 3:14-23. Ehud killed the king Elgon of Moab because he used his left hand to stab him, it was unseen; this allowed him access to the king.

God said to fear not, but to be strong and courageous. *(Joshua 1:6, 9)*

May I encourage you to learn to recognize the importance of the movement of each spirit. Learn to observe whether it is operating and infecting the person you are dealing with, or something within yourself. Take the time to study more in depth these spirits. I am only touching some key points to give you an insight into the importance of possessing this awareness. There is much to be said and learned in these spirits that affect your life daily.

Gate Keepers

Earlier we studied the importance of our words and the influence on our minds and how they damage our soul and spirit.

The devil is empowered in our agreement by our words. There is a gate in our minds as to what is permitted to enter.

"And I tell you, you are Peter, and on this rock, I will build my church, and the gates of Hell shall not prevail against it." (Matthew 16:18)

In recent weeks, I have experienced surgeries for the removal of a malignant tumor. Part of the process was to check to see if my lymph glands had been invaded. If the "gatekeeper" nodes were clear of cancer; then the likelihood was it had not invaded my body any further. This would determine if I was safe to leave them and proceed forward with maintenance treatments to block any further incidents.

The mind is the gatekeeper of the body. What invades your mind, if left unfiltered, will invade your soul. This is done intending to destroy your spirit, just as cancer destroys the body and leads to death if unattended.

That which comes into an agreement with things of this world, your natural wisdom isn't of God but a man. The gate is a place of access. Where our mind is focused is the area, we are drawing from whether it be God centered or man centered. Whatsoever, we think becomes a gate to either allow God to enter or the enemy to dominate our thoughts to kill, steal and destroy.

For as a man thinks in his himself, so he is… (Proverbs 23:7)

The renewal of our mind will bring us into new revelations. But if we don't experience it and apply the revelation, it will be lost. When this occurs, you have stopped the renewal of your mind.

When God revealed the power of joy as a tool of strength, by grasping hold of the revelation and applying it daily, the next step brought forth the understanding. It has allowed me to be supernaturally lifted above the battle with cancer. The revelation by God has created a joy unfathomable in the natural man. Yet, I am walking in His strength daily, applying the revelation.

In the weeks following, it doesn't mean I still don't battle or become exhausted. What it does mean is I possess a strength and power of dependency on God, knowing He is in control. During this trouble I have a peace and rest in spite of adversities.

Many talk the walk, but don't walk the talk! You can recite all the scriptures, yet if you don't change your thoughts and live them; they become words. You are sitting on the bleachers cheering. God wants you in the game of life, using His words as the game plan for your life.

You have your heads in your Bibles constantly because you think you'll find eternal life there. But you miss the forest for the trees. These scriptures are all about me! And here I am, standing right before you, and you aren't willing to receive from me the life you say you want. (John 5:39-40) (MSG-Peterson)

When Jesus was standing beside Mary and Martha, they didn't recognize him. Thomas had to see the nail scars to believe. How very sad to think often Jesus is here with us now, He attends over us, yet we fail to recognize the fact He is with us here the entire time.

Do not be conformed to this world (changed)... but be transformed by the (entire) renewal of your mind. (Romans 12:2 AMP)

<u>A. What does the mind of Christ mean?</u> It is to develop a mind and understanding of God's plan for the world. We understand He wants to establish His purposes in the world. The same things Jesus values you, as a believer, should value. (Isaiah 40:13). (1Corinthians 2:16)

1. A desire to bring glory to God (John 17:5) with a longing to provide salvation for sinners. (Luke 19:10)
2. An attitude the same as Jesus, (Philippians 2:5-8) you are to walk both in humility and in obedience to God.
3. A heart of compassion for the people. (Matthew 9:36)
4. A dependence on God through your prayers. (Luke 5:16)
5. Developing a spirit of surrender, yielding with obedience to God's way.

<u>B. How do you develop the mind of Christ?</u> You must first have the Holy Spirit. The Holy Spirit is received through saving faith in Christ. After you are saved the Holy Spirit, by following, His leadings will transform your mind to a Christlike mind.

1. *What area of your thoughts do you need to work on changing to become more Christlike in your mind?*
2. *How can you accomplish this?*
3. *What garbage have you been allowing to enter your thought life?*
4. *List five things you can immediately do to begin the process of renewal of your mind.*
5. *What spirit do you need to fight?*

AS THE MIND GOES, SO SHALL THE FOOTSTEPS OF THE MAN!!! *Proverbs 23:7 -Joyce Meyers*

WARRIOR'S ARMOR

- Discouragement   Deuteronomy 31:8
- Materialism   Matthew 6:19-24
- Self-worth   Genesis 1:26-27
- Doubt   Proverbs 3:8/ Matthew 21:21
- Gossip/Slander   Ephesians 4:29-32
- Fear   I John 4:18
- Depression   Deuteronomy 31:8/ Proverbs 12:25

- Oppression   Psalm 9:9/Psalms 146:7
- Anxiety   Philippians 4:6
- Worry   Matthew 6:25-27
- Hopelessness   Job 13:15/Psalm 25:3
- Evil Thoughts   Philippians 4:8
- Rejection   John 15:18
- Despair   Psalm 27:10 (NLT)/Isaiah 61:3
- Critical   Colossians 3:12-14
- Anger   Proverbs 19:11
- Guilt   Hebrews 10:22/Romans 3:23
- Shame   Isaiah 61:7/ Psalm 25:3
- Deception   Colossians 2:2-4
- Resentment   Leviticus 19:18
- Temptation   I Corinthians 10:13
- Bitterness   Romans 12:17-21
- Jealousy/Envy   Romans 13:13-14/ James 4:5-7
- Self-Pity   Romans 6:6-12
- Forgiveness   Ephesians 4:31

WHAT IS IN YOUR CERAMIC BOX?

In a conversation with a friend of mine, she related to me she had a dream. The dream was about a ceramic box; it was a big box, but no one had a key to open it! She added she felt her gifts were still in the box and were unobtainable. Perhaps the outcome of being held back by her former church, the spiritual gifts had not been acknowledged. She continued to write, she said, "I know the Lord has the Key!" I discerned the ceramic box relates to the Promises of God, and the Key is to the Kingdom of God! We activate it through faith to turn the Key and open His promises. The ceramic box is the Box of Wisdom, and the gift hidden within is the Gift of Understanding.

Wisdom is the principal thing, and with all thy getting get understanding. (Proverbs 4:7)

The value of wisdom is the ability to think and act using knowledge, experience, common sense, and insight.

We get wisdom from God by asking as we read the Bible, seeking His ways and walking in His plans and purposes in obedience. Wisdom takes a lifetime to gain; but as we learn and trust God daily, we will gain understanding and the ability to see and walk in His ways.

But if any of you lack wisdom, let him ask of God, who gives to all generously and without reproach, and it will be given to him. (James 1:5)

THE GIFT OF UNDERSTANDING

Are the spiritual gifts of my friend being held back? Is it possible that we need to develop our spiritual walk more? Or is it possible the delay may in fact be about the timing and understanding of the gift to be used? Personally, I've gone through years of spiritual preparation. There have been years of waiting, believing as I have trusted to develop my walk. This is all to gain wisdom and knowledge, just to glean a small perspective of our Heavenly Father.

For years now, I continue to wait for the answer of the promise spoken to me. I never have doubted the truth of His promise to me. There have been continuous battles and many encounters to tempt me with the appearance of the right answer. Only later for it to be recognized, it was the wrong answer. I needed to keep walking and trusting God.

Recently, I was talking to God about my uncertainty of whether I perceived what was spoken correctly. I totally trust Him, but I don't trust myself, flesh is flesh. and I can error. While I sat quietly listening and pondering the conversation, I was impressed to re-read Proverbs 4:7. Again I read the scripture and meditated on it when I realized how often I had prayed this verse and glided over the Word, *"with wisdom in all your getting get understanding."* The Holy Spirit stopped me, illuminating these words to me.

For days, I had felt this relentless need to search for a Word. But where and what was the Word? Now I know I am to pray for... *'and getting get understanding'!!!*

In my relentless searching for days, I had stared at the promise. I became much like one looking down the sites of a gun barrel while attempting to focus and hit the target's bull's eye. I know that I know the answer is there, real, and will come. God does not lie!

I need understanding!!! Let's take a look at understanding.

There are three mental models to compare:

1. **Knowledge** is a fact given; to possess the fact which was given and access the information.
2. **Understanding** is the ability to translate meaning from the facts. The illumination of this requires the Holy Spirit to bring the answer into our focus and produces the principles to apply to the fact.
3. **Wisdom** is knowing what to do with the fact, while applying the principle of the Word.

[131]A good explanation of the above is explained in this manner. We know the tomato is a fruit, not a vegetable. (Knowledge) It often is used in a salad. (Understanding) However, we know that we don't use it in a fruit salad. (Wisdom)

The simplicity of this statement is how you are to view these three principles. Knowledge is the fact. Understanding is how to apply the fact. Wisdom is the proper tool/principle to apply to the circumstances.

---

[131] Overcomer Dr. David Jeremiah Thomas Nelson Publisher, Nashville Tennessee

The who, what, when, why and how helps you see the fact gives information. The information then is used to attain the fact. When the understanding of the fact is determined. This then enables you how to apply the fact into the situation you are attempting to discern. It is impossible to have knowledge without having wisdom and understanding.

Exposing Darkness

And the evil spirit answered and said to them, *"I recognize Jesus, and I know Paul, but who are you?"* (Acts 19:15)

[132]Ginosko Greek/Hebrew is to recognize a person (Strong's #1997 BibleTools.org) to learn to know, get knowledge or perceive, to feel.

1. Jesus and Paul were both recognized by the demons. In a conversation with the Pharisees, they challenged Jesus to show them a sign (Matthew 16:1-5).
2. Jesus discussed with His disciples about the leaven of the Pharisees (v5-12).
3. Then conversation with them concerning Himself and concerning His church built upon him (v.13-20).
4. Another regarding suffering for them and theirs for him (v-21-28).

The conversation with the Pharisees, and Sadducees revealed they were in opposition with Christ. There was a difference of doctrine, because His doctrine did equally overthrow the errors and heresies of the Sadducees, who denied the existence of spirits. While the pride and hypocrisy of the Pharisees, were also imposters in their belief of the doctrine as well.

---

[132] Strong's 1097:ginosho Greek Hebrew definition

The intent of the demand for a sign from heaven was a pretense. Each one showing they would be satisfied and convinced, yet it was a guise this wasn't their true desire. They refused to acknowledge the signs at work about them which would relieve the needs of the sick but insisted upon a sign. This was a demand of the proud to satisfy their own curiosity. The evidence that was given was enough to satisfy an unprejudiced understanding, but was not intended to satisfy a vain contentment. The demand from them was a miracle from God to please their unbelief.

The motive was to tempt Jesus, not to be taught by Him but entrap Him. Israel challenged Christ in Matthew 16:1-4, in a similar manner demanding signs.

Jesus' reply to this demand, lest they be wise in their own conceit, He condemned them for looking at the natural signs that they had. We can recognize the red sky overnight indicates fair weather and a red sky in the morning is of foul weather. These are common rules, as is the movement of nature in the world we live in when the seasons change. We are able to tell countless things about weather, and believe the words of scientific studies, astrologers, seed time and harvest, but we are unable to see the hand of God about us. Let it suffice to say what the weather is to be, or the season belongs to God to say, not us and what pleases us.

It is a great shame we slight the signs of God who has provided countless details about us, to ask for a self-gratification, by His hands with signs of our own demands. Who are we but a piece of clay, merely dust to think so highly of ourselves to place such a demand on God?

Jesus will not tarry with those that tempt Him, but will depart leaving them to their own devises, nor should you tarry dear reader.

As you study the various spirits look back and examine the spirits we previously have studied. Notice to see how the spirits work to interrelate. See if you can recognize the demonic activity about you as we move forward.

Spirits of Accusations

To better identify the actions and voice of the Accusing Spirit you will find there is no love present rather a tone of condemnation. The attack may come as a correction. The Accusing spirit will insinuate you aren't good enough. You aren't right before God in an area of your faith walk, you need to make corrections, you are in error. This spirit will come as a friend using the law as a heavy burden and crush its victim. [133]The Accusing spirit will attempt to condemn you of your errors, faults, or failures. This is the actions of a religious spirit to condemn you while accusing you to repent, you are wrong. It will allude to a work-based performance instead of faith. This spirit will disregard the fact that the written Word states, *there is no condemnation to those who belong to Christ Jesus*, (Romans 8:1) while it ignores the cleansing blood of Jesus and that He is the law.

The attack may come in the form of a concern to better help you, the reality is this is an attack to destroy you. The words you speak, write, and every mistake present and past will be brought to your attention in an effort to convince you how very wrong you are. The deception is to get you to conform to the law totally with disregard of the works of Jesus.

Christ is become of no effect unto you, whosoever of you are justified by the law; you are fallen from grace. (Galatians 5:4)

The motivation of the accusing spirit is to cause you to fall from grace and stop trusting God's grace and mercy. The accusing spirit works with the religious spirit and stronghold, including legalism.

---

[133] www.MinisteringDeliverance.com/ The Accusing Spirit

The operation of the accusing spirit will work to wear you down spiritually. It will attempt in convincing you that you are a failure and rob you of your faith. The entire motive is to destroy you spiritually; while discrediting the works of Christ in our lives.

Accusing spirits may suggest you go back to all wronged and apologize; that is salvation by works. It is a finger pointing spirit, digging up your past and blaming somebody else. It works closely with the critical and judgmental spirits. It is hypocritical, two-faced and backbiting in its actions. This spirit also works in conjunction with the spirits of guilt, shame, condemnation and hopelessness.

Remember, the battlefield is always in the mind, and wrong thoughts destroy your obedience and trust in God. The accusing spirit will always point to the problem, while the Holy Spirit will point to the solution. If the true guilt has been repented of then once it is confessed, it is forgiven the guilt should no longer remain. Should guilt continue to occur, then the accusing spirit is at work and mentally they agree the sin has not been washed away. Once sin is repented, the Holy Spirit ends conviction.

After repentance to counter the attack fill your mind with the Word and that written regarding forgiveness. This spirit will attempt to build strongholds in your mind, it needs to be driven out by the renewing of your mind. The person with this spirit operates in deception.

Casting down imaginations, and every high thing that exalts itself against the knowledge of God and `bringing into captivity every thought to the obedience of Christ. (2Corinthians 10:5)

No Shame!

How often as a child have you been brought to believe you are bad? It was by either being told or insinuated you were worthless. Have you found yourself in a place feeling either unclean or unworthy to approach

God? You may have felt you can't have a personal relationship, that He wants with you. Shame is at work causing you to be distant, creating feelings of being unworthy to be in His presence. Countless believers struggle in their minds with thoughts of guilt and unworthiness.

[134]Guilt comes when you realize your failures. False guilt is from Satan where sin has been repented and forgiven, but the guilt lingers. You are reminded of your failures associated with your past. Repentance cleanses true guilt, while false guilt continues to badger you, eager to remind you of your past.

It is time to change your thoughts from the former to the fact it is a new day and beginning! Let go of the past failures, flaws and yesterday's sins. Your sins are removed upon your confession and repentance. Move your tent from the land of the former, let it go! God has when you confessed and said forgive me, I have sinned.

The Bible references shame as a vain imagination that must be cast down. The devil will attempt to wear you down and paint a distorted picture of who you are in God's eyes to create a sense of unworthiness and failures. Change your mind's lens to see the love your Heavenly Father has for you. You are washed in Jesus' blood and a new creation.

Shame and guilt are based on deception, which is the opposite of truth. So think about this, how are you worshipping God in spirit and truth if your imagination is hanging out with untruths about yourself? Lies from hell are being whispered, untruths. The word of God says to cast them down.

The former issues are dealt with; now is a time to worship and celebrate God, rejoice!

---

[134] www.MinisteringDeliverance.com/ Spiritual warfare: Defeating guilt and shame

Seasons of Faith

Beloved, think it not strange concerning the fiery trial, which is to try you, as though some strange thing happened unto you: (I Peter 4:12)

You see, the seasons change just as Jesus said in Matthew 16:3 when in conversation with the Pharisees and the Sadducees, we can tell by the face of the sky when it is red there will be rain. Hence, you look at the calendar day to recognize the time of season you are entering. We miss the hand of God or His purposes by rushing ahead, unobservant to what is happening about us behind the scenes.

Often, you pray, and an answer is delayed or answered in yet a different manner than you desire. The clarity you want; you do not stop to listen, to get understanding. Swiftly you move on, never waiting for the answer. Our tendency is to focus on the temporary, failing to wait to see the eternal purposes. While you long for the answer from God and His guidance remaining puzzled.

God told me to rejoice when diagnosed with breast cancer; "rejoice" was the furthest thought at first, to enter my mind. As I review the past seven plus years of recovery to find I am diagnosed with cancer, it would appear pointless…Why??? What is God's purpose and how can this possibly be to my good, as stated in Romans 8:28?

Consider this as a student the answers are given prior to the test. You first study, then you are tested. The significance of gaining understanding; is the knowledge to apply His answers to the situations, by application of the Word, therefore, you gain wisdom and a successful outcome. Often with God, we seem to have pop quizzes being seemly unprepared. Study His word to get the understanding required. Growth requires you to look higher than the mundane to the God of all creation.

[135]There are various tests/trials on the pathway of our journey.

1. The trial of faith is one of growth development with many challenges.
2. The discipline of faith trial is the development of your moral fiber.
3. The trial of patience of faith effects is to cause endurance.
4. The courage of faith trains you to face fear and overcome.

There are many stages of testing arriving at the fullness of faith.

5. The victory of faith is to receive the answer.

The discipline of faith comes when you are required to stand, waiting to follow a request by prayer, till the answer has arrived.

Like a soldier standing guard; you are to stand firm. Do not bend or flex from your position of belief remain fixed and positioned! With this discipline your power and strength are being developed as it deepens, as does the roots on a tree grow. You must remain standing firm when things appear contradictory to God's word in appearance. God's purpose in delays are to develop and equip you for what His destiny for you will require. Joseph was tested according to Psalms 105:19 it is written saying, "The Word of the Lord tried him." It wasn't a prison or difficulties, but the Word of the Lord.

"Like a caged bird", he remained in prison as he looked on as the just and the unjust were released; while he remained during this time that tried his soul is where he grew spiritually. Don't let go! When the release came, he was ready to deal with his wayward family with love and patience, only surpassed by God.

Where do you see yourself in the test of life?

---

[135] Streams in the Desert/L.B. Cowman Zondervan, Grand Rapids Michigan 49530 pg.191

If I had but one answer of how to overcome in adversity, it would all be summed up by saying, "But God!" In the days of tragedies, losses, or those of triumph learn to focus leaning on God. Life is a lesson of tests to develop you to become stronger in Him. When you gain strength, the reality is you are less, and He becomes more in His power within each one enduring a trial.

[136]A motto of Out Bound mountain climbers says, "If you can't get out of it, get into it!" Don't stand there no matter how small of a step of faith. Make that phone call, confront the situation you have dreaded. If you don't get up and try. Be willing to fail but know that God is in control no matter the outcome.

You will never win the battle if you never start the race. You will have chosen defeat; your fear of failure will keep you rooted to the spot. Get up, try, move forward. Go ahead take the step. you will not know until you face the giant called obstacle until you move.

As a reminder in an earlier discussion, the lion was but an illusion. Fear often creates terror in your mind; particularly, when you have been impacted in your life by many losses. Just as a climber is trained to look straight ahead, so must you. Don't look back nor down only onward and upward to God.

Trust God to give you both the strength and power to overcome.

Then He said unto me, Fear not, Daniel for from the first day that you set your mind and a heart to understand and to humble yourself before your God, your words were heard, and I have come as a consequence of (and in response) to your words (Daniel 10:12).

---

[136] IF YOU WANT TO WALK ON WATER YOU'VE GOT TO GET OUT OF THE BOAT, John Ortberg Zondervan Publishing House Grand Rapids, Michigan 49530

Heavenly Father,

I lift all those who are in a trial of faith enduring the testing of life. Each one of us have different challenges to overcome. Grant us Your grace and mercy with a sustaining strength, as we are brought through to a place of victory. Help us fix our focus, to stare into your face with each move we make, as we prepare to pursue, overtake and recover all. I speak peace, as we find rest in You, when we cast our cares upon you. Thank you now for the recovery of all in Jesus name. Amen.

I leave you with this thought. Turn on praise music; begin thanking God for all He has done in times past. Praise Him, giving thanks for all the ways He is working this out for your good.

Recognize just as you don't see the air, God is still with you. Psalms 22:3 states, God inhabits the praises of His people.

v.1 May the Lord answer you in the day of trouble! May the name of the God of Jacob set you up on high (and defend you); v2 Send you help from the sanctuary and support, refresh, and strengthen you from Zion. (Psalms 20:1-2)

ACKNOWLEDGEMENT

Once again, I have visited the corridor of times. The Lord has provided abundantly with untold care along my pilgrimage toward home. The Lord has continued faithfully to meet my every need. From the doctors, surgeons, specialist, medical staff teams that have cared for me. The countless prayer warriors, who have continued to pray and intercede for me through each stage of my recovery. Friends, who have lovingly been supportive, my production team who continue to aid me in all of my writings, to the supportiveness encouragement of readers. Great is His faithfulness unto me.

To each who have touched my world it is with sincere gratitude I say a heartfelt thank you for your love, prayers, supportiveness, and encouragement.

Diana Lynn Rogers
Celebrate Life! It is a daily gift from God!

INDEX REFERENCE

DAYS OF PLUNDER Volume I

Finding Light in the Darkness to Overcome and Recover All

Part I Corridor of Times	9
1. Goodbye	14
2. So Began The Journey	22
3. Who Am I?	24
4. Overcomer	25
5. Letting Go	31
6. Switched	32
7. Fixed Focus	34
8. Avoiding Confrontation	35
9. Anxiety	35
10. Come Out From Among Them	37
11. His Might And Power	40
12. Yielding And Surrendering	42
13. Because	45
14. The Lord Is My Shepherd	46
15. The Shepherd	47
16. All Things Work For The Good	49
17. My Grace Is Sufficient For You	50
18. Digging For Gold	57

19.	Jacob's Test	58
20.	Pathways Of Brokenness	61
21.	Hope	62
22.	Healing	64
23.	Reaching Your Destiny	66
24.	Identity	67

Part II Building Your Vision — 68

25.	The Principles Of God	68
26.	The Universal Laws Of Attraction	69
27.	Practice	69
28.	Law Of Thinking	70
29.	Law Of Supply	72
30.	Law Of Rhythm	72
31.	Law Of Receiving	73
32.	Law Of The Seed	74
33.	Law Of Gender	74
34.	Law Of Increase	74
35.	Law Of Compensation	75
36.	Law Of Non-Resistance	75
37.	Law Of Forgiveness	75
38.	Law Of Sacrifice	76
39.	Law Of Obedience	77
40.	Law Of Success	77
41.	Unlocking The Door Of The Vision	81
42.	Stepping Stones And Gaps along The Way	84
43.	Blocks	85
44.	Inability To Receive	86
45.	Self-Examination	86
46.	Setting Core Values	87
47.	Inventory	88
48.	Getting To Know You	88
49.	When Things Seem Impossible	89
50.	Reprograming Your Minds	89

Part III Pathways To Healing   90

    51. The White Alabaster Box   90
    52. Post-Traumatic Stress Disorder   91
    53. Anxiety   95
    54. Mary Did You Know   98
    55. Divine Encounter   99
    56. Paradigm Shift   100
    57. Letting Go Of The Former   100
    58. Golden Key   101
    59. Love Never Fails   104
    60. Eternity   106
    61. Validation And Confirmation   106

Part IV Poetry   108

    62. Would You Love Me?   108
    63. If I Could   109
    64. After The Rain   110
    65. Sands Of Time   111
    66. The Ancient Of Days   112

Epilogue   113

DIANA LYNN ROGERS

THE PROMISE Volume II

Finding Light in the Darkness to Overcome and Recover All

Prelude	117
Part I Corridor Of Times	119
1. Course Corrections God's Way/ Your Way	122
2. Patterns/Cycles	122
3. Sin Patterns	126
4. Sinful Patterns	126
5. Promises! Promises! A World Filled With Promises!	127
6. The Parrott	129
7. Pit To The Pinnacle	132
8. Mirror, Mirror, On The Wall Who Is The Fairest Of All?	135
9. Faith Barriers	138
10. Keeper Of The Vine	140
11. Stages Of Obedience	140
12. The Call to Obedience	143
13. ME LOVE COOKIES! From the Tales of a Cookie Monster	144
14. Peace	148
15. Endurance	149
16. Faithfulness/Faith	149
17. Mary, Mary, How Does Your Garden Grow	151
18. Joy	151

19.	The Seed Principles Of the Kingdom Of God	154
20.	The Gift Of The Holy Spirit	155
21.	Love	155
22.	Gentleness	159
23.	Words Matter	160
24.	If I Could	163
25.	Divine Order	164
26.	Divine Order And Protocol	166
27.	Who's God And Who Isn't God	168
28.	Honor	169
29.	Waters Of Transition	170
30.	Spiritual Laws Of Transition	172
31.	Preparation For The New Season	175
32.	Fruit Inspection	180
33.	Breaking Through	182
34.	God's Timing	185
35.	Belief	186
36.	Promises	186
37.	The Main Thing Is To Keep God The Main Thing!!!	187
38.	Wilderness To The Promise Land	188

Part II Covenant Talk   189

39.	Covenant	189
40.	The Creation Covenant	190
41.	The Noahic Covenant	190
42.	The Covenant Of Abraham	192
43.	Covenant With Israel	193
44.	Covenant With David	193
45.	The New Covenant	194
46.	Covenant Building 101	196
47.	Understanding	197
48.	Covenant Promises And Conditions	198
49.	Blood Walk	200
50.	Mingling of Blood Cutting	201
51.	Two Witnesses	202

52.	Exchanging Of Names	202
53.	Exchanging Of Gifts/Authority	203
54.	Covenant Of Feast	203
55.	Our Covenant With Jesus	204

Part III Warriors Battlefield   204

56.	Entry Into The Promise Land	205
57.	Something Old Something New Something Borrowed Something Blue	206
58.	Occupy God's Promise	207
59.	Territory Expanded	208
60.	Rest Is Required To Enter	208
61.	Let's Roll	208
62.	The Three Cord Agreement/Prayer	209
63.	A Review Of The Three Cord Agreement	213
64.	Overview Of The Three Cord Agreement	214
65.	Lord's Prayer	215
66.	Our Father's Heart	217
67.	Father's Love, Part I	219
68.	Father's Love, Part II	221
69.	Disappointments	222
70.	It Is The Lord	222
71.	The King's Kingdom	224
72.	A Vessel Of Honor For Your Glory	227
73.	Staking Claims	228
74.	Personal Promise Given	228
75.	As The Church Prays	230
76.	Abundance Of Rain	232
77.	Land Mines	233
78.	Waiting	233

Part IV Celebrate Life   236

79.	Building Memorials	236
80.	No Shame (Picture)	237
81.	Double Vision	239

82.	The Shepherd	240
83.	Valley Lesson	244
84.	Love	246
85.	God's Love	248
86.	Love Greek Style	248
87.	De-stressing Stressful Situations	249
88.	But God!!!	251
89.	Sustaining Grace	252
90.	Does No One Cry?	256
91.	So Now What?	258
92.	Giants In The Land	258
93.	How To Recognize Giants	262
94.	Gate Keepers	272
95.	Warrior's Armor	275
96.	What Is In Your Ceramic Box	275
97.	The Gift Of Understanding	276
98.	Exposing Darkness	278
99.	Spirits Of Accusations	280
100.	No Shame!	281
101.	Seasons Of Faith	283

dianalynnrogers.com

https://youtu.be/fuaLFSkZFoU

My Journey On the Edge of Eternity/ Diana Rogers

www.ingramcontent.com/pod-product-compliance
Lightning Source LLC
Chambersburg PA
CBHW020519080526
44583CB00013B/661